KV-731-572

Flourishing in the Early Years

If young children are to flourish and become happy, confident and motivated learners, they need to develop in an environment that gives them the opportunities and freedom to play and learn, along with the support of parents and practitioners who are flourishing themselves.

This invaluable text looks at the conditions that enable all those engaged in the early years sector to flourish, covering themes such as the outdoor environment, the curriculum, parent partnership, equality and ethical practice. Divided into three sections, each part covers:

- Concepts: A consideration of how flourishing is framed by political, historical and policy frameworks.
- Practices: Exploring the issues that early years practitioners are faced with when engaging with parents and multi-agent professionals within their setting.
- Futures: Examining some of the long-term issues that may need to be revisited on a regular basis to enable continual and flourishing development to occur.

With key points and reflective tasks, this book will be valuable reading for all students and practitioners working in the early childhood education and care sector who want to ensure that the children in their care are given the best possible start in life.

Zenna Kingdon is Principal Lecturer and Head of Early Childhood Education and Care at Newman University, UK.

Jan Gourd is Senior Lecturer and Programme Area Lead for Education at the University of St Mark and St John, Plymouth, UK.

Michael Gasper is an independent early years consultant, UK.

LIVERPOOL JMU LIBRARY

3 1111 01512 9594

Flourishing in the Early Years

Contexts, practices and futures

Edited by
Zenna Kingdon,
Jan Gourd and
Michael Gasper

Routledge
Taylor & Francis Group

LONDON AND NEW YORK

First published 2017
by Routledge
2 Park Square, Milton Park, Abingdon, Oxon OX14 4RN

and by Routledge
711 Third Avenue, New York, NY 10017

Routledge is an imprint of the Taylor & Francis Group, an informa business

© 2017 selection and editorial matter, Zenna Kingdon, Jan Gourd and Michael Gasper; individual chapters, the contributors

The right of the editors to be identified as the authors of the editorial material, and of the authors for their individual chapters, has been asserted in accordance with sections 77 and 78 of the Copyright, Designs and Patents Act 1988.

All rights reserved. No part of this book may be reprinted or reproduced or utilised in any form or by any electronic, mechanical, or other means, now known or hereafter invented, including photocopying and recording, or in any information storage or retrieval system, without permission in writing from the publishers.

Trademark notice: Product or corporate names may be trademarks or registered trademarks, and are used only for identification and explanation without intent to infringe.

British Library Cataloguing in Publication Data
A catalogue record for this book is available from the British Library

Library of Congress Cataloging-in-Publication Data
Names: Kingdon, Zenna, editor. | Gourd, Jan, editor. | Gasper, Michael, editor.
Title: Flourishing in the early years : contexts, practices and futures / edited by Zenna Kingdon, Jan Gourd and Michael Gasper.
Description: New York, NY : Routledge, 2016.
Identifiers: LCCN 2016024149 | ISBN 9781138841123 (hardback) | ISBN 9781138841130 (pbk.) | ISBN 9781315732466 (ebook)
Subjects: LCSH: Early childhood education—Textbooks.
Classification: LCC LB1139.23 .F65 2016 | DDC 372.21—dc23
LC record available at https://lccn.loc.gov/2016024149

ISBN: 978-1-138-84112-3 (hbk)
ISBN: 978-1-138-84113-0 (pbk)
ISBN: 978-1-315-73246-6 (ebk)

Typeset in Bembo and Helvetica Neue
by Florence Production Ltd, Stoodleigh, Devon, UK

Contents

Contributors

Editors

Zenna Kingdon is currently writing and researching independently. She was formerly Principal Lecturer at Newman University and Senior Lecturer at the University of St Mark and St John, UK. She was responsible for a range of Early Childhood Education and Care programmes, at both undergraduate and post-graduate levels, focusing on play, pedagogy and the impact that these have on the lives of young children.

Jan Gourd has worked in education for over 20 years as Head of Key Stage 1, Deputy Head and more than 10 years as a Headteacher in Plymouth, UK. She is currently Senior Lecturer at the University of St Mark and St John, leading a range of Education Studies programmes with an interest in creativity, children's writing and literacy and policy.

Michael Gasper is a published author and early years consultant. After working as a teacher and Headteacher for 27 years in total, he joined the Centre for Research in Early Childhood and co-ordinates research into the effectiveness of the Early Excellence Centre programme. He has worked on the National Professional Qualification for Integrated Leadership and currently delivers masters level programmes in Ireland to support the development of the early years workforce.

Contributors

Luke Reynolds graduated from the University of St Mark and St John and began to teach as a graduate assistant while completing his MA. While studying for a degree in Primary Education, he developed an interest in early years and also gained his Early Years Teacher Status.

He is currently spending time in practice and hopes to complete his PhD in the future.

Scott Buckler has taught at Newman University and the University of Worcester, UK. Prior to this he was a qualified primary teacher and taught at schools in London and the West Midlands. More recently, Scott gained recognition by the British Psychological Society and has also set up his own educational consultancy.

Bob Pilbeam has worked at the University of St Mark and St John for over 20 years. He is also a former centre manager for an outdoor pursuits centre and this has pervaded all of his work since. Bob is convinced by the transformational nature that outdoor education can have on individuals. More recently he has investigated Forest School and has given a number of papers at conferences on the work that he has been doing in embedding Forest School qualifications into degree programmes.

Leoarna Mathias is Lecturer in the department of Early Childhood Education and Care at Newman University, UK. Having worked in the early childhood sector for more than 10 years, she also continues to chair her local pre-school while engaging in doctoral research.

Sue Lea is an experienced manager and community educator who has worked across the public, private, voluntary and community sectors. She is working independently on a range of projects which engage her in both teaching and writing. Prior to this, she worked at the University of St Mark and St John in a range of roles which included Head of Early Years.

Introduction

Zenna Kingdon and Jan Gourd

In our first book, *Early Years Policy: The impact on practice*, we considered all aspects of policy within early years contexts and considered how these could be resisted and challenged in positive ways by utilising the concept of flourishing. We drew on Seligman's (2011) model of PERMA:

Personal Enjoyment: the pleasant life;

Enagagement: a flow state in which thought and feeling are usually absent;

(Positive) **R**elationships: relationships are key to the development of all humans;

Meaning: belonging to and serving something that is bigger than the self;

Accomplishment: the pursuit of success, achievement and mastery for its own sake.

In this second text we look more broadly at definitions of flourishing demonstrating that while the term may be new, the concept can be considered to be universal and has its roots in among other things the work of the ancient Greeks, particularly that of Aristotle. More recently we see that the work of some recognised early childhood pioneers, including for example, Margaret MacMillan, can be considered to support the development of flourishing in young children. Within this text we not only consider the flourishing of the children, but also those who care for them in early childhood settings as well as their parents and carers. Flourishing is examined in a range of contexts with consideration of how this can be facilitated.

This text is intended for students at both undergraduate and post-graduate level, as well as practitioners who are working in the early childhood education and care sector. All of the contributors to this text have taught at both undergraduate and post-graduate level, on a range of early childhood programmes; including foundation degrees, BA programmes and the new Early Years Teacher Status programme.

This text is divided into three sections: concepts, practices and futures. Within Part 1 Concepts, we consider flourishing as it is framed by political, historical and policy frameworks. Part 2 Practices, explores some of the issues that are faced by early childhood practitioners within their settings and when engaging with parents and wider multi-agency professionals. While Part 3 Futures, examines some of the issues that are longer term and may need to be re-visited on a regular basis in order that continual development can occur and to ensure that flourishing continues to be developed.

Part 1 Concepts

Chapter 1 'The conceptualisation of flourishing'. According to Seligman (2011) if you ask parents about what they want for their children they will discuss issues such as: confidence, happiness, self-esteem and contentment. These concepts are linked to concepts of flourishing. We consider the ways in which flourishing is linked to well-being and pleasure. The chapter begins to explore the concept of flourishing as a contextual dimension of childhood; we consider the practices that support children to flourish and the future of flourishing for our youngest children. These concerns are set against a policy background in which early years has yet again become the focus of political agendas in which school readiness rather than social and emotional development are what are considered as key. We refocus on the paradigm of early childhood that provides for children as agents in their own lives, capable beings who are able to participate and comment on their experiences, able to act, able to flourish (James and Prout 1997).

Chapter 2 'Constructs of the flourishing child' sets out to examine the 'flourishing child' as a recent iteration in the many social and educational constructions of the child throughout history. The flourishing child is contemplated at the heart of interrelated, and often competing, micro, meso and macro systems of influence; systems that inevitably impact on our understanding of childhood, and what it means to be a child. The chapter moves on to contemplate the child in the broadest sense, their holistic development is examined to fulfil the extensive meanings the term flourishing has come to represent. It progresses to consider constructs of the flourishing child; doing so in a critical sense to reaffirm the importance of acknowledging the unique child, while recognising the fluid, evolving nature of the construct of childhood. Rousseau's conception of childhood and his influence on early years pedagogy and play is discussed. The chapter closes with a focus on the child's home environment and a discussion of the ways in which cultural capital impacts on their ability to flourish.

Chapter 3 'The ecology of flourishing' critically explores the issues raised by the policy dichotomy of 'universal' and 'targeted' services. The move from universal to targeted services, such as the 'refocus' of Sure Start on low income families, is framed within a political and economic context rather than a social and welfare one exemplified by the loss of the ECM agenda. This discourse and policy focus has obscured the complexity of the reality of people's lives, focusing on what are essentially superficial symptoms, ignoring the causes of the causes and the ecological contexts (Bronfenbrenner 1994), and putting the blame for all difficulties faced by disadvantaged people on to the individual and most often the parents. This individual blame is highlighted by the plethora of policy initiatives under New Labour and the Coalition focusing on 'troubled families'. This chapter argues that in order for children and their families to flourish the dichotomy of universal and targeted provision must be challenged. Finally, this chapter revisits the concept of multi-agency working to support flourishing.

Chapter 4 'Risk taking, philosophy and ethical practice to facilitate flourishing'. Dahlberg and Moss (2005, p. viii) state that there is 'always more than one possibility, more than one answer to any question'. This means that early years professionals have to make responsible choices every day in practice. Many of these choices are intuitive and based on experience. This chapter discusses the balance between the ethics of practice, explicitly determining the notion of perceived risks versus potential benefits. At the same time the notion of compassion fatigue is explored, considering why it is so necessary for practitioners to flourish if they are to support children and families to flourish. With a developing field of research into risk-taking, this theme is explored in relation to early childhood settings. From this standpoint, a challenge issued to early childhood is that of developing revolutionary approaches and challenging the discourse of 'accepted' practice. Finally, the chapter explores how flourishing may be further facilitated within the early year's setting.

Part 2 Practices

Chapter 5 'Flourishing through Forest School' discusses the way in which Forest School is growing rapidly in popularity in the UK. Since its introduction as a concept in 1993 Forest School has grown from small beginnings at Bridgewater College to the point where many early years and primary settings now seek to include Forest School in their pedagogy or curriculum. The chapter seeks to explain some of this enthusiasm for a concept, which, some might argue, is a limited reinvention or re-packaging of pre-existing outdoor learning methods. The approach appears to have struck a chord with those educating younger age groups and with concerns for the moral panics of increasingly protected and sedentary lifestyles. The links between Forest School and opportunities for young children to flourish are considered.

Chapter 6 'Parent partnership for flourishing in an age of austerity' focuses on the value of partnerships with parents in identifying and nurturing characteristics that will enable them and their children to flourish. It uses reflection on case studies to draw out key features of successful partnerships between professionals, private, voluntary and independent agencies and parents as well as between agencies themselves and key challenges in these relationships. In reflecting on these challenges consideration is given to each perspective and particular attention will be given to ways in which successful partnerships can be supported at Local, Regional and National levels. It concludes with a juxtaposition of enabling and disabling factors for families, professionals and decision makers at all levels. The chapter develops the theme of flourishing, and draws on Bronfenbrenner, Wenger, Whalley and the Pen Green Team to demonstrate this in practice.

Chapter 7 'The creative curriculum: flourishing in the play environment'. This chapter explores the notion that while academics including Robinson (2016), Rosen (2014) and Waters (2013), continue to argue the necessity for a curriculum that supports young people to be creative, we appear to have a group of politicians and those in positions of politically conferred authority who are persistent in their refusal to acknowledge the research evidence that shows that children in early years settings do best when they are given opportunities to play and explore for themselves. This chapter explores how we need to provide an appropriate environment for young children, in which they are encouraged to: explore, to be curious and to develop the skills, knowledge and attitudes that will support their future development and their ability to flourish. The chapter concludes that in order for children in early childhood to be enabled to flourish there are a number of factors that need to be in place, these include: providing a creative curriculum, having a suitable environment, which includes access to indoor and outdoor spaces, allowing children to explore their own interests, and providing open ended and engaging materials with which they can investigate and explore.

Chapter 8 'Pedagogical documentation to support flourishing' explores the way in which the documentation of children's learning has gained prominence over the years and has in some instances become the primary occupation of practitioners. This documentation is created through ever increasing observations of children's activities. Foucaldian notions of the panoptican of power are at work (MacNaughton 2005). Likewise Greishaber and McArdle (2010) ask whom this surveillance of childhood is for. In the United Kingdom we create learning journeys, while in New Zealand they create learning stories and in Reggio Emilia pedagogical documentation is the main form of recording children's progress (Rinaldi 2006). In order to ensure that these records support the flourishing of the child we need to carefully consider how they are created and used. Carr (2011) spent time researching in a number of early years settings in New Zealand to consider how the learning stories were used with the children. These investigations focused on children's understanding not only of their learning, but also how the learning occurred. Rinaldi (2006: 63) demonstrates that in Reggio the documentation is used in, 'fostering learning and modifying the learning teaching relationship'. This chapter investigates whether there are more creative ways of using learning journeys in order to record children's progress, which benefits the children by incorporating our knowledge of formative assessment for lifelong learning and flourishing. We investigate what we can learn from New Zealand and Reggio practices to shift the balance from surveillance to assessment for flourishing.

Part 3 Futures

Chapter 9 'Equality for flourishing in the early years' shows that currently in England inclusion is defined by policy makers (DfE 2014) as responding to childrens' emerging needs and interests where practitioners respond to them and guide their development. The challenge in early years is that the range of diverse experiences, which exist for both children and for practitioners, may make inclusion something that is more easily talked and written about, than practiced. This chapter questions the hidden assumptions and mental models, which practitioners bring to their settings and explores the ways in which these might inhibit the flourishing of some children in their early years. It will argue that equality and inclusion are both central and fundamental to the development of all children. It will question why the early years' literature is often secure in terms of defining difference and dis/ability, but less secure in questioning the broader social, political and economic structures that limit the flourishing of all children. The chapter argues that early years practitioners have a duty and a responsibility to explore their own values and prejudices as part of their professional formation and in their ongoing professional roles. It will conclude that every child has a right to an early education in a cultural and educational space, which honours their unique experience, family background and community of origin, free from oppressive and judgemental language and practice.

Chapter 10 'Flourishing and quality' explores the current policy context of austerity, value for money and the education of pre-school children that has woven together notions of quality with techno-rational conceptions of professionalism within a performativity agenda (Moss 2014). This chapter deconstructs these concepts and questions the particular way in which policy has come to define what counts as quality in early years provision. It goes on to explore alternative conceptions of quality from the different perspectives of the child, the practitioner and the parent. This exploration will be located within the broader debates about the meaning and purpose of early years educational provision and will argue that a different professionally led discourse on quality offers an altered perspective of its importance and its relationship to the flourishing of the pre-school child. It will conclude that 'quality' re-framed can be used as an important conceptual tool to re-capture the elusive concept of educational excellence within the complex early years environment.

These final two chapters provide an opportunity to look at ways of being in the future that can support flourishing for the child, family and practitioner. We are not suggesting that these approaches are simple, in fact quite the opposite; we acknowledge many of the inherent challenges in these approaches. However, we conclude that we have attempted to examine flourishing from a range of perspectives and through a number of lenses. We hope that we provide thought-provoking challenges, which support those engaged in the early childhood sector in considering how they can provide a challenge to the neo-liberal techno-rational agenda of top-down approaches, that allow them and more importantly the children to flourish.

References

Bronfenbrenner, U. (1994) *The Ecology of Human Development*. London: Harvard University Press.

Carr, M. (2001) *Assessment in Early Childhood Settings: Learning Stories*. London: Sage.

Dahlberg, G. and Moss, P. (2005). *Ethics and Politics in Early Childhood Education*. Abingdon: RoutledgeFalmer.

DfE (2014) Statutory framework for the early years foundation stage: setting the standards for learning, development and care for children from birth to five. [Online] Available from: www.gov.uk/government/uploads/system/uploads/attachment_data/file/335504/EYFS_framework_from_1_September_2014__with_clarification_note.pdf [accessed 31 October 2015]

Greishaber, S. and McArdle, F. (2010) *The Trouble with Play*. Maidenhead: Open University Press.

James, A. and Prout, A. (1997) *Constructing and Reconstructing Childhood Contemporary Issues in the Sociological Study of Childhood*. London: Falmer Press.

MacNaughton, G. (2005) *Doing Foucault in Early Childhood Studies: Applying Poststructural Ideas*. London: Routledge.

Moss, P. (2014) *Transformative Change and Real Utopias in Early Childhood Education: A Story of Democracy, Experimentation and Potentiality*. London: Routledge.

Rinaldi, C. (2006) *In Dialogue with Reggio Emilia*. Abingdon: Routledge.

Robinson, K. and Aronica, L. (2016) *Creative Schools Revolutionising Education from the Ground Up*. London: Penguin.

Rosen, M. (2014) My professorial inaugural lecture at Goldsmiths, University of London: Humour in children's books, http://michaelrosenblog.blogspot.co.uk/2014/07/my-professorial-inaugural-lecture-at.html [accessed 05/05/15]

Seligman, M. (2011) *Flourish: A New Understanding of Happiness and Well-being and How to Achieve Them*. London: Nicholas Brearley Publishing.

Waters, M. (2013) *Thinking Allowed on Schooling*. Bancyfelin: Independent Thinking Press.

Wenger, E. McDermott, R. and Snyder, W. (2002) *Cultivating Communities of Practice*. Boston: Harvard University Press.

Whalley, M. and the Pen Green Team (2007) *Involving Parents in their Children's Learning 2e*. London: Paul Chapman Publishing.

Concepts

The conceptualisation of flourishing

Zenna Kingdon and Jan Gourd

Introduction

In our last book we looked at how early years policy contributed to flourishing in the early years. Previously we based our conceptualisation of flourishing on Seligman's PERMA. While this suited our purpose at the time, the aim of this book and this first chapter is to further explore how flourishing is conceptualised more broadly in the early years context. The linkages between flourishing, well-being, happiness and pleasure form the basis of this chapter. We will firstly look at a number of theories of flourishing and a number of theorists who do not necessarily discuss flourishing but its constituent attributes including happiness, resilience, self-esteem, interpersonal relationships and values. We then seek to relate each of those to common early years themes.

We open with a discussion of the notion of the theoretical foundations of flourishing. This includes a consideration of flourishing in the contexts of classical philosophy utilising the work of Aristotle. We then consider flourishing in terms of learning theory drawing on the work of Margaret McMillan and finally we consider flourishing through the lens of positive psychology examining the work of Seligman.

We move on to consider flourishing and well-being and the interrelatedness of these two concepts with a particular focus on mental health. We recognise that in order for individuals to enjoy good mental health particular conditions need to be in place. These are often also related to attachment theory (Bowlby and Ainsworth 1991), recognising that children need to be enabled to develop effective relationships with those around them in order to be able to flourish.

In looking at flourishing we then consider aspects of happiness as a significant contributory factor to long-term flourishing. Moments of happiness, however, do not necessarily lead to flourishing. Flourishing comes from values and relationships developed and deepened over time, which develop and strengthen the receptive capacities of the brain that enable an individual to respond appropriately and emotionally to life events. We investigate the emerging relationship between flourishing and neuroscience.

Greishaber (2008) and Murris (2013) provide challenge to some of the current educational practices in which there is a focus on norms and expected ways of developing and achieving, often at the detriment of other aspects of being that are linked to flourishing. Current educational practices are often focused on outcomes and achievements in the short term rather than on long-term activities that will support the flourishing of the individual child. These concerns are investigated in order that we can consider alternative educational practices that may support the development of flourishing.

Much of the developmental psychological approaches to education focus on a becomings model. More recently, sociology of early childhood has developed an integrated model in which children are seen as both beings and becomings. Cross (2011) takes this a stage further by integrating three selves: beings, becomings and having beens. This model is considered and its relevance to flourishing is explored.

Recent iterations of flow suggest that creative pedagogies that offer opportunities for self-direction and agency within stimulating environments maximise the opportunities for the development of flow within play. Subsequently, they influence the happy ethos of the childcare environment. We conclude by discussing the necessity to establish a positive ethos within all early childcare settings.

Foundations of flourishing: Aristotle, McMillan and Seligman

In considering flourishing in all its forms it is essential to try to establish the development of flourishing as the concept with which we are now familiar. In doing so we look back as far as the Ancient Greeks who were concerned with philosophical concerns of epistemology, the notion of how we develop knowledge and understanding and ethics, the notion that actions and pursuits should be moral and in the quest of some good (Aristotle 1925). He (ibid. 1925, p. 1) states that, 'every art and every inquiry, and similarly every action and pursuit, is thought to aim at some good.' Noddings (2012) suggests that almost all of Aristotle's Nicomachean Ethics were concerned with the good life – something that we can directly relate to the notions of flourishing. Watson *et al.* (2012)

equally suggest that Aristotle was concerned with what constitutes happiness and well living. Aristotle (1925, p. 11) states that in seeking good in one's life, 'we call that which is in itself worthy of pursuit more final than that which is worthy of pursuit for the sake of something else.' He argued that that something was happiness. He (ibid., p. 15) goes on to suggest that, 'the happy man lives well' Noddings (p. 152) further argues that Aristotle was concerned with seeking a better way than those that had come before, saying that, 'human beings are persistently seeking better ways than their ancestors'. She (p. 156) suggests that one of the strengths of Aristotle was that he sought to consider questions of everyday life and therefore had relevance for all, he did not, 'confine his philosophy to the analysis of abstruse language or the elaboration of a formal system'. Aristotle was concerned with the ethics of virtue in which individuals were concerned with the conduct of their everyday lives and the ways in which moral education should be developed.

Aristotle was not without his critics given that he argued in favour of a system that supported slavery and infanticide (Noddings 2012; Singer 1993). He supported the leaving of deformed newly born infants on mountainsides to die, suggesting this as a natural and humane solution for such sick and deformed babies (Singer 1993). He equally defended slavery because he felt that it was an essential element of a well-run society (Noddings 2012).

Despite these concerns it would seem that Aristotle is enjoying a renaissance and the ideas contained within his work are being used to support aspects of moral education including, citizenship, social and emotional learning, character education and positive psychology, the last being where current notions of flourishing are being developed (Kristjansson 2013). Kristjansson explores why Aristotle's philosophy is enjoying such resurgence and how it links with current concerns about flourishing and the good life. He (ibid. 2013, p. 51) suggests that many theorists have now, 'returned to the common-sense paradigm of the flourishing child, in Aristotle, where the simple and easily observable truths of the matter lie.' He (ibid. 2013) goes on to suggest that Aristotle's approach is appealing in that it addresses both human flourishing and a universal approach in which it is not possible to develop one's own virtues without at the same time benefitting others. Watson *et al.* (2012) support this idea suggesting that Aristotle introduced notions of morality and virtue from which value judgements needed to be made. Likewise, Noddings (2012) suggests that Aristotle addressed questions that concerned everyone and everyday life, his philosophy was therefore for everyone. Hence Aristotle's approach depends on an interrelated society in which happiness and flow occur as a result of individuals' happiness, well-being and pleasure.

- Aristotle's work is seen as common sense and it is for this reason it is enjoying a resurgence.
- Aristotle considered questions about everyday life and living well.

Margaret McMillan

Like Aristotle, McMillan can be considered to be having a renaissance and that her work has underpinned much of what is currently considered to be important in early years policy and practice. There are clear links between her concerns around diet and outdoor provision and aspects of the EYFS (DfE 2012). Margaret McMillan can be considered to be deeply concerned with flourishing, demonstrating concerns with children's 'physical, mental and moral well-being' (Read 2011, p. 423). Margaret was a Christian Socialist who became a member of the Independent Labour Party where her views were taken forward as the views of the party, focusing on the promotion of nursery education particularly for the children of the poor (Brehony 2009). In her early career she worked with older and privileged children, however, Du Charme (1992) suggests that having been influenced by a Russian revolutionary she became interested in the plight of the poor. From then on her career was spent firstly in Bradford and later in London concentrating on the children who were growing up in slum situations considering how their lives could be improved (Giardiello 2013). In Bradford she was elected as the ILP member of the school board, where she worked closely with Dr James Kerr, the School Medical Officer. She became interested in the physiology of growth. She campaigned for improved ventilation in schools, for correct breathing to be taught, for school baths and for the provision of wholesome school dinners (Bradburn 1989).

In 1897, the first school in Bradford had its own swimming bath and 12 slipper baths were seen. McMillan was concerned about how the children's' opportunities to get clean, something that her research allowed her to understand, impacted on children's health and well-being (Bradburn 1989). On returning to London McMillan concerned herself with the development of outdoor nurseries and night camps for children in Stowage Deptford where the children were once again living in extreme poverty.

> To let them live at last and have the sight of people planting and digging, to let them run and work and experiment, sleep, have regular meals, the sights and sounds of winter and spring, autumn and summer . . . to get these things we sacrificed everything else.
>
> (McMillan 1919 cited in Bradburn 1989, p. 142)

McMillan sensed, and her research evidence supported this, that children would flourish when they were well fed and clean, when they engaged in an environment that was appropriate for them and met their needs, when they were enabled to gain a sense of the seasons and were able to understand the relationship between what was sown in the ground and what they cooked in the kitchen. These holistic and cyclical relationships with those around them and with nature were at the heart of McMillan's work. These relationships extended to those who cared for them in the nurseries. McMillan believed that the staff should be well qualified and trained to work with young children. She stated that:

> The new thinkers, the psychologists . . . Began to show why the first five years of life are the most important of all . . . They told us how the first five years was the time of swift events and that destiny was settled then.
>
> (McMillan 1932, cited in Bradburn 1989)

McMillan's pedagogical approach included three notions that set her work apart from others, which was training women to work with young children. Firstly, she stated that young children needed teachers, secondly, that the staff working with the children should be immersed in their lives in such a way that they could understand the childrens' experiences, this included living within close proximity of the nursery settings in order that they were able to visit the children in their homes. Thirdly, practice needed to precede academic work. McMillan was insistent that the women who worked with the young children were vocationally inclined to do so. Through these three principles she felt that she would be enabled to develop practitioners who were in turn enabled to support young children to flourish; physically, emotionally and intellectually through both education and care (Giardiello 2013).

- McMillan was concerned that young children were well fed, clean and in a suitable environment.
- These three aspects when taken together appear to support flourishing.

Seligman

Seligman initially studied philosophy before undertaking postgraduate research in animal psychology before, at his students' behest, undertaking a two-year psychiatric residency (American Psychological Association 2006). He has now been concerned with what he refers to as positive psychology for more than 20 years. During that time, he published a number of papers and books that explored his notions of well-being. Positive psychology has not been without its opponents and in 2001 Eugene Taylor, whose own work concerns the history and philosophy of psychology, published a damning attack on Seligman's work under the guise of a response to Seligman's assertion that Humanistic Psychology was not Positive Psychology. Taylor (2001) argues that Seligman's assertions are not appropriately researched and that a simple undergraduate literature review would demonstrate the extent to which Humanistic Psychology is grounded in scientific research and generates a research tradition. Taylor (2001), however, does not appear to be the overriding voice within the American Psychology sector. Instead in 2006 Seligman was awarded the Distinguished Scientific Contributions Award by the American Psychology Society for among other things his, 'creation of a new field – positive psychology' (American Psychology Association 2006, p. 772).

- Seligman has developed the field of positive psychology.
- Flourishing and well-being are central to his work.

Flourishing and well-being

Health and well-being are much more than merely physical states, they also represent the mental and emotional health of the individual. Eaude (2009) looks at the Mental Health Institutes list of contributing factors to children's mental health. The Mental Health Foundation (Fraser and Blishen 2001, p. 9) highlights the following attributes in children's mental health: self-esteem; physical, emotional, social and spiritual growth; resilience; the ability to make good personal relationships; a sense of right and wrong; the motivation to face setbacks and learn from them; a sense of belonging; a belief in their ability to cope and a repertoire of problem-solving approaches. Much of this reflects the work of Bowlby and Ainsworth (1991) who believed that effective attachment was essential in the active development of an individual and in their inter-personal relationships, all of which impact on their self-esteem, their ability to demonstrate resilience, and ultimately to flourish. More recently Rose and Rogers (2012) have considered the role of the adult in early childhood settings as seven selves who support children through differing roles in order that children are given opportunities to develop and flourish. Narvaez (2015) suggests that not enough attention is given to the crucial and critical periods of children's development, which lay down the foundations of flourishing in later life.

De Ruyter (2007, p. 27) cites Ryan and Deci (2001) as arguing, 'that there are three innate psychological needs or nutriments that are functionally essential to a person's flourishing: (1) the need for autonomy or self-determination, (2) the need for competence or effectiveness, and (3) the need for relatedness or affiliation'. As much as adults, children need to have a sense of autonomy that they are enabled to make decisions for themselves and that their ideas are heard and acted upon (James and Prout 1998, Corsaro 2011). Likewise, they need to be considered to be competent; this is both in making comment on their lives as well as in achieving in the activities with which they engage. Finally, children need to feel a sense of belonging or being part of a family, a setting or a community. When children have these three aspects met they are likely to achieve a sense of well-being and be enabled to achieve. De Ruyter (2007, p. 27) adds to this by suggesting that, 'humans are happy if they believe they are, and only when they believe they are happy do they experience well-being'. Children need to be supported in early years settings by both the policy and by the pedagogical practice of the staff in order to be enabled to develop a sense of well-being. McLauglin (2008) suggests that promoting mental well-being among pupils requires a holistic pedagogy that incorporates all the qualities that 'good' teachers exemplify particularly taking an individual interest in their pupils. Huppert (2007, p. 308) cited in Maclaughlin (2008) suggests that a person's basal level of happiness is not genetically determined and supports the notion that certain constituents or habits of flourishing do have a place in the school curriculum. These she suggests are:

> developing good habits, particularly the habits of regular exercise and being kind to others; developing positive ways of thinking, such as savouring the moment; and being motivated, i.e. having the energy to make things happen.

McLaughlin (2008, p. 358) further comments that 'the implications for how teaching, learning and relating are conducted are very profound'.

She clearly states that it is the integration of what we know about psychology, neuro-science, counselling within a teacher's pedagogy that makes the difference to a child's flourishing and developing resilience.

- Adults in early childhood settings impact on the child's ability to flourish.
- Positive habits and behaviours support flourishing.

Flourishing and happiness

There is some debate as to whether happiness and flourishing are one and the same thing or at least whether it is possible to have one without the other. Scoffham and Barnes (2011, p. 537) present a working definition of happiness, which they suggest is 'a state of flourishing, that involves a sense of personal fulfilment within a shared moral framework'. Likewise, Narvaez (2015, p. 256) suggests that flourishing 'includes not only an individual's well-being but his or her sociomoral capacities and networks'. Furthermore, Noddings (2003) suggests that happiness needs to be combined with issues of social conscience in order to satisfy social relationships within all aspects of an individual's life. This suggests that happiness is relative rather than an absolute. It can occur in different environments in response to different events and experiences. Scoffham and Barnes (2011, p. 537) suggest that happiness 'can include calm reflection, curiosity, fascination, exhilaration, and ecstasy'. It would appear that there is neurological research, which demonstrates that flourishing is dependent on the development of neuronal and hormonal systems that underpin the development of later networks (Narveaz 2015, and Scoffham and Barnes 2011). The development of positive emotions developed through happiness or living in a happy state allow for the development of positive states of mind and according to Scoffham and Barnes (2011, p. 540) create 'a greater willingness to accept difference', and individuals' abilities to explore, imagine, be playful and inquisitive are all increased. They suggest (ibid. 2011) that we concentrate on developing a pedagogy of happiness and well-being, they argue that early years practitioners should create happy environments in which they nurture children and that this in turn will allow them to flourish. Therefore, it would seem that children need agency within their environment in order to challenge, stimulate and feed their need to explore, play, be curious and investigate. The EYFS (DfE 2012/14) recognises and provides for this through the overarching principle of Enabling

Environments, however, given the predominance of developmental approaches practitioners are often challenged to provide the environment described. Scoffham and Barnes (2011, p. 547), state that 'there is no direct route to happiness so it makes little sense to separate it from day-to-day teaching and the development of habits of mind'. If an early childhood education and care setting prioritises happiness it would seem that the flourishing of both the individual and the community would follow. Furthermore, Noddings (2003, p. 1) argues that 'happiness should be an aim of education', and, as Scoffham and Barnes (2011, p. 547) note, 'happy people are rarely mean, violent or cruel'. Therefore, it would appear that while happiness and flourishing are not one and the same it is unlikely that an individual or community can flourish with an absence of happiness.

- Happiness and flourishing are not one and the same thing but they are interrelated.
- A child will not be able to flourish without being happy.

Flourishing and educational practices

Grieshaber (2008) suggests that developmental norming means that development takes precedence over learning and that practitioners will seek to see what they need to see and ignore the expanse of maybe unintentional learning, which might be richer and beyond that which was sought. Murris (2013, p. 253) notes that 'The highly influential paradigm of developmental psychology is still pervasive in educational practice, despite decades of serious academic critique and challenge'. Matthews (1994) considers that children have been dealt great injustices by developmental psychologists 'whose regimes of truth' have dominated current educational practice and continue to do so. The current obsession with neo-liberal techno-rational assessment techniques is almost solely down to the ideologies of the developmental psychologists. The 'dangerous rise of therapeutic education' (Ecclestone and Hayes 2008) also comes from the same discipline. The dominance of developmental psychology on education continues to be challenged. Murris (2013) suggests that the dominance is immoral as it limits the possible in education. Developmental psychology treats children as 'becomings and not beings' (Murris 2013, p. 254). The calls for attention to the individual within education and not the 'developmental norm' have been dominant in the discourse of Robinson and Aronica (2016) for some time. This individualised approach to education should be the dominant discourse of the early childhood curricula and the documentation of learning.

Flourishing as being, becoming and having been

Notions of being and becoming have been identified by sociologists in the consideration of children and their position in society. Until the 1970s there was no consideration of childhood as a paradigm or an interest in its own right. However, from the latter half of the twentieth century onwards the rights of children and their position in society appeared to change. Prout and James (1997, p. 7) argue that the emerging childhood paradigm includes, 'an actively negotiated set of social relationships within which the early years of human life are negotiated'. They further argue that childhood is both de and re-constructed by and for children. The emerging paradigm allows us to reconstitute childhood, to consider how it has changed over time. As part of the new approach, 'we are saying that children are in and of the social world, part of the broader pattern of social change' (Wyness 2006, p. 84). These notions of children as part of the world around them, not simply as investments in the future, but also capable of commenting on their lives through their activities including their play has given children a new social status. Historically children were constructed as becomings or what they would be in the future, with an emphasis on adulthood as an ultimate goal or pinnacle of success. From the 1970s onwards children began to be constructed as beings, part of society in the moment (Corsaro 2011). Uprichard (2008) suggests that an either or approach is problematic; instead she suggests an integrated approach one in which children are considered to be framed by both their being and their becoming. Cross (2011) begins with the work of Uprichard (2008) stating that she appears to have developed a useful complexity model in considering the construction of children. Cross (2011) takes this a stage further arguing that children need to be considered as not simply beings and becomings but also as having beens; with their past experiences framing who they are now and how they will respond in a range of situations. Cross (2011, p. 31) suggests that, 'in bringing this third term into consideration, it is important to also consider children's own capacity to experience themselves as a human having been'. It would appear reasonable to argue that any interaction in the present will be influenced by what has occurred in the past. While very young children may not be able to effectively articulate their understanding of what prompts them to behave in particular ways in a given situation, it would appear though that their previous experiences will impact on their behaviours. A recognition of children as engaging with the world through all three of these states links with their ability to flourish. The flourishing child is able to comment on who they are now, who they may wish to become and what has influenced them.

- A becomings model of children does not support notions of flourishing.
- A recognition of the child engaging in their social world as being, becoming and having been actively supports their ability to flourish.

Flourishing: flow and play

Play can be argued to demonstrate opportunities for children to engage with the world as beings, becomings and having beens. Similarly play allows children to demonstrate flow. It enables them to be themselves and to demonstrate agency in the here and now, within their own social worlds. Broadhead (1997, 2001 and 2006) developed what she calls the, Social Play Continuum (SPC) an observational tool that can be used to gain insight into and to categorise learning processes while looking at; language, action and interaction. The research was developed across three phases, the first phase of data collection occurred in nursery settings, while the data for the second two phases was collected in Foundation Stage classes. Observations focused on specific activities, including: water, sand, role-play, small and large construction as well as small world play. Broadhead (1997, 2001 and 2006) used the continuum to identify characteristics of play in socio-cultural contexts. Her research builds on the social constructivist traditions of Vygotsky. She argues that language is the most powerful tool that children use to change themselves and to stimulate thought and learning. She believes that children learn in socio-cognitive contexts in which they, 'engage with learning in communities of learners' (ibid. 2006, p. 192). As such she sees that adults and more-able others hold a vital role in supporting learning within the zone of proximal development. She emphasises the early years literature that supports children's learning in an environment where they can learn together in creative and investigative ways. In a more recent piece of research she discusses the work of Piaget suggesting that it was his work that led the way in promoting active learning during the 1970s and 1980s, where play was seen at the core of the curriculum (Broadhead and Burt 2012). Broadhead (2001, 2006) goes on to suggest that the work of Vygotsky contextualises children's learning, recognising the impact of social interactions on cognition. It is as a result of his work that researchers have focused on childrens' interactions with each other. She argues that children need to be observed at play in order to conduct appropriate research that explores the cognitive development that occurs while children are engaged in a play-based curriculum. Such curricula provide opportunities for children to flourish as they are enabled to be themselves in the moment and to interact developing positive relationships with peers and adults.

Czikszentmihalyi (1990) suggests that when individuals are engaged in a flow like state they are absorbed, deeply concentrating in such a way as to make them unaware of their surroundings. They are usually challenging themselves by engaging in tasks that are stretching their abilities. Vygotsky (1978, p. 102) suggests that while a child is engaged, 'in play it is as though he were a head taller than himself', this shows how play offers the child the chance to develop and maximise their engagement. Likewise, both Vygotsky (1978) and Czikszentmihayli (1990) suggest that play or flow is not necessarily directly linked to pleasurable experiences, Vygotsky (1978) argues that pleasure cannot be seen as a defining characteristic of play that can lead to sharper experiences of pleasure. However, both Vygotsky (1978) and Czikszentmihayli (1990) would argue that flow and play can lead to longer term gains, which in turn will link clearly with the concepts that we are defining as flourishing. Others have used flow as the starting point for considering childrens' levels of engagement within an activity. As in the Social Play Continuum (Broadhead 1997, 2001, 2006) the Leuven Scales of Well-being and Involvement are concerned with children's involvement with their learning and their relationships with those around them (Laevers 2004). The Leuven Scales of well-being and involvement were developed out of work that was initiated in 1976 when a number of Flemish pre-school teachers working with two advisory teachers began to investigate and critically reflect on their practice (Laevers 2004). The concepts drew on the work of Czikszentmihayli's notions of flow, a state in which the participant is deeply involved and engaged in an activity (Laevers 2004). The initial research led to the development of the EXE-theory, Experiential Education, which was an approach that suggested that the most economic and effective method to assess the quality of a setting was to focus on two areas, 'the degree of "emotional well-being" and the level of "involvement"' (Laevers 1994 cited in Laevers 2004, p. 5).

Both the scales operate on a five-point system:

> from level 1 (no activity) through level 3 (child is engaged in an activity, but is functioning at a routine level) to level 5 (continuous, intense activity of the child, with purpose and pleasure).
>
> (Leavers 2004, p. 6)

He (ibid. 2004) goes on to explain that the scales have been used with high levels of reliability and validity throughout the world, but places particular emphasis on the Effective Early Learning project that was conducted in the UK by Pascal and Bertram (2000). Pascal and Bertram explain that they adopted the Leuven scales as part of the project because they felt that they were effective and focused on the processes of learning while being appropriately theoretically underpinned. The Leuven Scales were intended to support the development of quality in terms of content and outcomes (Laevers 2011). In terms of early years education and care they support a pedagogical approach that values play as an effective method of engaging children and supporting their learning and development. Both the SPC and the Leuven Scales consider play from the adult perspective, there is little opportunity for children to comment on their experiences. These three approaches to cognitive development and play demonstrate a pedagogy in which the child is at the centre of the process, where the concern is for the child and their ability to flourish.

- Play and play-based learning provides opportunities for children to flourish.
- Play and other activities can lead to longer-term benefits that support flourishing.

Flourishing in contexts

Within early childhood education and care settings, such as schools, little explicit attention has been paid to the flourishing of the children or communities. Cherkowski and Walker (2014, p. 202) suggest that, 'this is a significant gap in our field of study'. The early childhood sector is diverse within England and Wales, however, most children will attend some form of early childhood setting prior to entry in school. This can include, pre-schools settings within the community, private day nurseries, childrens' centres, maintained nurseries, childminders and a range of outdoor provision, which is currently on the increase. In all of these contexts the curricula that is delivered to the children is the same, but the ways in which they may receive it will be different.

Childminders who mainly operate within the home setting are often seen to give more nurturing familial care than those providing care in larger settings. Childminders historically were seen to provide for gaps in the childcare market, they were not particularly seen as a quality aspect of the early childhood sector. Fauth *et al.* (2013) suggested that parents saw placing their child with a childminder as being the next best thing to being at home with them. This was due to the individualised care that the childminder is able to offer, given that they can only have three children under the age of five including their own. The family, along with experience and the flexibility of the provision, are attractive aspects of the offer to many parents. Brooker (2016) has recently investigated parents' reasons for choosing childminders over other forms of early childhood provision and notes that happiness was seen as the first priority of parents who placed their children with childminders, believing that children's emotional security was the single most important concern for young children. Furthermore,

> A childminding environment was widely believed to be more con-ducive to children's emotional security than was nursery care, particularly for younger children, and some participants made this point forcefully.
>
> (ibid. 2016, p. 78)

Vincent *et al.* (2008) discuss the ways in which different groups of parents make choices about the childcare provision that they use looking at a group of middle class and a group of working class mothers. The middle class mothers prioritised the risk of emotional neglect in their choices whereas the working class mothers were more concerned about the physical safety of their children. These different groups appeared to perceive that their children needed different things in order to flourish. Therefore, it would seem that the context in which the child finds itself may well be determined not simply by the offerings with the locality but dependent on social class.

- Children in the early childhood sector in England follow the same curriculum, but may experience it very differently dependent on the type of setting that they are in.
- It would seem that little research has been done into the flourishing of the setting or community.

Conclusion

It would seem that the value that we place on differing aspects of child-care provision and how we construct that provision within a values base will have profound long-term consequences for the future flourishing of children. Consideration of the values and ethos created within a setting are of utmost importance, if we wish to develop the antecedents of a flourishing life. These aspects of ethos can often be forgotten in our attempts to survive a neo-liberal techno-rational world predicated on meeting developmental norms.

We believe that too great an emphasis is placed on the outcomes agenda, too much practitioner time is given to placating external agendas, attention is diverted away from the core values, which will engender flourishing leading to enhanced attainment. It would seem that happiness is central to this agenda and that when children are happy attainment and well-being follows. Happiness is a serious goal, not measurable, not recordable and reportable in any quantitative sense, but qualitatively a priority. The development of flourishing is holistic and all aspects of a child's life contribute to their ability to flourish. In terms of early childhood settings, it is essential that there is an ethos within the setting and the community that values this approach. If the practitioners are not supported to flourish themselves then they cannot authentically deliver this agenda.

REFLECTIVE QUESTIONS

■ Why should we be concerned about flourishing rather than attainment?
■ How does the way in which children are seen or constructed, impact on their ability to flourish?
■ In what ways can settings be supported to flourish?
■ Is a consideration of theorists such as: Aristotle, McMillan and Seligman, key to our current understanding of flourishing?

References

American Psychologist (2006) 'Martin Seligman Award for Scientific Contributions' in *American Psychologist*, 61(8), 772–774.

Aristotle (1925) *The Nicomachean Ethics*, Oxford: Oxford University Press.

Basford, J. and Bath C. (2014) 'Playing the assessment game: an English early childhood education perspective' in *Early Years*, 34(2), 119–132.

Bowlby, J. and Ainsworth, M. (1991) 'An ethological approach to personality development', *American Psychologist*, 46, 331–341.

Bradburn, E. (1989) *Margaret McMillan: Portrait of a Pioneer*. London: Routledge.

Brehony, K. (2009) 'Transforming theories of childhood and early childhood: child study and the empirical assault on Froebelian rationalism', *Paedagogica Historica*, 45(4), 585–604.

Broadhead, P. (1997) Promoting sociability and cooperation in nursery settings. *British Educational Research Journal*, 23(4), 513–531.

——. (2001) 'Investigating sociability and co-operation in four and five year olds in reception class settings' *International Journal of Early Years Education*, 9(1), 23–35.

——. (2006) Developing an understanding of young children's learning through play: the place of observation, interaction and reflection. *British Educational Research Journal*, 32(2), 191–207.

Broadhead, P. and Burt, A. (2012) *Understanding Young Children's Learning Through Play*. London: Routledge.

Brooker, L. (2016) 'Childminders, parents and policy: Testing the triangle of care', *Journal of Early Childhood Research*, 14(1), 69–83.

Cherkowski, S. and Walker, K. (2004) 'Flourishing communities: re-storying educational leadership using a positive research lens' *International Journal of Leadership in Education*, 17(2), 200–216.

Corsaro, W. (2011) *The Sociology of Childhood* 3rd ed. London: Sage.

Cross, B. (2011) 'Becoming, being and having been: practitioner perspectives on temporal stances and participation across children's services'. *Children and Society*, 25, 26–36.

Csikszentmihalyi, M. (1990) 'FLOW: The psychology of optimal experience', in *Global Learning Communities*, New York: Harper and Row.

De Ruyter, D. (2007) 'Ideals, education, and happy flourishing', in *Educational Theory*, 57(1), Illinois: University of Illinois.

DfE (2012) *Statutory Framework for the Early Years Foundation Stage*. Runcorn: DfE.

DuCharme, C. (1992) *Margaret McMillan and Maria Montessori: Champions of the poor*, Paper presented at the National Association for the Education of Young Children, New Orleans, LA, November 12–15, 1992.

Eaude, T. (2009) *Children's Spiritual, Moral, Social and Cultural Development*. Exeter: Learning Matters.

Ecclestone, K. and Hayes D. (2008) *The Dangerous Rise of Therapeutic Education*. London: Routledge.

Fauth, B. Renton, Z. and Solomon, E. (2013) *Tackling Child Poverty And Promoting Well-being: Lessons from abroad*. London: NCB.

Fraser, M. and Blishen, S. (2001) *Supporting Young People's Mental Health*. London: The Mental Health Foundation.

Giacdiello, P. (2013) *Pioneers in Early Childhood Education*. London: Routledge.

Grieshaber, S. 2008. 'Interrupting stereotypes: teaching and the education of young children' *Early Education & Development*, 19(3) pp. 505–518.

James, A. and Prout, A. (1997) *Constructing and Reconstructing Childhood Contemporary Issues in the Sociological Study of Childhood*. London: Falmer Press.

Kristjansson, K. (2013) 'There is something about Aristotle: the pros and cons of Aristotelianism in contemporary moral education', in *Journal of Philosophy of Education*, 48(1), 48–68.

Laevers, F. (2004) *Starting Strong Curricula and Pedagogies in Early Childhood Education and Care.* OECD.

Laevers, F. (2011) *Experiential Education: Making Care and Education More Effective Through Well-Being and Involvement.* Leuven: CEECD.

McLaughlin, C. (2008) 'Emotional well-being and its relationship to schools and classrooms: a critical reflection', Faculty of Education, University of Cambridge, Cambridge, UK.

Matthews, J. (1994) '. . . if radical education is to be anything more than radical pedagogy', in *Discourse*, 15(1), 60–72.

Murris, K. (2013) 'The epistemic challenge of hearing child's voice'. *Studies in the Philosophy of Education*, 32: 245–259.

Narvaez, D. (2015) 'Understanding flourishing: Evolutionary baselines and morality' *Journal of Moral Education*, 44(3), 253–262.

Noddings, N. (2003) *Happiness and Education.* Cambridge: Cambridge University Press.

——. (2012) *Philosophy of Education 3e*, Boulder: West View Press.

Pascal, C. and Bertram, T. (2000) *Further Memorandum from the Effective Early Learning Project (EY 81)* [online] Available from: www.publications.parliament.uk/pa/cm199900/cmselect/cmeduemp/386/0061406.htm [accessed] 16/06/14.

Prout, A. and James, A. (1997) 'A new paradigm for the sociology of childhood? Provenance, promise, problems'. In James, A. and Prout, A. (1997) *Constructing and Reconstructing Childhood Contemporary Issues in the Sociological Study of Childhood.* London: Falmer Press, pp. 7–33.

Read, J. (2011) 'Gutter to garden: historical discourses of risk in interventions in working class children's street play', *Children and Society*, 25(6), 421–434.

Robinson, K. and Aronica, L. (2016) *Creative Schools.* St. Ives: Penguin.

Rose, J. and Rogers, S. (2012) *The Role of the Adult in Early Years Settings.* Maidenhead: McGraw-Hill.

Scoffham, S. and Barnes, J. (2011) 'Happiness matters: towards a pedagogy of happiness and well-being' *The Curriculum Journal*, 12(4), 535–548.

Singer, P. (1993) *Practical Ethics 2e*, Cambridge: Cambridge University Press.

Taylor, E. (2001) 'Positive psychology and humanistic psychology: A reply to Seligman', *Journal of Humanistic Psychology*, 41(1), Winter 2001, 13–29.

Uprichard, E. (2008) 'Children as "being and becomings": children, childhood and temporality', in *Children and Society*, 22(4), 303–313.

Vincent, C., Braun, A. and Ball, S. (2008) 'Childcare, choice and social class: Caring for young children in the UK' *Critical Social Policy February*, 28, 5–26.

Vygotsky, L. (1978) *Mind in Society.* London: Harvard University Press.

Watson, D., Emery, C. and Bayliss, P. (2012) *Children's Social and Emotional Wellbeing in Schools a Critical Perspective*, Bristol: Policy Press.

Wyness, M. (2006) *Childhood and Society: An Introduction to the Sociology of Childhood.* Basingstoke: Palgrave Macmillan.

2 Constructs of the flourishing child

Luke Reynolds

Introduction

Initially considering the notion of flourishing and the ambiguity of childhood, as encompassed in its social construction, this chapter will examine the notion of the flourishing child as a fluid, evolving conception, which is influenced by social, political, cultural and historical parameters. With reference to children's play, creativity, critical thinking and early years policy, a critical stance will be adopted to affirm the understanding that the flourishing child can be constructed in a multiplicity of ways depending on who is defining it. As such, the flourishing child will be contemplated at the heart of interrelated, and often competing, micro, meso and macro systems of influence; systems that inevitably impact on our understanding of childhood, and what it means to be a child.

This chapter will consider the flourishing child in terms of the fulfilment of objectively identifiable *goods* and the way the child makes sense of these to flourish. From this perspective, the child will be contemplated in the broadest sense, whereby their holistic development will be examined to fulfil the extensive meanings the term flourishing has come to represent. It will progress to consider constructs of the flourishing child; it will do so in a critical sense to reaffirm the importance of acknowledging the unique child, while recognising the fluid, evolving nature of the construct of childhood. Initially, Rousseau and his influence on early years pedagogy and play will be discussed. However, before progressing to consider constructs of the flourishing child, it is firstly pertinent to explore the social construction of childhood.

Understanding flourishing

When considering human *flourishing*, De Ruyter (2007) distinguishes between eudaimonic and hedonistic theories, and the way they can be utilised to describe the quality of a person's life in terms of objective and subjective characteristics. Eudaimonic theories, concerning the objective characteristics of flourishing, suggest that human flourishing occurs through the acquirement of a set of fundamental *goods*, which are founded on the biological characteristics of human beings. For instance, it is difficult to argue that health, physical activity, safety, social relations, and intellectual and creative development are not essential to the notion of flourishing. This is not dissimilar to Maslow's (1970) hierarchy of needs, where it is claimed that in order to reach a state of self-actualisation, it is a necessity for a person to firstly satisfy their physiological, safety, social and esteem needs. This notion is also considered in Aristotle's (1980) *Nicomachean Ethics*, where it is stated that flourishing for animals occurs only when they are functioning well according to their natures. In this case, the term *nature* could be used synonymously with the aforementioned eudaimonic *goods* to imply the fundamental physiological and biological characteristics required for flourishing to occur. However, Aristotle (1980) also claims that in order to function well according to their nature, human beings must act with reason in accordance with moral and intellectual virtue. As such, it can be seen here that flourishing must not only be considered in terms of eudaimonic theories, but should also be examined in terms of those subjective, hedonistic theories, whereby human beings flourish only if they feel or are aware of their flourishing. For example, De Ruyter (2007) suggests that humans only exist in a flourishing state if they actually believe they are flourishing; a hedonistic view that emphasises the importance of acknowledging the possibility of an individual experiencing a positive state of mind regardless of what is invoking the positive feelings. As such, the individual is capable of constructing his or her own interpretation of what makes them flourish, according to what they value, what is advantageous to them, and the satisfaction they receive. From this, it would be an over-simplification to consider the flourishing child in terms of two binary, conflicting categories; eudaimonic and hedonistic. However, before progressing to consider constructs of the flourishing child, it is firstly pertinent to explore the social construction of childhood.

- ■ Flourishing is underpinned by a number of fundamental requirements including; being healthy, having affective social relationships and having their physical needs met.

■   At the same time they can only flourish when they are aware that they are flourishing.

Childhood: a social construction

As an amateur historian, Aries (1962) sought to prove that the model of the traditional twentieth-century family was not in decline as conservative claims were suggesting, and embarked to map the role of the child in family relations throughout history. Having attempted this, Aries (1962: 125) controversially concluded that, 'in medieval society the idea of childhood did not exist'. He argued that during the Middle Ages, children, although existing as young members of the human species, were not categorised, differentiated or classified as anything distinctive to adults. Concisely, rather than being seen in the social category of 'childhood', children were merely observed as existing as under-developed adults. Although Aries' (1962) assertions provided a platform to critique the current thinking about children and their relation to society, his work is not without critique (Heywood 2001). For example, Aries' methodology relied on the analyses of diaries found in literate aristocratic homes to make sweeping claims about childhood, with his reliance on generalising and his use of limited sources forming the basis of such critique (De Mause 1976; Pollock 1983; Shahar 1990). Yet, in spite of this, his affirmation of 'childhood' being fluid and relative, while evolving in time and place, is still respected today. Moreover, the shifting, evolving nature of the 'child' and 'childhood' is repeatedly demonstrated in the works of numerous key thinkers in education. For example, Thomas Hobbes (1558–1679) observes children as innately evil, having been born unruly and anarchistic; John Locke (1632–1704) suggests children are born as blank slates, who can be moulded and shaped by their environments and adults; while Jean-Jacques Rousseau (1712–78) portrays children as being naturally good, with childhood being a time of innocence. In short, childhood, and flourishing, must be considered as social constructs.

According to May (2011: 7), social constructionism analyses 'how a particular way of defining something came about, and why it continues to be so'; a theoretical orientation, which considers ways of seeing and analysing social reality by acknowledging the processes and relationships that produce lived reality. Involving evolving human interaction at the micro, meso and macro levels of society, Gergen and Gergen (2003: 2) describe social constructionism as an

> unfolding dialogue among participants who vary considerably in their logics, values and visions.

Such a depiction emphasises the aforementioned construct of childhood flowing and progressively changing across time and place, with any attempted definition being bound by these contextual parameters. The main tenets of social constructionism themselves, as outlined by Gergen (1985 cited in Burr 2003), act to reaffirm the understanding of the fluidity of childhood.

- Aries claims that a concept of childhood did not exist in medieval times and that it is a construct that has been developed much more recently.
- Childhood is a fluid state and has been described in a variety of different ways across the centuries.

The unique child

Thus far, the argument has been made that childhood does not exist in a natural, essential state, where undeniable facts and unquestionable truths concerning its definition enable us to definitively 'know' about the child and how the child flourishes. Alternatively, the case has been made to suggest that the term 'childhood', and its interpretations, arise from our collective meaning-making and the way discourses allow such meaning to be articulated and represented in society. After all, Hall and Geiben (1992: 295) describe discourses as 'ways of talking, thinking or representing a particular subject or topic. They produce meaningful knowledge about the subject. This knowledge influences social practices, and so has real consequences and effects'. However, care has to be taken to avoid, what James and James (2004: 15) refer to as, conceptual slippage. In this, it is described how the concept of the 'child' is being mistakenly used as a generalised representation for the collectivity of 'children'; an assertion that suggests what is collectively and culturally 'normal' for children, can be comfortably applied to the individual child. In spite of this, 'best interests' for children are culturally and structurally specific, and therefore fail to recognise the unique child.

Rousseau on the developing child

According to Darling and Nordenbo (2003), Jean-Jacques Rousseau is one of the 'intellectual giants' of the Western world, being considered the primary philosopher to advance the notion of progressive education by advocating a child-centred approach founded in naturalism and romanticism. For Grieshaber and McArdle (2010), Rousseau's ideas of children existing as 'naturally good' beings – experiencing healthy development if guided by nature – are highly influential in the way we view and understand early childhood pedagogy and play today. O'Hagan (2001) describes Rousseau as a romantic naturalist, where his ideas initiated a stream of thinking based upon the metaphors of health and growth. As part of this, Rousseau rejected the Christian notion of 'original sin' and instead promoted the view of innate human goodness. Barrow and Woods (2006) explain how Rousseau believed children would most likely experience healthy development if they were guided by nature rather than society. With children being naturally good, their education should allow their inherent goodness to unfold without societal interferences, which would lead to their corruption (Carr 2003; Matheson 2008). If not interfered with, the innate goodness within children would unfold to create a society that was more harmonious and less restrictive (Carr 2003; O'Hagan 2001). To outline such concepts, Rousseau wrote of the life of a fictional character, *Emile*, detailing the educational programme that a young boy should follow through to adulthood (Trohler 2012).

In openly opposing the Christian notion of 'original sin' in *Emile*, Rousseau was essentially advocating themes of freedom, naturalism and originality (Scholz 2010). Ideas such as the child being naturally good, lead to Rousseau reasoning that play is a natural thing and children should have freedom to play (Grieshaber and McCardle 2010). This is clearly demonstrated where Rousseau states, 'let them [children] eat, run and play as much as they want' (Rousseau, 1762/2007: 2003 cited in Grieshaber and McCardle 2010: 3). For Wood and Attfield (2005), it is the work of Rousseau that initially underpins the strong regard for which play is observed in early years education, with play being noted across the sector as an essential attribute to any child's learning and development. For example, the statutory framework for the Early Years Foundation Stage (DfE 2014: 9) states that 'Each area of learning and development must be implemented through planned, purposeful play ... Play is essential for children's development, building their confidence as they learn to explore, to think about problems, and relate to others'. Although the wording in this statement may be in conflict with other definitions of play, which emphasise its spontaneity and impulsiveness (Bateson and Martin 2013; Brown and Patte 2012; Frost 2010), it is clear that play is of significance to the flourishing child and will now be deliberated in greater depth.

- Rousseau is described as a romantic naturalist who believed that children were naturally good.
- According to Rousseau children learn best away from society in a natural environment.

Flourishing and play

The term 'play' is of great difficulty to define. Not only does it exist as a noun, verb and adjective, but its meaning is ambiguous and subjective, whereby a multiplicity of understandings and interpretations have been applied to this singular, yet powerful, word. Smidt (2011) defines play in terms of problem solving, exploration and experience, and expression and communication, with each of these elements combining to make the play purposeful for the child. Bateson and Martin (2013: 2), however, describe play as being spontaneous and rewarding to the individual; actualising from the child's intrinsic motivation; occurring in a safe, protected context; observed as being exaggerated or incomplete when compared to non-playful adult behaviour and performed repeatedly. Conversely, Brown and Patte (2013) acknowledge the observation of some classic and contemporary scholars that play exists in opposition to work, where play is thought of as trivial and frivolous in comparison to work of a more serious nature, be that in school or adult life. Encompassing the far-reaching meanings play has come to represent, Moyles (1994:5 cited in Andrews 2012: 10) suggests that, 'Grappling with the concept of play can be analogised to trying to seize bubbles, for every time there appears to be something to hold on to, its ephemeral nature disallows it being grasped!'. Yet in spite of the varying definitions, there is generally an accepted consensus that play is an essential contributor to a child's flourishing; specifically, promoting a child's personal, social, emotional and physical development. It is therefore not surprising that the statutory framework for the Early Years Foundation Stage (DfE 2014) suggests that purposeful play should be used as a vehicle to promote development in three prime areas: communication and language; physical development; and personal, social and emotional development.

Be that as it may, Brown and Patte (2012) claim that policy, as outlined above, is resulting in play being utilised in early years settings as a mechanism to encourage children to achieve specified learning outcomes as a form of early academic preparation. In doing so, settings are failing to provide children with adequate opportunities for unstructured, spontaneous play. As such, it is proposed that children are missing out on the freedom to engage in and direct their play around their own interests and curiosity; an essential component of their development and flourishing. However, this seems to be at odds with the statutory framework for the Early Years Foundation Stage, where it is stated that:

> Children learn by leading their own play, and by taking part in play which is guided by adults . . . As children grow older, and as their development allows, it is expected that the balance will gradually shift towards more activities led by adults, to help children prepare for more formal learning, ready for Year 1.
>
> (DfE 2014: 9)

From this, it can be seen that there is the expectation that children have the opportunity to engage in their own unstructured play. Simultaneously, there is also an undertone of early years education being about the preparation of children for school. This is further emphasised in the Early Years Teachers' Standards (National College for Teaching & Leadership 2013), where in all eight standards, the word 'play' is not mentioned once, even though there are two standard indicators dedicated to the understanding of teaching early mathematics and systematic synthetic phonics! As such, a deficiency in opportunities for unstructured play is likely to be the product of the performativity and accountability agendas.

- Play; unstructured and freely chosen can be considered to be an essential element of flourishing.
- Play as described in the EYFS (2012/14) appears to be underpinned by an agenda that is focused on attainment and outcomes.

Flourishing and the neo-liberal agenda

According to Bauman (2012), it is the recklessness of neo-liberalism and consumer markets that seeks to capitalise on any human problem, with the ability to transform every protest and countervailing force into its advantage and profit, with this being responsible for the creation of a culture of performativity and accountability in education, which seeks to hold individuals responsible for educational outcomes (Headington 2000). For Ellyatt (2011) the performativity and accountability agenda existing in today's education system is responsible for the creation of a generation of children who are profoundly disengaged from the joy of learning; with conformity, standardisation and credentialisation acting to substitute an educational experience that could embrace diversity, complexity, critical thinking, multiple perspectives and subjectivity.

As such, this chapter has reached a stage where the flourishing child can be considered in two distinct ways. According to the literature on children's play, the flourishing child is one who has opportunities to explore, indulge their curiosities and interests, while developing intellectually, physically, socially and emotionally through the unfolding of their unstructured play. Alternatively, neo-liberalism and its associated performativity and accountability agenda(s) frames the flourishing child as one who is competently acquiring the dispositions, skills and appropriate knowledge to be able to successfully secure employment in adulthood. From a Foucauldian perspective, this requires normalising judgement to occur during the child's education, whereby children are compared and differentiated in accordance with a desired norm in order to establish homogeneity (Foucault 1979). Yet, in spite of the dichotomous way these two notions of flourishing have been portrayed, the attributes and characteristics that constitute the flourishing child, from both perspectives, are not mutually exclusive.

- The neo-liberal agenda is hijacking education and leads to children being disengaged from the joys of learning.
- Performativity and flourishing are not necessarily mutually exclusive, however, it is the way in which children are given opportunities to develop which is essential.

Flourishing and creativity

According to Jesson (2012), it is difficult to define creativity as it does not exist as quality or an outcome, but is involved with the people, processes or products included in its inception. To overcome this, she instead refers to a set of behaviours, which constitute creativity, drawing from the contents of a Qualifications and Curriculum Authority (2004, cited in Jesson 2012: 5) report titled '*Creativity: Find it! Promote it!*'. Adapted from this, creativity is defined in terms of five creative behaviours:

> Creativity is much more than an exploration of artistic ideas, and should involve questioning and challenging, making connections and seeing relationships, envisaging alternatives/seeing things in new ways, exploring ideas and keeping options open, and reflecting critically on ideas and outcomes.

This definition sits in stark contrast to what McArdle (2003 cited in Grieshaber and McArdle 2010: 42) describes as 'bunny-bum art', whereby school children are required to glue cotton wool on the tail section of template rabbits, each producing a near-identical end result as part of an art project; a process that meets none of the criterion for creativity as outlined above. Yet, this does act to highlight the often-accepted notion that creativity is synonymous with art, whereby cutting, sticking, painting and gluing often take place within a designated 'creative area' in some early years settings. Yet, for Bateson and Martin (2013: 3), creativity, as 'developing a novel form of behaviour or novel idea, regardless of its practical uptake and subsequent application', can be inspired through children's play. As part of this, play is considered to produce innovative ways of thinking and behaving when the child has to interact with and negotiate their environment in order for their play to develop and evolve. This notion is emphasised in *Development Matters* (The British Association for Early Childhood Education 2012: 5), whereby it is suggested that characteristics of effective learning include playing and exploring, active learning and creating and thinking critically; all of which could be encompassed in the above definitions of creativity.

Furthermore, Fisher (2004) suggests that the only way to fully engage children with their learning is to promote creative thinking, with those children whom are encouraged to think creatively showing increased levels of motivation and self-esteem. This is observed to be the result of the children actively questioning, making new connections, challenging ideas, representing ideas in different ways and applying imagination in finding new or innovative outcomes (Wegerif 2010; Usher and Kober 2013). Through participating in this form of learning, it is thought that children develop a sense of ownership and responsibility for their learning, which not only increases motivation, but also allows for deepened conceptual understandings to develop (Fisher 2004).

Moreover, Jones and Wyse (2004) suggest that children's aptitude for creative thinking can be supported by valuable opportunities for experiential learning, where pupils can actively experiment to develop their own predictions, ideas, meanings and concepts. For example, Kolb and Kolb (2005) put forward a model of experiential learning in which concrete experience, reflective observation, abstract conceptualisation and active experimentation complement one another in forming a learning cycle. Concrete experience occurs when the child experiences something new. The child is then able to reflect on the experience through analysing the events and any inconsistencies between the experience and understanding. Opportunity for reflection provides the child with new ideas or reasoning for the modification of existing concepts, which could subsequently be applied and tested in future scenarios through active experimentation. By claiming all learning is relearning, Kolb and Kolb (2005) suggest that the learning cycle facilitates children in drawing out their own ideas and beliefs so that they can be examined, tested and integrated with new, more refined ideas. Although this may seem aspirational in the early years, it is certainly achievable with adult support.

For example, stemming from the Researching Effective Pedagogy in the Early Years (REPEY) study (Siraj-Blatchford *et al.* 2002), *sustained shared thinking* is advocated for its significance in enhancing early years performance; an episode in which children can work with other children, or more commonly adult(s), to advance and broaden their thinking.

Siraj-Blatchford *et al.* define it as:

> An episode in which two or more individuals 'work together' in an intellectual way to solve a problem, clarify a concept, evaluate activities, extend a narrative etc. Both parties must contribute to the thinking and it must develop and extend.
>
> (2002: 8)

Using this definition as the base for discussion, Brodie (2014) deconstructs its meaning to appreciate its implications. Here it is discussed how working together often refers to the working partnership between an adult or a child, or a child and child, where one member is considered to be more knowledgeable than the other. The term 'work' refers to an active and creative process; one which can be considered in similar terms the characteristics of effective learning as outlined in *Development Matters* (The British Association for Early Childhood Education 2012: 5) – playing and exploring (engagement), active learning (motivation), and creating and thinking critically (thinking). In this, the practitioner and child work in partnership, whereby the practitioner is responsible for clarifying and developing concepts for the child's understanding through conversational learning. Perhaps here it is useful to make reference to Bloom's Taxonomy (Bloom *et al.* 1956) as a way of effecting this advancing dialogue.

According to Bloom *et al.* (1956), knowledge and the development of intellectual thought, can be considered in terms of a hierarchy of cognitive processes, which range from lower to higher orders of cognitive thinking. The suggested orders of thinking begin at the knowledge level, and progress through comprehension, application, analyses, synthesis and evaluation, from lower order to higher order thinking skills. Using this as a framework for sustained shared thinking, it is possible for practitioners to develop and extend a child's thinking progressively in accordance with the taxonomy. In practice, this may be achieved through suggesting, reminding, recapping, modelling, speculating, questioning, reciprocating and clarifying as part of the ongoing dialogue with the child. In essence, Brodie (2014) proposes that developing children's critical thinking skills is core to sustained shared thinking, whereby children begin to develop the capacity to consider their own thinking through meta-cognition. The importance of doing so is emphasised by Cropley (2001), where it is claimed that the dominant characteristic of modern life is that it is subject to unprecedented rapid change. Past transmissive approaches to education defined a child's intelligence in terms of their ability to acquire socially relevant and valued information, rapidly and accurately recall this when required, and then apply it to already known situations (Tucker 2012). Cropley (2011) suggests that such an approach to teaching and learning is no longer acceptable, as the knowledge and skills needed for the future remain unknown. Instead, education should prepare children to be flexible and display openness and adaptability in the face of the unexpected; an acknowledgement that reiterates the importance of fostering creativity and critical thinking in children in order for them to flourish. However, this notion is neither original nor novel.

- Creativity is an essential element of flourishing but is not confined to activities associated with art.
- Creative thinking is an essential skill, which supports flourishing and that children can be supported to develop.

Troubling play, power relationships and flourishing

Up until this point the assumption has been made that play is the pre-dominant vehicle in the construction of the flourishing child and, indeed, this chapter has provided evidence to suggest this. Yet, in recognition of James and James' (2004: 15) aforementioned notion of conceptual slip-page – where the concept of the child is mistakenly used as a general-ised representation for the collectivity of children – it is pertinent here to discuss what Grieshaber and McArdle (2010) title 'the trouble with play'. As part of this, it is suggested that, even though play is often depicted as a fun and innocent engine for the development, learning and flourishing of all children, it is also a complex element of childhood where 'power relations are played out in terms of "race", class, socioeconomic status, gender, age, size, skin colour, sexuality, heteronormativity, proficiency with English, and more' (Grieshaber 2008 cited in Grieshaber and McArdle 2010: 8). For example, through a practitioner's observa-tion of 'block play area' in an early years setting, MacNaughton (1997) acknowledges the gendered power-relations that exhibit themselves in such play. In this case, focus was given to the way in which boys domineeringly acquired and territorialised this space, and the failure of practitioners in recognising the significance gender holds in children's play and their everyday lives. A similar observation has been made by Stephenson (2011), where it is described how, through superhero play, many boys strive to define themselves by gender, often using threatening behaviour as an expression of control and power over girls.

In spite of this, to disengage the gender power relations in play, Broadhead and Burt (2012) suggest the use of open-ended play, where adults create and sustain an environment that allows children's interests and experiences to emerge and develop, while the adults systematically look for ways to extend these opportunities. As part of open-ended play, it is claimed there is the potential for matching the respective interests arising from the gendered preferences of both boys and girls. Broadhead and Burt (2012) continue to state that this can result in mixed gendered groups working together to reach joint goals and achievements, instead of being preoccupied with meeting gendered expectations. Further-more, MacNaughton (1997) outlines the necessity for practitioners to reconstruct their pedagogical gazes in order to observe and acknowledge the gendered child. Although both of these suggestions are centred on gendered power relations, there is nothing to suggest that the skilled practitioner could not use open-ended play as an opportunity to engage and inspire all children, regardless of the power relations that may exist. Even though such relations may never be wholly disengaged, through skillful planning and a restructuring of practitioners' pedagogical gazes to recognise the children's exercise of power, some of the existing 'dark play' (Sutton-Smith 1997 cited in Grieshaber and McArdle 2010: 8) might be mitigated.

- Children can use power inappropriately in their play in order to demonstrate their notion of self.
- Practitioners need to carefully consider how such power is managed.

Flourishing and the home

Yet, this chapter has highlighted a prominent dichotomy in the understanding of children's play. On the one hand, the flourishing child is observed as being curious, and independent; capable of directing their own play in line with their individual interests and discoveries. This is commensurate with Rousseau's understanding of the child being 'naturally good' and experiencing healthy development if guided by nature. Conversely, there appears to be a continuous appetite for adult intervention and guidance. According to Robinson (2013), this could be explained by the construction of childhood innocence as a regulatory tool. In this, the historical construction of childhood innocence – that referring to simplicity, naiveté and lack of knowledge and understanding – is responsible for the dualistic relationship between childhood and adulthood, whereby adults supposedly possess the appropriate knowledge a child should acquire, and childhood is concerned with the child amassing such knowledge; this acting to preserve relations of power in the Western world. Be that as it may, this chapter has attempted to consider the role the early years practitioner or teacher has in enabling a child to flourish. However, it is now appropriate to consider the role of the child's upbringing.

In his understanding of *habitus*, Bourdieu (1977) attempts to provide challenge to existing notions of human agency as being reliant on consciousness, or human choice, being located within an independent, non-partisan autonomy. As part of this, it is suggested that our thoughts, perceptions and feelings are fashioned and moulded from the deposited remains of our prior experiences, which we remain widely unaware of. Therefore, human behaviour is reliant on improvisation, where our dispositions result in practices that are considered ordinary without being directed by consciousness – the admission of a social learning process that involves the norms and rules of society becoming internalised by the habitual repetition of professed bodily, affective and cognitive repertoires (Chandler 2013). For Bourdieu (1977: 45) the habitus is a means of conceptualising 'conditioned and conditional freedom' in a way that departs from freedom being observed as the result of chance or the development of critical consciousness, as outlined by Freire (1972), which can bring about liberation. Instead, the habitus is considered 'beyond the grasp of consciousness . . . cannot be touched by voluntary, deliberate transformation, cannot even be made explicit' (Bourdieu 1977: 93–94). It assimilates the consequences of one's social background, and controls the way in which information and resources are used to inform human action (Crossley 2005). Having an appreciation for the role of the habitus is necessary for understanding the way a child can flourish in terms of what Bourdieu (1986) refers to as 'capital'.

When one considers the term capital, it is likely to conjure images of economics, monetary value and property (Crossley 2005). Yet for Bourdieu (1986), the term capital refers to forms of resources that are available to individuals, which are not necessarily reducible to money. The term capital represents the different resources that individuals utilise in their everyday lives, and in which individuals actively seek in recognition of their worth (Moore 2004). It defines the parameters in which individuals are compared against each other, and how they are considered advantaged or disadvantaged in relative positions to those who occupy more or less capital (Coleman 2007; Moore 2004; Layder 2006). Asides from economic capital, which denotes an individual's accumulated wealth, Bourdieu (1986) designates three other distinct forms: social capital, cultural capital and symbolic capital. Cultural capital is concerned with the cultural assets one acquires, which regulate social mobility, distinct from economic capital (Bennett and Savage 2004; Modood 2004). Social capital refers to the social networks and relationships the individual belongs to (Moore 2004), while symbolic capital recognises the high regard of societal status and its value in obtaining advantages for oneself (Bourdieu 1992).

According to Bourdieu and Passeron (1977), the education system comprehensively characterises specific traits and dispositions as respected and valued, while others remain underrated and undermined. This is achieved by the cultural capital explicitly corresponding to the cultural field, or in this case schooling, whereby the system approves certain dispositions and knowledge at the detriment of others (Bourdieu 1986). Here it is admissible to frequent the aforementioned idea of Apple (2013) that schools maintain and disseminate 'legitimate knowledge' in ways that give cultural legitimacy to the knowledge of specific groups in society. As part of this, the ability of a group to effectively share their knowledge widely is reliant on that group's power in the larger political and economic arena, with power and culture being seen as inseparable entities interwoven with existing economic relations in society (Apple 2013). Bourdieu and Passeron (1977) suggest that the education system operates as to reproduce the class structure in society by favouring and rewarding the forms of cultural capital that are concentrated within the middle classes. Schools and teachers aid in cultural reproduction by rewarding the possession of elite cultural capital in pupils from middle-class and privileged backgrounds. Thus, through socialisation and parents endowing their offspring with economic, social, symbolic and cultural capital, the social class system is preserved and emulated (Tzanakis 2011; Webb *et al.* 2002). Furthermore, Winkle-Wagner (2010: 18) claims that working-class children are indigent in the superior forms of cultural capital, with schools making little attempt to lessen its obscurity:

> Pedagogic actions in education may require an initial familiarity with the dominant culture. Yet education does *not* transmit an explicit understanding of dominant culture . . . Thus, education requires of everyone what it does not give.
>
> (Winkle-Wagner 2010: 18)

As such, it is possible for the flourishing child to be observed in terms of their acquired capital through childhood, and the ways they are able to utilise this in their education; or more specifically, the ways in which it is recognised and rewarded in the education system. Therefore, the child's flourishing cannot be assumed to take place in a vacuum, but rather transpires as part of a complex system of interrelated parts. This is commensurate with Bronfenbrenner's ecological model of childhood (1979). In this, varying environmental systems are considered and the way in which these impact on child development. At the microsystem level, the family is highlighted as the context for the child's earliest experiences, which are influenced and impacted on by all the surrounding systems. These include mesosystems, where interaction occurs between microsystems; the exosystem, which contains the community and localised context; the macrosystem, in which political ideologies and social structures are located; and finally the chronosystem, which acknowledges the historical changes that impact on all other systems. In short, McDowall Clark (2013: 14) claims that the model can 'help us understand and recognise the different contexts which impact on childhood. This can help support understanding of what childhood is, what it means and the ways we behave towards children as a result'. Once again, this emphasises the inherent complexity associated with determining the flourishing child, whereby the construction of childhood is fluid, relative, and evolving in time and place.

- The capital that the child is endowed with in the home environment will impact on their experiences of education and this can occur both positively and negatively.
- The child is not growing up in a vacuum but will be impacted by a range of experiences many of which are beyond the control of either the home or the setting.

Conclusion

Although it is often expected for a chapter to reach a conclusion based on its findings, in this case, the word 'conclusion' seems inappropriate. A word that signifies closure, completion and certitude – its use appears impertinent in this context, having spent considerable time formulating the argument that understandings of the flourishing child are fluid and relative in nature, and cannot be defined in terms of facts, certainty and inevitability. This has certainly been emphasised through discussion of the social construction of childhood, and the culminating understanding that the child exists at the heart of a complex arrangement of interrelated, impacting systems. Even though the chapter has attempted to examine some constructs of the flourishing child, such interpretations are but a few of the innumerable understandings of what this actually means or looks like. As such, this chapter has demonstrated the complexity associated with early childhood; a stage of the life course, which is so embedded in cultural and social norms that its complications and intricacies dissolve into common-sense assumptions and understandings.

REFLECTIVE QUESTIONS

- In what way is childhood a social construction?
- How does Rousseau's notion of a natural childhood influence current thinking?
- Why is creativity a central component in supporting flourishing?
- What are the responsibilities of practitioners in relation to a child's *cultural capital* and their ability to flourish?

References

Andrews, M. (2012) *Exploring Play for Early Childhood Studies*, London: Sage.

Apple, M. (2013) *Can Education Change Society?* Abingdon, Oxon: Routledge.

Aries, P. (1962) *Centuries of Childhood: A Social History of Family Life*. London: Jonathan Cape Ltd.

Aristotle (1980) *Nicomachean Ethics*; translated with an introd. by David Ros; rev. by J. O. Urmson. Oxford: Oxford University Press.

Barrow, R. and Woods, R. (2006) *An Introduction to Philosophy of Education 4e*. Abingdon: Routledge.

Bateson, P. and Martin, P. (2013) *Play, Playfulness, Creativity and Innovation*. Cambridge: Cambridge University Press.

Bauman, Z. (2012) *On Education: Conversations with Riccardo Mazzeo*. Cambridge: Polity Press.

Bennett, T. and Savage, M. (2004) 'Introduction: Cultural capital and cultural policy', in *Cultural Trends*, 13(2), 7–14.

Bloom, B., Engelhart, M., Furst, E., Hill, W. and Krathwohl, D. (1956) *Taxonomy of Educational Objectives, Handbook I: The Cognitive Domain*. New York: David McKay.

Bourdieu, P. (1977) *Outline of a Theory of Practice*. Cambridge: Cambridge University Press.

——. (1986) 'The forms of capital', in Richardson, J. (ed.) (1986) *Handbook of Theory and Research for Sociology of Education*. New York: Greenwood.

——. (1992) *Language and Symbolic Power*. Cambridge: Polity Press.

Broadhead, P. and Burt, A. (2012) *Understanding Young Children's Learning Through Play: Building Playful Pedagogies*. London: Routledge.

Brodie, K. (2014) *Sustained Shared Thinking in the Early Years*. Abingdon: Routledge.

Bronfenbrenner, U. (1979) *The Ecology of Human Development*. Cambridge, MA: Harvard University Press.

Brown, F. and Patte, M. (2012) *Rethinking Children's Play*. London: Bloomsbury Academic.

Burr, V. (2003) *Social Constructionism 2e*. London: Routledge.

Carr, D. (2003) *Making Sense of Education: An Introduction to the Philosophy and Theory of Education and Teaching*. Abingdon: Routledge.

Chandler, B. (2013) 'The Subjectivity of Habitus', in *Journal for the Theory of Social Behaviour*, 43(4), 469–491.

Coleman, J. (2007) 'Social capital in the creation of human capital', in Sadovnik, R. (ed.) (2007) *Sociology of Education: A Critical Reader*. Abingdon: Routledge.

Cropley, A. (2001) *Creativity in Education and Learning: A Guide for Teachers and Educators*. Oxon: RoutledgeFalmer.

Crossley, N. (2005) *Key Concepts in Critical Social Theory*. London: Sage.

Darling, J. and Nordenbo, S. (2003) 'Progressivism' in Blake, N., Smeyers, P., Smith, R. and Standish, P. (eds) (2003) *Philosophy of Education*. Oxford: Blackwell.

De Mause, L. (1976) *The History of Childhood*. London: Bellew.

De Ruyter, D. (2007) 'Ideals, education, and happy flourishing', in *Educational Theory*, 57(1), 23–35.

DfE. (2014) Statutory framework for the early years foundation stage: setting the standards for learning, development and care for children from birth to five. [Online] Available from: www.gov.uk/government/uploads/system/uploads

attachment_data/file/335504/EYFS_framework_from_1_September_2014__
with_clarification_note.pdf [accessed 31 October 2015]

Ellyatt, W. (2011) 'The Democratization of Learning', in House, R. (ed.) (2011) *Too Much, Too Soon? Early Learning and the Erosion of Childhood.* Stroud: Hawthorn Press.

Fisher, R. (2004) 'What is Creativity?' in Fisher, R. and Williams, M. (eds) (2004) *Unlocking Creativity: Teaching Across the Curriculum.* London: David Fulton.

Foucault, M. (1979) *Discipline and Punish: The Birth of the Prison.* London: Penguin Group.

———. (1989) *The Order of Things: Archaeology of the Human Sciences.* London: Routledge.

Freire, P. (1972) *Pedagogy of the Oppressed.* Harmondsworth: Penguin.

Frost, J. (2010) *A History of Children's Play and Play Environments: Toward a Contemporary Child-Saving Movement.* New York: Routledge.

Gergen, M. and Gergen, K. (2003) 'The social construction of the real and the good', in Gergen, M. and Gergen, K. (eds) (2003) *Social Constructionism: A Reader.* London: Sage.

Grieshaber, S. and McArdle, F. (2010) *The Trouble with Play.* Berkshire: Open University Press.

Hall, S. and Geiben, B. (1992) *Formations of Modernity.* Cambridge: Polity Press.

Headington, R. (2000) *Monitoring, Assessment, Recording, Reporting and Accountability.* London: David Fulton.

Heywood, C. (2001) *A History of Childhood.* Cambridge: Polity Press.

James, A. and James, A. (2004) *Constructing Childhood.* Basingstoke: Palgrave Macmillan.

Jesson, J. (2012) *Developing Creativity in the Primary School.* Berkshire: Open University Press.

Jones, R. and Wyse, D. (2004) *Creativity in the Primary Curriculum.* London: David Fulton.

Kolb, A. and Kolb, D. (2005) 'Learning styles and learning spaces: enhancing experiential learning in higher education', in *Academy of Management, Learning and Education*, 4(2), 193–212.

Layder, D. (2006) *Understanding Social Theory 2e.* London: Sage.

McDowall Clark, M. (2013) *Childhood in Society for the Early Years.* London: SAGE.

MacNaughton, G. (1997) 'Feminist praxis and the gaze in the early childhood curriculum', in *Gender and Education*, 9(3), 317–326.

Maslow, A. (1970) *Motivation and Personality.* New York: Harper & Row.

Matheson, C. (2008) 'Ideology in education in the United Kingdom', in Matheson, D. (ed.) (2008) *An Introduction to the Study of Education 3e.* Oxon: Routledge.

May, V. (2011) *Sociology of Personal Life.* Basingstoke: Palgrave.

Mills, S. (2003) *Routledge Critical Thinkers: Michel Foucault.* London: Routledge.

Modood, T. (2004) 'Capitals, ethnic identity and educational qualifications', in *Cultural Trends*, 13(2), 87–105.

Moore, R. (2004) *Education and Society: Issues and Explanations in the Sociology of Education.* Cambridge: Polity Press.

National College for Teaching & Leadership (2013) *Teachers' Standards (Early Years): from September 2013.* [Online] Available from: www.gov.uk/government/uploads/system/uploads/attachment_data/file/211646/Early_Years_Teachers__Standards.pdf [accessed 31 October 2015]

O'Hagan, T. (2001) 'Jean-Jacques Rousseau', in Palmer, J. (ed.) (2001) *Fifty Major Thinkers on Education: From Confucius to Dewey*. London: Routledge.

Pollock, L. (1983) *Forgotten Children: Parent-Child Relations from 1500–1900*. Cambridge: Cambridge University Press.

Robinson, K. (2013) *Innocence, Knowledge and the Construction of Childhood: The contradictory nature of sexuality and censorship in children's contemporary lives*. Abingdon: Routledge.

Scholz, S. (2010) 'That all children should be free: Beauvoir, Rousseau and childhood', in *Hypatia*, 25(2), 394–411.

Shahar, S. (1990) *Childhood in the Middle Ages*. London: Routledge.

Siraj-Blatchford, I., Sylva, K., Muttock, S., Gilden, R. and Bell, D. (2002) *Researching Effective Pedagogy in the Early Years*. [Online] Available from: www.ioe.ac.uk/REPEY_research_report.pdf [accessed 1 November 2015]

Smidt, S. (2011) *Playing to Learn: The Role of Play in the Early Years*. Abingdon: Routledge.

Stephenson, A. (2011) 'How children's collective interests influence their curriculum experiences: developing relationships, differentiating by gender, and defying adults', in *Australasian Journal of Early Childhood*, 36(4), 139–146.

Tahko, T. (2008) 'A new definition of a priori knowledge: in search of modal basis', in *Metaphysica*, 9(1), 57–68.

The British Association for Early Childhood Education. (2012) *Development Matters in the Early Years Foundation Stage (EYFS)*. [Online] Available from: www.foundationyears.org.uk/files/2012/03/Development-Matters-FINAL-PRINT-AMENDED.pdf [accessed 1 November 2015]

Trohler, D. (2012) 'Rousseau's Emile, or the fear of passions?' in *Studies in Philosophy and Education*, 31(5), 477–489.

Tucker, L. (2012) 'Re-calling, re-membering, and re-imagining education', in *Encounter*, 25(2), 16–23.

Tzanakis, M. (2011) 'Bourdieu's social reproduction thesis and the role of cultural capital in educational attainment: A critical review of key empirical studies', in *Educate*, 11(1), 76–90.

Usher, A. and Kober, N. (2013) 'Student motivation: an overlooked piece of school reform', in *Education Digest*, 78(5), 9–16.

Webb, D. (2013) 'Pedagogies of hope' in *Studies in Philosophy and Education*, 32(4), 397–414.

Webb, C., Ackerly, D., McPeek, M. and Donoghue, M. (2002) 'Phylogenies and Community Ecology' in *Annual Review of Ecology and Systematics*, Vol. 33: 475–505.

Wegerif, R. (2010) *Mind Expanding: Teaching and Creativity in Primary Education*. Berkshire: Open University Press.

Winkle-Wagner, R. (2010) 'Foundations of educational inequality: cultural capital and social reproduction', in *ASHE Higher Education Report*, 36(1), 1–21.

Wood, E. and Attfield, J. (2005) *Play, Learning and the Early Childhood Curriculum 2e*. London: Paul Chapman Publishing.

Zangwill, N. (2013) 'A priori knowledge that I exist' in *Analytic Philosophy*, 54(2), 189–208.

3 The ecology of flourishing

Michael Gasper and Leoarna Mathias

How the balance between the relative and proven benefits of universal and targeted services can contribute to flourishing is the focus of this chapter. Does separation by 'either, or', enforced by financial constraint, produce the most effective contribution to flourishing or is this distinction false? We suggest that it is. To separate universal and targeted services is a misunderstanding of their interdependence, like asking if the rear wheels of your car are more essential than the front wheels: both are essential parts of a properly functioning whole. Seligman suggests:

> As our ability to measure positive emotion, engagement, meaning, accomplishment, and positive relations improves, we can ask with rigor how many people in a nation or in a city or in a corporation are flourishing.
>
> (2011, p. 12)

The dilemma that faces all in early years is how to make the best use of reducing resources while trying to convince Government of the validity of such measurements and their equal validity with the current, narrowly defined, outcomes focused measurements? A key factor in challenging the current 'harder' measurements lies in the debate over universal and targeted services. This chapter sets out how such a dilemma came about, explores the nature and value of both universal and targeted services, their interdependent relationship and the need to consider how to maintain both in a context of: financial constraint, limited perceptions and political priorities shifting towards increased austerity, in order to encourage flourishing of families and children.

How this dilemma came about – background and historical context

The New Labour administration (1997–2011) set up and developed Sure Start, a system of early intervention focused on children and families in need. 'Need' was defined by existing state norms and indices of poverty. Children's Centre staff worked to identify and prioritise need and to provide specific multiagency support to families 'in need' and with a range of different needs of Sure Start delivered through Sure Start Local Programmes (SSLPs). The intention was not to do things *for* individuals and families or to provide services to perpetuate or create dependency, rather to *work with them* to help them shift from hopelessness and helplessness towards confidence and self-sufficiency. Williams and Churchill (2006, p. 56) showed how improving well-being and self-belief were critical factors in achieving this:

> Overall, we found substantial evidence for experiences of individual parent empowerment in all the case study areas. This was usually expressed in terms of feeling less isolated, more valued (especially as mothers), and more confident in their parenting activities

The system was grounded in existing early intervention practice and evolved further from various initiatives, including Early Excellence Centres and Neighbourhood Nurseries, and grew into an effective, locally-based programme, which achieved measureable success over time.[1]

Sure Start Centres worked with a wide range of need sometimes identified by partner agencies, in particular Health Visitors and Social Care. Fundamental to any success was the establishment of initial contacts. Centres provided services, which were focused on identified individual needs – *targeted services* – as well as more general services applicable to all and open to all – *universal services*. Targeted services were derived from contacts with individual families and their children and referrals from other agencies, and provided small numbers attending a more tailored series of sessions over a limited time with an assessment of their situation, feelings and aspirations at the start and end of the programme. Universal services operated in a similar way, but covered areas of knowledge and practice, which were more widely and generally applicable, for example, healthy eating, safety in the home and play activities, and were successful when offered in inviting, non-judgemental and accessible ways (ibid., 2006). Whereas targeted programmes worked for families after an initial relationship had been established through their key worker, universal programmes encouraged contact with a wider range of families, including those who lacked the confidence to attend on their own but were able to attend with friends or with initial support from their key worker or other professionals. Many of the individuals and families reached in this way were shy of engagement and included those who were 'hard to reach' – a phrase that included individuals and families who specifically avoided contact with officialdom. Universal services increased the potential reach of Sure Start Centres and frequently enabled them to successfully open a relationship with isolated or vulnerable individuals, which they would not otherwise have been able to do:

> Often, the encouragement to use services and to join groups gave parents the support of others in similar situations. Where SSLPs provided a supportive and valuing environment for parents to articulate their concerns, these parents reported increased self-esteem and greater confidence and knowledge about parenting as well as improvements in their relationships with their children, in their children's well-being and learning skills.
>
> (Williams and Churchill 2006, p. 35)

Sure Start Children's Centres leaders and staff were no strangers to change. From their inception Centre staff and leaders were at the cutting edge of accountability and measurement and subject to constant adjustment and adaptation. Assessing their own effectiveness, maintaining a finger on the pulse of local needs, predicting new needs and adapting services to meet them, were all part of the Sure Start Children's Centres' brief. The initial funding of Sure Start Local Centres (SSLP) was protected and this enabled the establishment and development of local networks of centres, which flourished. But the high aspirations and successes achieved began to come under increasing pressure. A report in June 2007[2] attempted to assess changes in SSLP areas over a five-year period, but was inconclusive in identifying directly attributable improvements. However, a 2008[3] report by Jay Belsky and Ted Melhuish, while cautious in many respects, did indicate some significant gains including, less negative parenting, 3-year-olds in SSLP areas having '*better social development with higher levels of positive social behaviour and independence/ self-regulation*', more positive social behaviour and families using more child and family related services in their area.

The subsequent Memorandum to Parliament, a memorandum submitted by Professor Edward Melhuish, March 2010: 13[4] noted:

In the longitudinal investigation of thousands of children and families, comparisons were made of children and families in Sure Start areas with those in similar non-Sure Start areas; revealing beneficial effects for children and families living in Sure Start areas.

Despite the positive indications, a significant limiting factor was the emergence of the full programme just as the downturn in the economy took effect. Subsequent political change increased pressure, particularly after the 'ring fence' protection was taken away from funding, and as austerity measures were introduced Local Authorities were pressurised into reducing spending dramatically. Initially, public opinion forced some Local Authorities, such as Stoke-on-Trent, to re-assess closure decisions, but over time larger reductions could only be met by reorganisation forcing Local Authorities, which valued Sure Start Centres, into creating larger groups of centres that had previously stood alone, disguising staff reductions and appearing to avoid wholesale closures. These new groups and 'localities' combined with reductions in staffing, required significant changes in structure, leadership, and type and delivery of services. In this context the primacy of targeted over universal services was presented as logical, inevitable and the best way forward.

- Sure Start was set up to work with families in need.
- Austerity led to the reduction of many of these universal services that had been evidenced as being of benefit.

The nature and value of targeted and universal provision and their interdependent relationship

While social, educational and psychological research has come to recognise complexity, variability, lack of certainty and how to value the positive potential this brings, political thinking and practice is stuck in the past. Short term, 'quick fix' initiatives have been reinforced by the need for new ministers to be seen to be 'doing something'. This has led to a continuation of short-term decision making often contradicting any initiative of the preceding administration. A shift towards private enterprise and away from public funding was epitomised by Michael Gove, then Secretary of State for Education, and his reforms and wholesale destruction of the structure of education in the name of private enterprise, while shifting curriculum content back to a narrow core reminiscent of the 1950s.

There has been a fundamental shift in priorities away from the aspiration of free health care for all, from social support and care and from broad-based education for all. 'Universal' has given way to 'targeted' in more than one area. And targeting has come to mean top down, imposed targets with narrowing criteria, rather than bottom up, identified from local or individual needs. The arguments of economics are prevailing and steering hard won social gains onto a pathway of limited vision with no clear sense of direction or purpose beyond the day to day. Political support has been generated by playing on fears: a blame culture focused on benefit fraud has been the excuse for drastic changes to social security and benefit payments; a bedroom tax, which was most damaging to less well-off families created anxiety among many families and new challenges for Local Authorities to find more social housing and more housing for single occupancy; dilemmas over immigration policy have sparked fears over job losses to cheap labour provided by migrant workers, refuelling racist agendas. The same period of time has witnessed a significant increase in food bank use in many cities and towns as even those in work find it hard to make ends meet.

In this context it is even more important to see the bigger picture and grasp the interdependence of both universal and targeted approaches. The focus on Sure Start provides insights into the value of less myopic, more considered approaches and how these relate to wider vision and encourage our flourishing as a nation. If we look at the economic perspective from a purely pragmatic view the simplistic shift in service provision from universal to targeted does not make sense because it denies the complexity of the real world.

- There has been a shift from universal provision to targeted services.
- Targeting has often meant that decisions have been taken without consideration of the local need.

Political perspectives

In 1999 Tony Blair spoke optimistically about his hopes of eradicating child poverty within a generation (White 1999). Two years into his tenure at this point, Blair had by this time already set in motion the Sure Start Local Programmes, drawing upon strands of evidence stretching back as far as the Head Start programme in the US (conceived during the Kennedy and Johnson administrations of the early 1960s), which itself was rooted in the work of Bronfenbrenner (2005) and his ecological model of child development. During the late 1960s and early 1970s there was considerable cross-pollination of ideas between US and UK academics, and the establishment of the Education Priority Areas through the Plowden Report (1967) had been an early experiment in working with disadvantaged families, and an attempt to engage with real world complexity. However, political will for such work weakened during the latter half of the 1970s and was not reignited in the UK until the election of New Labour in 1997 (Welshman 2008). However, initial enthusiasm for the project waned by 2005, albeit on the basis of somewhat shaky evidence (DfE 2013; Hall *et al.* 2015) as it failed to be the rising tide that would lift all boats up off the mud (ibid., 2015). As the decade progressed, and the global recession approached, a new language of more targeted services focusing on social exclusion sailed into view, as did the need to encourage parents (mothers) back to work via the provision of more childcare. Nevertheless, the New Labour project of tackling the multi-layered causes of poverty, drawing upon the evidence base it had helped to create, for example EPPE (2004) altered the policy landscape substantially, by at least attempting to hold in mind at all times the complex range of factors that combine to bring about deep and persistent poverty for some.

In sharp contrast, the Coalition Government refocused reduced funding on a much more closely defined group of families in the greatest need, with complex and persistent issues. This recidivistic group were to be reached through the Troubled Families Programme (TFP). The justification for this refocus was twofold. Firstly, the stated economic imperative of austerity politics, which in turn was used to defend the necessity of the Coalition's policy priorities in relation to welfare provision. And, secondly, a desire to tackle, on explicit ideological terms, the more enduring problem of conceptualising and solving the issues faced by a small but persistent group within society enduring high levels of deprivation on many fronts (Welshman 2013).

New Labour's language of encouraging social mobility and tackling poverty and social exclusion quickly, after 2010, gave way to a rather different approach from the Coalition. Many commentators in the field argue convincingly that the riots that occurred in a number of English cities during the summer of 2011 'helped to create additional impetus' (Hayden and Jenkins 2014: 632) for a change of policy direction in relation to such families. Throughout that summer, a more pernicious discourse of 'feral parents' and fatherless children permeated the news media and Cameron's speeches (De Benedictis 2012; Jensen 2013). Any residue of attempts to identify the *structural* factors that trap some families in cycles of hardship, left by the end of the New Labour government, was briskly swept aside. A more ominous narrative, targeting and individualising the problems of such families, and implicitly apportioning blame, became prevalent (Churchill 2014; Hayden and Jenkins 2014).

- New Labour appeared to want to work with a range of families to provide universal support but also to encourage mothers, in particular, back into the workplace.
- The coalition appeared to focus only on those families that they perceived to be in the greatest need with complex or what they referred to as persistent issues.

The troubled families initiative

Louise Casey, who had previously held a number of high profile roles during both the Blair and Brown administrations, was now appointed as Director General of the Troubled Families Programme, publishing her own report, *Listening to Troubled Families*, in July 2012.[5] Criticised for being evidence-light, Casey's report nevertheless confirmed that yet another re-conceptualisation of the problem family as the 'troubled family' (which simultaneously has problems and causes problems to others) had taken place. Such re-conceptualisations occur regularly throughout the history of welfare provision in England, and despite a thin evidence base, prove to be 'resistant to sociological rebuttal', as MacDonald has observed (2015: 199). By 2012, a figure of 120,000 families, who were draining the budgets of police, health services, social services and education services in the areas they resided in and, therefore, requiring intervention, was firmly established in the public mind. A direct consequence of such targeting was the disappearance of the notion that society would benefit if social mobility was open to all, replaced by resentment on the part of 'hard working families' and 'strivers' (Patrick 2014) that a select few were using up so much of the finite tax payer resource (Jensen 2013; Butler 2014).

Having acquired a budget top-sliced from the budgets of a number of other government departments, Casey quickly set about target setting for English local authorities.[6] Her team estimated the numbers of troubled families that could potentially be identified in each local authority, and a Payment by Results framework that would drive the programme forward was made available.

Excavating beneath the surface of Casey's report, however, one finds a problematic evidence base. Blair's government had concluded that 2.5 per cent of every generation were 'deeply excluded' (Welshman 2013: 200) and by 2008 New Labour were suggesting that approximately 140,000 families were experiencing five or more disadvantages from a 'basket' of indicators, that included 'no parent in the family is in work', 'family has a low income (below 60 per cent of the median)' and 'no parent has any qualifications', among others. In *Families At Risk* (2008), the Brown administration now pledged itself to tackling the multiple and entrenched problems of these deeply disadvantaged families, albeit in a more targeted way than had been seen earlier in the administration.[7] The data used in this Cabinet Office report was drawn from the work of the Family and Children Study (FACS), which was in turn managed by the Department for Work and Pensions.

The focus of FACS and of *Families at Risk* was squarely upon indices of deprivation, as were the Family Intervention Projects (FIPs), developed at a local level across England, that were borne out of the Cabinet Office's report. While the number of families identified as in need of further intervention – 140,000 – is strikingly similar to the 120,000 figure presented during 2011–12 by the Coalition government, it is in the management of the Payment by Results framework that we can most clearly grasp the criticisms made of Casey's evidence and approach, which remain as concerns for targeting. Local authorities would be financially rewarded for tackling three issues in particular: '*worklessness, anti-social behaviour and crime*' and '*non-school attendance*' by the children within the targeted families: a very different definition of targeting. As financially incentivised targets, these three issues are at odds with the broader focus on deprivation inherent in the pages of both the FACS and *Families at Risk* and New Labour policy approaches. This prior-gathered research data was newly reconfigured, or 'constructed to fit the political priorities near the start of a new government, with a focus that . . . ignored the child welfare, social and health issues' (Hayden and Jenkins 2014: 645) contained within that original data.

This reconfiguration of the data, accompanied by a persuasive rhetoric, described by Levitas as, 'policy making by anecdote' (2012), combined to create a particular, individualistic discourse of blame around families facing multiple challenges (Crossley 2015[8]). The Coalition era has been defined by such discourse, with David Cameron calling upon us to tackle a 'culture of disruption and irresponsibility that cascades through the generations' (Lambert 2015: 1). This, despite the fact that, there are 'quite other ways' (Levitas 2012) to interpret the substantial body of research that focuses on the lives of these families. MacDonald, Shildrick *et al.* (2012) have argued persuasively that the structural causes of poverty are being ignored in favour of an ideologically-rooted 'separating off' from society of this small yet supposedly disruptive group. In reality, these families are subject to an 'accumulation and multiplicity' of challenges that overwhelm them (ibid.) and through 'a process of economic decline and neighbourhood sorting, the least advantaged areas become populated by the least advantaged people' (Lupton and Power 2004: 133). To speak in terms of 'benefit cheats' or 'shirkers', as numerous members of the Coalition cabinet did at this time, serves only to divide people into simplistic categories, and demonstrates a failure to govern society using a 'responsible civic language' (Ellison 2014: 8).

Nevertheless, professionals on the ground were now called upon to embrace the TFP. In many local authorities, much of the innovative work taking place under the umbrella of the previously discussed FIPs, was simply re-branded and tweaked to bring it in line with the expectations of the TFP. Prior to 2010 it is clear that the then Department for Children, Schools and Families saw Sure Start as a provider of more generalist, or universal, services and the more recently introduced FIP programmes as more targeted and structured in nature.[9] Within the FIPs there was a sense that by being allowed to work in genuinely creative ways, and in meaningful multi-agency contexts, effective work with these deeply excluded families could be done (Davies 2015). Some of this feeling has carried over into the reconstituted TFP projects at local level (Hayden and Jenkins 2014), and they are not without their successes. Indeed, 4Children's 2014 Census of Sure Start Children's Centres[10] recommends both the reinvigoration of the universal offer of Sure Start *and* the continued strengthening of the TFP at a sensible rate. Where both professionals and the research community take issue with the TFP is at the point where 'outlandish claims' (Hayden and Jenkins 2014: 645) are made about its achievements. These act as justification for a considerable ramping up of the project under the Conservative Government of 2015, extending the work to a further 400,000 potential families. At the same time, the budgets of Sure Start, and other local authority provision, were substantially curtailed. Stewart describes a 32 per cent decrease in funding for Sure Start over the life time of the Coalition government, and reports the closure of a fifth of all centres during the same period.[11] Others argue that the Payment by Results approach gives local authorities a reason to both identify more families than actually genuinely meet the criteria, to maximise their potential income from the project. Beyond this, local authorities may focus only on those families whose particular challenges closely match the three primary targets of the programme: increased employment, reduced criminal or anti-social behaviour and improved school attendance. If these are the families, as the TFP implies, who are troublesome to others, then there are other truly troubled families, outside this particular criteria, who are not the focus of TFP help (Davies 2015).

The Troubled Families Programme is thus unashamedly targeted by nature, and by virtue of its particularly narrow focus on increasing employment, reducing crime and improving school attendance, is at odds with the more holistic intentions of both the original Sure Start ethos and wider international ideas around flourishing, as defined by Forgeard *et al.* (2011) and others. In particular, it fails to acknowledge the more subjective constructs of well-being present in the concept of flourishing (Gasper 2010). It also falls short of reflecting the inter-related complexity of the problems experienced by the target families. Instead, it is an example of 'policy-based evidence' (Hayden and Jenkins 2014: 638) in which the data was moulded to fit the very particular landscape of post-recession, post-riot, new-era austerity Britain. We are witnessing the 'increasingly conditional, targeted and punitive strategies of a new welfare regime' (Jensen 2013: 60). The parenting of the next generation has become a site of public interest, and, somehow, society has consented to government intervening in family life on the thin evidence that such feral families not only exist, but are wholly responsible for their perceived failures (De Benedictis 2012; Butler 2014; Jensen 2013; MacDonald *et al.* 2013). As Wacquant (2010: 214) has argued, governments who fully embrace the neo-liberal project, while affording those who hold social, economic and cultural capital with a substantial degree of freedom, are 'anything but laissez-faire at the bottom'. Instead they reveal themselves to be 'fiercely interventionist' (ibid., 2010) as they attempt to bring such families in line. Such intervention does not have flourishing at its heart, rather it is a project focused on encouraging compliance and saving money. As such,

> [F]amilies with tense or divergent relationships with the state are [now] to be governed in the context of a state and a set of social attitudes that represents a decisive break with the post-war welfare consensus.
>
> (Butler 2014: 415)

- The Troubled Families Programme appears to construct a group of families in a very particular way, not necessarily based on evidence.
- The aims of the TFP agenda: employment, involvement in crime and school attendance are not necessarily the key issues for those families facing poverty and deprivation.

Arguments for retaining both universal and targeted services

Separating universal and targeted services, particularly where the definitions guiding targeting exclude so many in the greatest need, is a misconception. The economic arguments used to justify a reduction of support are spurious and the pernicious labelling of those targeted, harmful.

Universal services, provided pathways to far more aspects of need than the three focus aspects of the TFP. A wider definition of need in the past allowed more needs to be addressed in the first instance and wider access to greater numbers of families 'in need'. Universal services often provided pathways to more focused, targeted services. The value in economic, social and personal terms is obvious. In social and personal developmental terms, the services provided a means for those in need to acknowledge those needs, and a pathway to begin to take ownership and address them. Losing universal contacts makes no sense practically or ideologically. The less stringent time constraints on universal services also meant that a lasting, rather than a temporary, change could be achieved.

Targeted services were previously identified in a variety of ways: through the needs of children and often revealing wider family needs and vice versa; through personal contacts with other service users, often leading to self-referral once relationships were established; through contacts with other agencies, and, through the awareness of staff involved.

Successive reports produced by the evaluations of Early Excellence Centres (EECs) and Sure Start identified the following characteristics of both universal and targeted services:

1   their specialised, coordinated and planned application to professionally identified need;

2   their individualised nature, being shaped and created in response to the particular needs of a family or individual;

LIVERPOOL JOHN MOORES UNIVERSITY
LEARNING SERVICES

3   their non-judgemental, respectful and empowering character, acknowledging cultural and social diversity, and encouraging agency and responsibility within the family (Bertram *et al.* 2002: 10).

The same report recognised the advantages of the broad base of services provided by settings highlighting the following characteristics of use identified from case study analysis:

1   Adult family members often access support services for their own needs only after, and often through, an acknowledgement of their children's needs.

2   The nature of the first contact with a family is critical in determining how a family will access and benefit from the EEC services.

3   The wide range of services provided through the EECs, particularly those which might be perceived as being of a more unusual or specialist nature for an early years' service e.g. legal, financial or housing advice, can provide much needed support at a critical point in a family's history.

4   The pattern of use of EEC services varies as a family history develops, with families needing and accessing services more or less intensively at different points in their life cycle. Centres needed to be able to respond flexibly to this dynamic of need[12] (Bertram *et al.* 2002: 11).

Sure Start evaluations showed similar positive benefits of approaches that were both universal and targeted, with the universal often leading to more targeted provision, with occasionally the reverse also being found. Successive reports showed the value of flexibility in approaching the identification of need and how best those needs could be met and also recognised the strength in providing bespoke services for individuals and groups within different areas locally and nationally. The shift towards a strategy offering less flexibility, tighter definitions of need, and towards 'one size fits all' provision demonstrates a degree of austerity that is minimalist in the extreme and that risks abandoning many families who could have been better supported by approaches combining both universal and targeted approaches.

The following vignette based on the writers' experiences of many examples illustrates the kind of achievements that are possible by using such a combined approach.

A parent ('Aisha') attending a 'Healthy Eating' programme confides in a member of the family support staff ('Jasmine') that she knows a lone mother ('Mary') who is afraid of leaving her flat. Aisha thinks Mary has a young child. The family support worker contacts colleagues in Social Care and Health to ask if this person is already receiving support. They confirm she isn't. Jasmine suggests that Aisha encourages Mary to come with her to one of the Healthy Eating sessions. At first Mary is reluctant to do so but eventually she agrees. Mary freezes at the doorway. The family support worker talks with her, reassures her and coaxes her until gradually she is drawn into the activity. Over time she develops friendships and asks if she and her child can attend the 'drop in' sessions she has heard others in the group talk about.

The principles described in this vignette will be recognised by anyone who has worked in Family Support over the last 16 years. Such examples can still happen but are increasingly rare as the pressure imposed by targets take priority over identified local needs that do not match the reduced criteria. The reductions in Government funding for Care and Welfare, for Benefits and for Local Authorities have brought reductions in staff and re-configuration, which now limits communication and the ability for organisations to work together. Services such as Health Visitors, which have seen an increase in overall staffing, have also seen shifts in operational strategy moving staff away from first hand, face to face practice contacts towards more distant information dissemination. Despite Government moves to encourage Health and Social Care to work more closely together, the unintended consequences of austerity have created pressures that mediate against this. The organisation and structure, which underpinned universal and targeted services in the past, is threatened and in its place is a system that can at best deliver a reduced level of support to a very specific group. The Chancellor would argue we cannot afford both universal and targeted services. If there are to be meaningful early intervention services we cannot afford not to have both.

- Universal and targeted services are not the same, they provide different services to children and their families with different intended outcomes, both of which are important.
- Austerity has led to choices being made about service provision, these choices are often imposed in a top-down model.

Conclusion

Following the May 2015 election, the Troubled Families Programme confirmed its place in the Conservative government's policy offer, having supposedly 'turned around' the lives of 99 per cent of the original 120,000 cohort (DCLG 2015). It was then expanded to reach a further 400,000 families during the parliamentary term. That figure represented 6.5 per cent of all families in England; Crossley (2015) observes that nearly every family who might be referred to non-universal services will be included in the TFP by virtue of this sizeable increase in programme size. Furthermore, Prime Minister Cameron spoke of applying the TFP model to other entrenched problems within society (ibid., 2015). Commentators are now significantly more cautious, however, arguing that '[t]he government's "troubled families" story is, in short, too good to be true' (ibid., 2015: 7), while others continue to forcibly assert that the very idea of persistent problem families who 'transmit their poverty' to the next generation remains 'unsupported by scientific evidence' (Gordon 2011[13]). At the same time, Cameron has started speaking of taking Sure Start back to its original purpose of 'early intervention', while at the same time presiding over substantial cuts to Sure Start funding, and ignoring the argument that Sure Start was never intended to be an early intervention tool. Rather, as Eisenstadt (2012: 46) concludes in her assessment of Sure Start for the Child Poverty Action Group, Sure Start taught us that, 'a service meant for everyone must reach out to those least likely to use it, while remaining welcoming to all'. If a changed version were to emerge with the punitive constraints of TFP, this is unlikely to be achieved.

Throughout this chapter we have argued that to separate universal and targeted services through notions of 'either, or' is false and unproductive. In order to do meaningful work with the most vulnerable in our society we must open the doors of our services to *every* citizen. Universal and targeted services belong together on a continuum, not being pitched against each other by policy makers, 'who are often removed from the visceral effects of poverty' (Lea 2014: 24). The present policy focus of the Conservative government, which favours the targeted approach and underfunds the universal, is very likely to 'miss some of the non-poor families who may need them' (Eisenstadt 2012: 46). To employ narrow access criteria and use a payment by results framework, as the TFP does, is to deny the complexity of the real world, to misunderstand the sometimes circuitous and tangential routes vulnerable families take towards sources of support.

In tracking the policy trajectories of both Sure Start and the TFP, this chapter poses wider questions about the relationship between policy makers, policy 'implementers' (the professionals delivering front-line services) and the policy 'recipients' (in this case, families in receipt of either Sure Start or TFP 'interventions'). Diagrammatically the relationship between these three groups appears in Figure 3.1 (below).

In this model, there is the opportunity for genuine exchange between the three groups:

■ Policy makers can gather together 'stories' about the experiences of the lives of recipients, and use this information to inform their policy making; we have come to call this process *evidence-based policy making.*
■ Policy implementers can consider the implications of policy, can interpret, translate and 'mediate the interface' (Lea 2014: 15) between the policy and the client, as well as being able to feed back to the policy makers the successes or challenges contained within the policy initiative for them as professionals.
■ Policy recipients can explore the impact of policy on their lives with the implementers, and positively contribute to the refining of professional practice as they do so.

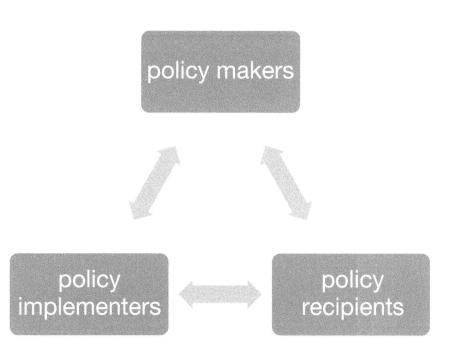

FIGURE 3.1

In the numerous reviews of Sure Start that have been documented within this chapter, there is a clear suggestion that, to a greater or lesser extent, policy makers, implementers and recipients have been allowed to 'communicate' in this way and shape the delivery of services.

While criticisms of the short comings of New Labour's approach to evidence-based policy do exist (Biesta 2010), we can at least say that during the early part of the twenty-first century, there was genuine political will to understand the experiences of vulnerable citizens, and to reflect upon the insidious effects of poverty on communities. We might argue that the multi-directional 'discussions' about policy, that are represented by this model – and were part of the New Labour approach to policy making – have at their heart the politics of recognition (Williams 1989), in that they allow all parties to be heard in the policy-making process. Each party to the discussion has rights and responsibilities, and there is a genuine space in which the principles of 'opportunity, reciprocity and participation' (Spoonley *et al.* 2005) might characterise the debate.

Consider, by contrast, this approach, as shown in Figure 3.2.

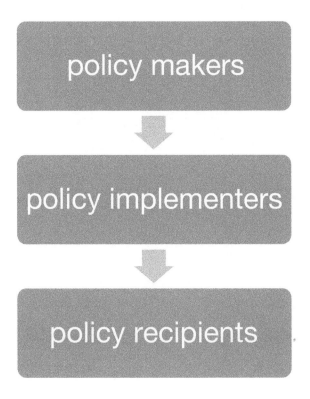

FIGURE 3.2

In this model, the politics of redistribution (Williams 1989), and its patriarchal overtones, are visible, and the opportunity to discuss, refine and consider the evidence in favour of continuing a policy initiative is denied; there is now a lack of reciprocity and participation. The commentaries surrounding the inception and continuation of the TFP speak of policy making 'by anecdote' (Levitas 2012), and of the de-professionalisation of the front line workers, as they force families to jump through the hoops of the programme's requirements in order that their local authority gets the funding. Any wider commitment to the flourishing of the client group is potentially lost in such a results-driven climate, which appears to deny any modification or adaptation to local or individual needs.

Yet there may be a chink of light shining through the gloom of this picture. Within *both* models, in as much as they represent differing ways of understanding how policy is implemented, there is scope for action, particularly on the part of the implementers. They can move from being 'street-level bureaucrats', who act as mere conduits of the state (Lipsky 2010) to 'policy entrepreneurs' (Lea 2014) who develop a capacity to critique, interpret and modify policy, along ethical lines. Through a consideration of the question, 'whose interests am I serving, harming or ignoring?' (Ibid) they can begin to find the spaces between policy initiatives that allow them to operate in accordance with their value base, and thus promote the genuine flourishing of their client group through both universal and targeted delivery.

REFLECTIVE QUESTIONS

1   What ethical issues arise from the dilemma of a belief in autonomy and equal partnership with parents and the principles and practice of early intervention that requires outside agencies imposing change? What principles should lead intervention in practice?

2   What does the term 'agency' imply when applied to young children? How does this balance with notions of professional knowledge and duty?

3   What does the adoption of the construction of the 'street level' professional bring to early years practice?

4   What similarities and differences can we discern in the services available to families with problems during the period 1997–2015, and what do they tell us about the relationship between research evidence and policy making?

Notes

1   National Evaluation of Sure Start local programmes: An economic perspective. See also: http://webarchive.nationalarchives.gov.uk/20100113210150/dcsf.gov.uk/everychildmatters/research/evaluations/nationalevaluation/ness/ness publications/

2   Barnes, J., Cheng, H., Howden, B., Frost, M., Harper, G., Lattin-Rawstrone, R. and Sack, C. and the NESS Team (2007) Changes In the Characteristics of SSLP Areas between 2001/01 and 2004/05 http://webarchive.national archives.gov.uk/20100113210150/http://dcsf.gov.uk/everychildmatters/publications/0/1908/

3   Belsky, J. and Melhuish, E. (2008) *The Impact of Sure Start Local Programmes on Three Year Olds and their Families* http://webarchive.nationalarchives.gov.uk/20100113210150/http://dcsf.gov.uk/everychildmatters/research/publications/surestartpublications/1974/

4   www.publications.parliament.uk/pa/cm200910/cmselect/cmchilsch/130/9110202.htm

5   http://dera.ioe.ac.uk/14970/1/2183663.pdf

6   The programme did not extend to other members of the Union.

7   http://webarchive.nationalarchives.gov.uk/20100416132449/http:/www.cabinetoffice.gov.uk/media/cabinetoffice/social_exclusion_task_force/assets/families_at%20_risk/risk_data.pdf

8   www.crimeandjustice.org.uk/sites/crimeandjustice.org.uk/files/The%20Troubled%20Families%20Programme%2C%20Nov%202015.pdf

9   http://webarchive.nationalarchives.gov.uk/20130401151715/www.education.gov.uk/publications/eOrderingDownload/DCSF-00264-2010.PDF

10 www.4children.org.uk/Resources/Detail/Children-Centres-Census-2014

11 http://sticerd.lse.ac.uk/dps/case/spcc/WP12.pdf

12 http://dera.ioe.ac.uk/4667/1/RR361.pdf

13 www.poverty.ac.uk/working-papers-policy-response-social-mobility-life-chances-children-parenting-families-uk/social

References

Barnes, J., Cheng, H., Howden, B., Frost, M., Harper, G., Lattin-Rawstrone, R. and Sack, C. and the NESS Team (2007) *Changes in the Characteristics of SSLP Areas between 2001/01 and 2004/05* http://webarchive.nationalarchives.gov.uk/20100113210150/http://dcsf.gov.uk/everychildmatters/publications/0/1908/ (accessed December 2015).

Belsky, J. and Melhuish, E. (2008) *The Impact of Sure Start Local Programmes on Three Year Olds and their Families* http://webarchive.nationalarchives.gov.uk/20100113210150/http://dcsf.gov.uk/everychildmatters/research/publications/surestartpublications/1974/ (accessed December 2015).

Bertram, T., Pascal, C., Bokhari, S., Gasper M. and Holtermann, S. (2002) *Early Excellence Centre Pilot Programme Second Evaluation Report* DfES: Research Report RR361 http://dera.ioe.ac.uk/4667/1/RR361.pdf (accessed December 2015).

Biesta, G. (2010) 'Why "What Works" Still Won't Work: From Evidence-Based Education to Value-Based Education', in *Studies in Philosophical Education*, 29, pp. 491–503.

Bronfenbrenner, U. (2005). *Making Human Beings Human: Bioecological Perspectives on Human Development*. Thousand Oaks: Sage.

Butler, I. (2014) 'New families, new governance and old habits', in *Journal of Social Welfare & Family Law*, 36(4), pp. 415–425.

Cabinet Office (2008) *Reaching Out: Think Family Analysis: Themes from the Families At Risk Review*. London: Social Exclusion Task Force.

Central Advisory Council for Education (England) (1967) *Children and their Primary Schools*. London: HMSO.

Churchill, H. (2014) 'Turning lives around? The Troubled Families Programme'. *In Defence of Welfare* www.social-policy.org.uk/wordpress/wp-content/uploads/2015/04/07_churchill.pdf

Crossley, S. (2015) *The Troubled Families Programme: The perfect social policy?* Online: Centre for Crime and Justice Studies, Briefing 13 www.crimeandjustice.org.uk/sites/crimeandjustice.org.uk/files/The%20Troubled%20Families%20Programme%2C%20Nov%202015.pdf (accessed December 2015).

Davies, K. (2015) *Social Work with Troubled Families: A Critical Introduction*. London: Jessica Kingsley.

DCLG (2015) PM Praises Troubled Families Programme Success, Press Release, London: DCLG 22.06.15.

De Benedictis, S. (2012) ' "Feral" Parents: Austerity parenting under neoliberalism', *Studies in the Maternal* 4: 2. www.mamsie.bbk.ac.uk/articles/abstract/10.16995/sim.40/ (accessed January 2016)

Department For Education (1967) *Children and Their Primary Schools: v. 1: Plowden Report* London: HMSO Department For Education (2011) *National evaluation of Sure Start local programmes: An economic perspective* DFE-RB073 www.gov.uk/government/publications/national-evaluation-of-sure-start-local-programmes-an-economic-perspective (accessed September 2015)

DfE (2013) *National evaluation of Sure Start local programmes: An economic perspective*. Research Report London: DfE.

Eisenstadt, N. (2012) 'Sure Start and child poverty: what have we learned?' in Judge, L. (ed.) Ending Child Poverty by 2020: Progress made and lessons learned Online: CPAG www.cpag.org.uk/sites/default/files/CPAG-ECPby2020-1212.pdf (accessed December 2015)

Ellison, N. (2014) Introduction to *In Defence of Welfare 2* Online: Social Policy Association www.social-policy.org.uk/wordpress/wp-content/uploads/2015/04/IDOW-Complete-text-4-online_secured-compressed.pdf (accessed December 2015)

Forgeard, M., Jayawickreme, E., Kern, M. and Seligman, M. (2011) 'Doing the right thing: Measuring wellbeing for public policy', in *International Journal of Wellbeing*, 1(1), pp. 79–106.

Gasper, D. (2010) 'Understanding the diversity of conceptions of well-being and quality-of-life', in *Journal of Socio-Economics*, 39, pp. 351–360.

Gordon, D. (2011) Consultation response; social mobility and child poverty review poverty and social exclusion in the UK. www.poverty.ac.uk/working-papers-policy-response-social-mobility-life-chances-children-parenting-families-uk/social (accessed December 2015)

Hall, J., Einstadt, N., Sylva, K., Smith, T., Sammons, P., Smith, G., Evangelou, M., Goff, J., Tanner, E., Agur, M. and Hussey, D. (2015) 'A review of the services offered by English Sure Start Children's Centres in 2011 and 2012', in *Oxford Review of Education*, 41(1) pp. 89–104.

Hayden, C. and Jenkins, C. (2014) '"Troubled Families" Programme in England: "wicked problems" and policy-based evidence', in *Policy Studies*, 35(6), pp. 631–649.

Jensen, T. (2013) 'Austerity parenting', in *Soundings: A Journal of Politics and Culture*, 55, pp. 60–70.

Lambert, M. (2015) '"Bridge over Troubled Water": what we don't know about those 80,000 post war "problem families"' [Conference Paper] Social Policy in the Spotlight: Change Continuity and Challenge Belfast 6–8th July 2015 Social Policy Association.

Lea, S. (2014) 'Early years work, professionalism and the translation of policy into practice' in Kingdon, Z. and Gourd, J. (2014) *Early Years Policy: The Impact on Practice*. London: Routledge.

Levitas, R. (2012) Still Not Listening Poverty and Social Exclusion. www.poverty.ac.uk/articles-families/still-not-listening (accessed December 2015)

Lipsky, M. (2010) *Street Level Bureaucracy: Dilemmas of the Individual in Public Service* (30th ed.) New York: Sage.

Lupton, R. and Power, A. (2004) 'What we know about neighbourhood change: a literature review: CASE report 27'. London: Centre for the Analysis of Social Exclusion; London School of Economics and Political Science.

MacDonald, R. (2015) *Review of* Welshman, J. (2013) 'Underclass: A history of the excluded since 1880 2nd edn London: Bloomsbury', in *Academic Journal of Social Policy*, 44(1), pp. 198–200.

MacDonald, R. and Shildrick, T. (2015) '"Rough Turf": "Troubled Families" as the intergenerational persistence of extreme, socio-spatial class disadvantage', [Conference Paper] *Social Policy in the Spotlight: Change Continuity and Challenge*, Belfast 6th–8th July 2015, Social Policy Association.

MacDonald, R., Shildrick, T. and Furlong, A. (2013) 'In search of "intergenerational cultures of worklessness": Hunting the Yeti and shooting Zombies', in *Critical Social Policy*, 34(2), pp. 199–220.

MacDonald, R. and Shildrick, T. (2015) 'Rough Turf: "Troubled Families" as the intergenerational persistence of extreme, socio-spatial class disadvantage', [Conference Paper] Social Policy in the Spotlight: Change Continuity and Challenge Belfast 6–8th July 2015 Social Policy Association.

NESS, Melhuish, E. Memorandum to Parliament, October 2009 www.publications.parliament.uk/pa/cm200910/cmselect/cmchilsch/130/9110202.htm (accessed December 2015)

NESS, Williams, F. and Churchill, H. (2006) 'Empowering parents', in *Sure Start Local Programmes*, 6(1), p. 56.

Patrick, R. (2014) 'Rhetoric and reality: exploring lived experiences of welfare reform under the Coalition', in *Defence of Welfare* [online]: Social Policy Association www.social-policy.org.uk/wordpress/wp-content/uploads/2015/04/06_patrick.pdf [Accessed December 2015].

Seligman, M. (2011) Flourish: *A New Understanding of Happiness and Well-being and How to Achieve Them*. London: Nicholas Brearley Publishing.

Spoonley, P., Peace, R., Butcher, A. and O'Neill, D. (2005) 'Social cohesion: A policy and indicator for assessing immigrant and host outcomes', in *Social Policy Journal of New Zealand*, 24, pp. 85–110.

Sylva, K., Melhuish, E., Sammons, P., Siraj-Blatchford, I. and Taggart, B. (2004) *The Effective Provision of Pre-school Education (EPPE) Project: Final Report.* Nottingham: DfES.

The National Archives: http://webarchive.nationalarchives.gov.uk/2010011321 0150/dcsf.gov.uk/everychildmatters/research/evaluations/nationalevaluation/ness/nesspublications/ [accessed September 2015].

Wacquant, L. (2010) 'Crafting the neoliberal state: workfare, prisonfare and social insecurity', in *Sociological Forum*, 25(2), pp. 197–220.

Welshman, J. (2008) 'The Cycle of Deprivation: Myths and Misconceptions' in *Children and Society*, 22(2), pp 75–85.

Welshman, J. (2010) 'From head start to Sure Start: Reflections on policy transfer', in *Children and Society*, 24, pp. 89–99.

——. (2013) *Underclass: A History of the Excluded since 1880* 2nd edn London: Bloomsbury Academic.

White, M. (1999) 'PM's 20-year target to end poverty', *The Guardian* 19.03.1999.

Williams, F. (1989) *Social Policy: A Critical Introduction – Issues of Race, Gender and Class.* Polity Press: Cambridge.

Williams, F. and Churchill, H. (2006) *Empowering Parents in Sure Start Programmes*, Research Report for the National Evaluation of Sure Start, Department for Education and Science, Research Publication, London.

Risk taking, philosophy and ethical practice to facilitate flourishing

Scott Buckler

Introduction

The previous chapters have advocated the following: the need to facilitate and the benefits of flourishing. As discussed, flourishing provides many advantages for the developing child through the various domains of being such as their physical, mental, emotional and spiritual health.

This chapter extends these themes while issuing a warning. Fundamentally enabling flourishing is to be championed, although the 'shadow' side of enabling flourishing is discussed in relation to the practitioner working within what may be deemed a constrictive framework of burdensome bureaucracy, an over-emphasis on organisation at the expense of originality, or the tension between accountability and autonomy.

This chapter discusses the balance between the ethics of practice, specifically ascertaining the notion of perceived risks versus potential benefits. With a developing field of research into risk-taking, this theme will be explored in relation to early childhood settings. From this perspective, a challenge is issued to early childhood, that of developing anarchistic approaches and challenging the discourse of 'accepted' practice in an attempt to continue developing what we may deem best-informed practice without the screening of successive layers of political dogmatic operation. Finally, this chapter will explore how flourishing may be further facilitated within the early years setting.

Flourishing and positive psychology

Seligman's model of well-being is the culmination of a lifetime's commitment to psychology and research. Back in the late 1960s, Seligman developed the model of 'learned helplessness' (Seligman *et al.* 1968), whereby, if a person felt trapped and could not escape a distressing situation, they would in essence give up trying. His famous experiment of sending electric shocks to caged dogs after a warning light flashed indicating the impending jolt conditioned dogs to realise they could step over a barrier and not receive the shock. In essence, the dog learned how they could seek safety through their action. Yet the experiment was similarly conducted where no matter what side of the barrier the dog moved to, they could not escape the impending shock once the light flashed. Although it did not take long for the dog to give up trying to prevent the shock, sitting resignedly waiting for the jolt, it took far longer to recondition the dog to understand that they could escape the shock on another occasion. Such learned helplessness experiments were similarly conducted with humans, however opposed to electric shocks, there was an inescapable noise, yet the same learned helplessness could be instilled (Miller and Seligman 1975).

In what may be deemed an archive of psychology's negative past lay the foundation for Seligman's partnership with Csikszentmihalyi (pronounced 'chick-sent-me-hi-yi', which thankfully Csikszentmihalyi explains how his name is phonetically sounded in his books) and the development of 'Positive Psychology'. Although Maslow (1954/1987) was the first to use the term 'positive psychology', an approach he advocated focused on fully functioning and healthy human beings, the term has become synonymous since the turn of the new millennium with Seligman.

Although many attempts have been provided to define positive psychology, Linley *et al.* (2006) suggest that the term remains a lucid concept: Hart and Sasso (2011) discuss that positive psychology has become as much a popular culture movement as an academic subject, while Sheldon and King (2001: 216) refer to it as 'the scientific study of ordinary human strengths and virtues'. However, from the original inception of the term, Seligman and Csikszentmihalyi (2000) identify three pillars of positive psychology: positive subjective experiences, personality traits of thriving individuals and the enhancement of social institutions.

Hart and Sasso (2011) assert that the majority of research within positive psychology has centred on the first two pillars, while other authors have discussed the limited research on the third pillar of enhancing social institutions (Gable and Haidt 2005; Martin 2006). To this extent, although the benefits of enabling children to flourish, has been previously advocated, the question is 'at what expense to the practitioner'?

At first glance of the last sentence, we may advocate that it does not matter about our subjective well-being within children's settings: after all, we are there for the children and that alone is the joy we derive, that feeling of worth where we are transforming lives. However, if, as practitioners, we do not look after ourselves, who in turn will support the flourishing of children? If we carry the tensions inherent in the modern early childhood workforce, are we not putting ourselves in danger, or is this purely a selfish assertion? Indeed, this 'shadow' of facilitating flourishing of others at the expense of ourselves can result in what is known as 'compassion fatigue'.

- The three pillars of positive psychology are: positive subjective experiences, personality traits of thriving individuals and the enhancement of social institutions.
- The third pillar, enhancing social institutions, such as early childhood settings (among others) requires further research.

Compassion fatigue

Compassion fatigue was originally defined by Joinson (1992) as a form of burnout within the nursing profession, although it has been more commonly aligned to professionals within a range of professions. Originally Maslach and Jackson (1986: 1) defined burnout as, 'a syndrome of emotional exhaustion, depersonalisation and reduced personal accomplishment that can occur among individuals who do "people work" of some kind'. They specifically highlighted professionals who work with students, pupils, clients, patients, consumers, and so forth: in essence, anyone associated with the helping professions of education, health care or human services. An alternate perspective is provided by Pines and Aronson (1988: 9) who described burnout in relation to physical symptoms, specifically that burnout is 'a state of physical, emotional, and mental exhaustion caused by long-term involvement in situations that are emotionally demanding'.

Burnout and the associated concept of compassion fatigue are discussed by Joinson (1992) as relating to the personality traits, which encouraged a person into the profession, but at the same time put the person at risk for compassion fatigue. Rank et al. (2009) suggest that compassion fatigue is the result of a depletion of internal emotional resources within the caring professions, whereby support is offered to respective 'client groups' (e.g. children, patients, etc.) with poor self-care by practitioners and little, if any, emotional support within the workplace. One of the causes of compassion fatigue is the concept of burnout on a physical, mental or emotional level due to the perceived demands significantly outweighing the perceived available resources, also the effect of remaining empathetic in light of such tensions (Gentry, Baggerly and Baranowsky 2004). Gentry, Baranowsky and Dunning (2002) developed a 30-item Compassion Fatigue Scale (Revised) to assess burnout, which consisted of items scored on a ten-point Likert Scale, for example, 'I feel that I am a 'failure' in my work', 'I have frequently felt weak, tired or rundown as a result of my work as a caregiver', 'I feel I am unsuccessful at separating work from my personal life'.

According to Merriman (2015), unattended compassion fatigue can result in a range of undesirable outcomes, for example, ethical violations and the risk of potential harm to make sound decisions, or premature exit from professional practice. Consequently, in a time of unprecedented change within early childhood, is compassion fatigue currently on the agenda to enable a thriving, flourishing workforce? If not, why not?

As professionals we may deem that we are selfless in our approach to working with children, providing their well-being before ours, however, if we are at risk of burnout, with the associated harm that this may cause to children or ourselves, should we not strive to address the third pillar of positive psychology through enhancing social institutions such as early childhood settings? In essence, this tension between those we support and the lack of support we provide ourselves may be deemed the 'shadow' side of early childhood, a concept related to Carl Jung's archetype of the hidden components of ourselves (or indeed, our institutions or professions) that we supress, but in supressing, in turn damage ourselves (Jung 1964).

How then do we redress this balance? How can we find that essence, which enables us as practitioners to flourish at the same time as those we support to ensure a vibrant, successful, flourishing setting specifically when we may feel impeded by the range of tensions that govern early childhood through what Moss refers to as the dominant discourse of the institutionalisation of childhood (Moss 2006)?

Moss (2006) discusses the institutionalisation of childhood being at a period of intensification, entering such institutions earlier and remaining in them for longer. He progresses to discuss that although this provides potential opportunities, there are similarly risks to be acknowledged, in the same way I have discussed the 'shadow' side of the profession. Specifically, Moss (2006) highlights the Anglo-American narrative about early childhood education and care as a 'regime of truth' to facilitate social stability and economic success through early childhood institutions being places of technical practice. Through this, Moss discusses how children may be deemed as agents to be programmed by technicians in response to certain problems arising from competitive market capitalism. Given that this regime is highly instrumental, that there is a technical skill to be achieved, public policy is developed to emphasise control and regulation of the early childhood context.

Moss (2006: 129) extends this assertion, suggesting that this results in denaturalisation whereby other possibilities and ways of thinking are dismissed, opposed to imagining other possibilities such as 'a worker who is a learner, a researcher, a critical thinker, and a reflexive as well as dialogic practitioner'. Furthermore, he (ibid. 2006: 133) discusses how this can be addressed through a 'resistance to power', through developing a politics that confronts:

1   'Regimes of truth' that govern what we can think and do;
2   Processes of subjectification, by which we are created as a particular type of subject; and
3   Certain dimensions or forms of injustice, in particular domination and oppression.

Such a form of politics can help resist the dominant discourse through envisioning alternatives and possibilities in order to think and act differently, through the early childhood field to be more adventurous and willing to cross borders into other areas, and to resist neo-liberal discourses, which separate individuality from solidarity, while promoting democracy, mutuality and collaboration. Such an approach may be deemed 'anarchistic' with the associated negative implications associated with that term, however the concept of anarchy is central to early childhood education and care: not the black flag waving, anti-capitalist protestors we occasionally see on news reports, but that of an academic anarchy, one that celebrates challenging accepted norms.

- Burnout and compassion fatigue are evident in the caring professions.
- There is a dominant discourse in early childhood, which may not resonate with our perspectives, which can challenge us.
- Solidarity, democracy, mutuality and collaboration are core factors to be advocated to help our professional settings develop and redress the balance of the dominant discourse. These factors resonate with the concept of anarchism.

A challenge to early childhood: anarchism

Although 'anarchy' derives from the Greek word 'anarchia' (ἄναρχος), ('an' meaning 'not' or 'without' and arkhos 'ruler', thus 'absence of a ruler'), further exploration of the concept is problematic. As Suissa (2006: 7) noted, the term 'is anti-canonical in that there is no one single body of work which defines the principles or nature of the anarchist position', furthermore, the term is open to academic simplifications, distortions and misunderstandings.

Despite the perceived lack of principles, Mueller (2012) identifies three recurrent themes through various anarchistic texts: liberty (an essence of freedom), equality (everyone treated as equals through a true democracy) and solidarity (working together for the common good). Taking each of these in turn, in relation to liberty Guérin (1970: vii) defines this as 'not an abstract philosophical concept, but the vital concrete possibility for every human being to bring to full development all the powers, capacities and talents with which nature has endowed him [sic], and turn them to social account'. Similarly, Goldman (1979) asserts that anarchy should enable a person to grow to their full stature, cultivating what is within them. In relation to equality, this is the rejection of social or institutional hierarchy and domination, which as Kropotkin (1988: 83) notes, 'hierarchy brutalises and warps those who rile by being corrupted by their relative power, and those who are ruled by their servile attitudes and deference to authority'. Consequently, equality of both conditions and opportunity are perceived as necessary conditions for everyone to develop and express their individuality (Mueller 2012). In relation to solidarity, the concept of cooperation and free association between individuals to provide mutual aid is deemed, a natural and important phenomenon, which as Kropotkin (1972: 28) outlines, 'cooperation and empathy have been a factor in the evolution of many species opposed to domination, competition and destruction'.

Despite the overuse of quotations in defining the values of anarchy, I invite you to read the further quotations from Emma Goldman (1911: 62), which summarises her position on anarchism:

> Anarchism, then, really stands for the liberation of the human mind from the dominion of religion; the liberation of the human body from the dominion of property; liberation from the shackles and restraint of government. Anarchism stands for a social order based on the free grouping of individuals for the purpose of producing real social wealth; an order that will guarantee to every human being

free access to the earth and full enjoyment of the necessities of life, according to individual desires, tastes, and inclinations.

. . . if education should really mean anything at all, it must insist upon the free growth and development of the innate forces and tendencies of the child. In this way alone can we hope for the free individual and eventually also for a free community, which shall make interference and coercion of human growth impossible.

(Goldman 1906: 13–14)

Despite these quotes being over 100 years old, to what extent does this resonate within you as a professional? To what extent do they resonate with facilitating flourishing children? Where do such anarchistic values relate to other theories and practice within the domain of early childhood? Would you suggest that Reggio Emilia or other such beacons are centres of anarchistic practice? Goldman (1906, 1911) is, however, one of a number of anarchists who have advocated the importance of such freedom to enable children to flourish: others include William Goodwin, Max Stirner, Mikhail Bakunun, Francesc Ferrer i Guardia, Ivan Illich, Paul Goodman, Colin Ward, Leo Tolstoy, Paulo Freire, among others.

The purpose of the discussion on anarchism is to provide a justification to continue to challenge what is either accepted or imposed. Only through continually questioning and daring to ask questions such as 'why?' then assessing whether the answers relate to our understanding and the context of where we work, can we then either accept or refute top-down approaches. Of course, asking 'why?' can be deemed as a dissenting voice, especially if you are the only person within a group to ask this, yet collectively we should be encouraging more questioning. In the same way, it is by questioning our practice through the concept of reflection, as discussed further on in this chapter, that we develop. Therefore, should we not similarly ask such questions to those, whatever their role, within early childhood opposed to being passive recipients?

This discussion of anarchism in turn provides the basis for considering how best to support flourishing not only within children but also within the setting. Paramount to the discussion of anarchism is that of challenging accepted norms or what was previously referred to by Moss (2006) as the dominant discourse. Such challenging within early childhood has been gathering momentum, in what Dahlberg and Moss (2005) refer to as a 'critical mass' despite the opposing continued focus on qualification levels within the workforce with frameworks which favour measurable features and which can be correlated with child outcomes that are deemed desirable through the predominance of technocratic approaches (Georgeson and Campbell-Barr 2015). If the early childhood workforce is deemed as technocratic programmers of children, this appears to challenge the very notion of what is meant to be a professional.

- Anarchism has been actively encouraged by a number of academic thinkers specifically working with children.
- Although anarchism does not have a central approach, three themes resonate: liberty, equality and solidarity.
- By adopting an anarchistic perspective, we can continue to challenge dominant discourses to further professional practice.

Defining the professional: philosophy

We need to consider how is a professional defined and whether it relates to; the skills they possess, their qualifications, their experience, the ability to conform to what is the accepted Government 'norm'. Is it all of these, some of these or none? After all the term 'professional' is ascribed to numerous vocations, yet what really defines professional practice? Perhaps it is a person who continually questions: questioning what they do, how they do it and why they do it. Such questioning facilitates reflection, which in turn promotes further learning. Models of reflection such as those advocated by Kolb (1984), Brookfield (1995) among others are a cornerstone of many professional courses: indeed, the concept of reflection has become synonymous with professional practice (Dimova and Loughran 2009; Kinsella 2009), yet I would argue that such reflection is only part of the jigsaw that contributes to professional identity. Central to our professional practice is securing a philosophy of practice, one which resonates within us, not one which is imposed.

Central to the concept of philosophy is the ability to question in order to seek values through which we operate (Craig 2005; Honderich 2005; Nagel 1987; Strangroom 2006). While Craig (2005) defines philosophy through asking three questions, these relate to Honderich's (2005) identification of branches within philosophy, summarised in Table 4.1.

Philosophy as a subject needs to be applied: by itself, it is just an intellectual folly. Consequently, we need to turn our philosophy into action in order to make sense and navigate our way through competing

Table 4.1 Defining philosophy of professional practice

Three branches of philosophy (Honderich 2005)	Three questions of philosophy (Craig 2005)
Metaphysics (the theory of existence, or the general nature of the world)	What is there?
Epistemology (theory of knowledge, or the justification of belief)	How do we know?
Ethics (theory of values, or the conduct of life)	What should we do?

demands and tensions, beliefs and preferences, theories and policy. As such, should we base our practice on what we need to do to conform, or should we seek to create innovative practice based on a wider perspective informed through our philosophy? Such innovation may be deemed as risk-taking, an area to which we will return further in this chapter.

According to Buckler and Castle (2014), there are four core philosophies that apply to our profession: essentialism, realism, progressivism and existentialism. Essentialism is based on the 'essential' knowledge that needs to be conveyed to children in a systematic way, ensuring children have the requisite skills and knowledge to function effectively while conforming to accepted standards. Realism focuses on the development of meaning through the assumption of natural laws and proven facts: by this, children are equipped with principles in order to solve problems. Progressivism is based on experience that children make sense of the world depending on the experiences they have and how these are guided by more experienced others through careful questioning to enable the child to plan their course of action. Finally, existentialism is based on the importance of individual experience, whereby children are encouraged to focus on their values through being encouraged to make choices and ask (then answer) their own questions to establish conclusions.

It is unlikely that any professional subscribes to just one of these approaches: it depends on the situation or the context, the learner and a range of other decisions. Therefore, a mixture of approaches is required, or what is known as the idiosyncratic or eclectic philosophical approach. Given that this will differ depending on the variety of factors, the professional has to determine the best course of action, or what Craig (2005) questions, 'What should we do?' Related to Craig's concept is that of ethics as identified by Honderich (2005).

- As professional practitioners, we should be aware of our philosophy and how this relates to our professional context.
- As professionals, we should continually question what we are doing, how we are doing it and why we are doing it.

Ethics: risks versus benefits

At a simplistic level, ethics is concerned with the 'right' and 'wrong' way of solving problems or achieving things, however, who defines what is actually the correct way to achieve? Although ethical codes of conduct are evident within the profession, with research, and so forth, ultimately it is us, alone, who make that decision. Exploring ethics further, it may be deemed as a careful balancing act between the potential benefits of pursuing a course of action against the potential harm that may be caused through that course of action. Indeed, Dahlberg and Moss (2005) refer to such ethics as the choices that occur in practice, specifically that there are always different possibilities in answering a question. Take for example the theme from this book about encouraging flourishing within children. How best should this be achieved? Are we informed by what we have read, discussed and experienced to make an informed decision, or rather, is this based on what we are told to do by others? Should flourishing become a prescriptive set of activities in the same way that Forest School has become, or rather, is it about a philosophy of allowing experimentation by both practitioners and children?

Given the framework of accountability, are you prepared to take that risk? Indeed, the notion of risk-taking has generated a developing field of research, yet this notion of risk has been discussed for a century through the work of Dewey (1916) though suggesting that there is a relationship between thinking and risk. Specifically, through reflecting on a problem, this can result in a degree of uncertainty, which in turn relates to ascertaining the risks involved. Consequently, the practitioner needs to engage with seeking information, trying different strategies and drawing conclusions, which in turn fosters learning. As Reio (2007) comments, by taking risks, we can try out new ideas and approaches, creating and fostering learning within environments.

With the promotion of standards and qualifications, there is a danger of seeking perfection although as Wain (2006) notes, such perfection-orientated learners are risk-adverse, afraid to take risks seeking the safety of performance, rather than striving towards mastery. As Reio (2007) suggests, it is only through taking risks that innovation can develop.

- Ethics concerns the balance of potential benefits versus potential risks, whereby the benefits should outweigh the risks.
- As professionals, we should continue to take measured risks to further our understanding and contribution to early childhood.

How can we progress flourishing within our settings?

As discussed earlier, one of the pillars of positive psychology is to develop flourishing institutions. Although I have discussed the barriers that prevent places flourishing, in returning to a theme in Chapter 1, a core way to promote such flourishing is through self-determination theory, a theory of intrinsic motivation. Intrinsic motivation is a form of motivation, which engages people through being of personal interest, of providing free choice, providing the person with a sense of control, and not necessarily providing any rewards except from being involved in the activity (Deci and Ryan 1985).

Yet for too long, the prevalent form of motivation has been through the behavioural approach that relates to extrinsic motivation. Here, either rewards or punishments are provided from an external agency: a parent, a teacher, society and so forth. Take a look around almost any early years setting and there will be reward charts, a milieu of assorted stickers that can be earned, praise, all provided by another person if the child meets an expectation. If the early years sector is to enable children to achieve their potential and function within the wider society, this wider society is similarly motivated extrinsically. If I drive too fast, or the wrong way, down a road, I am punished. If I work hard in my job, I receive the reward of payment and possibly holidays. It is, however, possible for extrinsic motivation to lead to intrinsic motivation through what Deci et al. (1991) refer to as regulation, for example, a child may initially be motivated to read through the use of rewards or punishments, yet in time, the child may internalise the motivation to read, reading for enjoyment rather than an extrinsic reward.

Consequently, if the self-determination theory is to be facilitated with children, why can this not be used within our own context? As a review, self-determination theory encompasses three related strands remembered through the acronym CAR: Competence, Autonomy and Relatedness.

In terms of competence, learners should perceive themselves as competent in their activities. Autonomy is where the learner should have a degree of choice within their learning. Such choice should not be a 'forced choice', for example, either eat your peas or your beans before you leave the table, but rather more along the 'what type of vegetable would you like to eat?' Relatedness refers to the learner relating well with their peers and others, also with the learning context.

Expanding self-determination theory to the early childhood setting, if a practitioner is able to discuss their planning with others and they feel that they can discuss honestly and openly their choices and decisions without judgement, but in a supportive atmosphere, this would promote the concept of relatedness. From the planning, if the practitioner can exert a degree of freedom in deciding how best they bring the planning into action, this would facilitate autonomy through choice. The practitioner then utilises their planning through their personal skills with the children, capitalising on her or his own strengths to engage with the children, which in turn relates to competency.

As a suggestion for operating with the next top-down directive that will come out within the coming month (yes, I am taking a gamble here depending on when you are reading this . . . it could be tomorrow!) then self-determination theory can be used to facilitate a flourishing setting. Opposed to disseminating the new directive through a meeting, an alternate way would be to bring together the practitioners, outline the directive, allowing open and honest questioning about where the directive has come from and what has promoted it. From here, practitioners could be encouraged to work with a partner to discuss how they could oper-ationalise part of the directive. As such, each group could use their autonomy to select what they work with, how it could be developed through identify their own SMART targets (Specific, Measurable, Achiev-able, Realistic, Time-restricted), then engage and reflect on the action.

Self-determination theory has a tradition of strong research to support the concept, whereby positive correlations have been demonstrated between this way of facilitating intrinsic motivation and positive emotions within the learning environment through enjoyment and greater achievement (Brouwer 2012; Daniels and Perry 2003; Gottfried 1990; Guay *et al.* 2010). Personally, I feel that self-determination theory is one of the best-kept theories within early childhood education and care: it makes sense, has a strong research background, it resonates as a way of promoting how things could operate rather than the dominant discourse of top-down initiatives, thus enabling an anarchistic approach of freely working together on an equal basis. How can this not be cherished within the sector as a way forward?

■   Self-determination theory relates to competence, autonomy and relatedness.
■   Self-determination theory should be encouraged within our professional settings as a way to promote an anarchistic philosophy of liberty, equality and solidarity, which in turn would enable a more intrinsically motivating working environment that enables flourishing of professional practitioners, children and others.

A critique of positive psychology

This chapter started through providing an overview of positive psychology, while progressing to explore the shadow side as can be manifested through compassion fatigue. Indeed, the field of positive psychology has been questioned in relation to the value system it appears to 'impose' in relation to American ideals, which may not be equally shared by other cultures, along with the impartiality of an empirical research tradition (Held 2002; McDonald and O'Callaghan 2008; Sundararajan 2005). Additionally, McDonald and O'Callaghan (2008) discuss how positive psychology has produced and defined what are deemed 'positive' human experiences by establishing a prescriptive set of constructs, through an almost dogmatic approach. Take for example Csikszentmihalyi's concept of flow: is 'flow' always good questions Boniwell (2008)? By this, Boniwell (2008: 28) warns that pursuing the state of flow may not necessarily be desirable and that flow may be found in activities, which 'can be morally good or bad', such as with addictions, workaholics, or indeed, any activity taken to extremes that may harm the self or others. Leontiev (2006: 50) further warns that positive psychology 'is an ideology rather than a theory' due to a lack of a unified theoretical model. Yet despite such criticisms, which may be allied at any developing theory, this chapter has encouraged personal and professional reflection as to whether this approach resonates with the reader and practitioner.

Conclusion

Enabling flourishing within children is of utmost importance, yet similarly we need to consider how the early childhood setting facilitates flourishing for practitioners to avoid burnout and compassion fatigue. Through exploring our professional practice while considering that taking measured risks is beneficial to our professional development, while challenging the accepted norms adopted through a paradigm of anarchism, we can in turn empower the early childhood sector opposed to conforming to what may be deemed the accepted norm.

As children engage and play, being true innovators in their world, should we as practitioners similarly model such innovative approaches to enable that same level of excitement, or awe and wonder, to truly progress our profession and our settings? I issue you the challenge to be more anarchic in your approach, to identify what your philosophy of practice is, to champion diversity of approaches, to enjoy the many rewards on offer and to flourish.

REFLECTIVE QUESTIONS

- What are the advantages and limitations of positive psychology?
- What are the three values of anarchism and how does this relate to your professional context?
- How could you implement the three principles of self-determination theory (competence, autonomy, relatedness), within your professional context?
- Ethics has been defined as a balance between potential benefits and potential risks, where the benefits should outweigh the risks. Consider three examples from your professional practice as to where such ethics relate.

References

Boniwell, I. (2008) *Positive Psychology in a Nutshell: A Balanced Introduction to the Science of Optimal Functioning*. London: PWBC.

Bookchin, M. (2005) *The Ecology of Freedom: The Emergence and Dissolution of Hierarchy*. Edinburgh/Oakland: AK Press.

Brookfield, S. (1995) *Becoming a Critically Reflective Teacher*. San Francisco, CA: Josey-Bass.

Brouwer, K. (2012) 'Writing motivation of students with language impairment', in *Child Language Teaching and Therapy*, 28(2), pp. 189–210.

Buckler, S. and Castle, P. (2014). *Psychology for Teachers*. London: Sage Publications Ltd.

Craig, E. (2005) 'Philosophy', in N. Warburton (ed.), *Philosophy: Basic Readings 2e*. Abingdon: Routledge.

Dahlberg, G. and Moss, P. (2005). *Ethics and Politics in Early Childhood Education*. Abingdon: RoutledgeFalmer.

Daniels, D. and Perry, K. (2003) '"Learner-centred" according to children', in *Theory into Practice*, 42(2), pp. 102–108.

Deci, E. and Ryan, R. (1985) *Intrinsic Motivation and Self-Determination in Human Behaviour*. New York: Plenum.

Deci, E., Vallerand, R., Pelletier, L. and Ryan, R. (1991) 'Motivation and education: The self-determination perspective', in *Educational Psychologist*, 26(3–4), pp. 325–346.

Dewy, J. (1916) *Democracy and Education*. New York: Free Press.

Dimova, Y. and Loughran, J. (2009) 'Developing a big picture of understanding of reflection in pedagogical practice' in *Reflective Practice*, 10(2), pp. 205–217.

Gable, S. and Haidt J. (2005) 'What (and why) is positive psychology?' in *Review of General Psychology*, 9(2), pp. 103–112.

Gentry, J., Baggerly, J. and Baranowsky, A. (2004) 'Training-as-treatment: Effectiveness of the certified compassion fatigue specialist training', in *International Journal of Emergency Mental Health*, 6, pp. 147–155.

Gentry, J., Baranowsky, A. and Dunning, K. (2002) 'ARP: The accelerated recovery compassion fatigue', in Figley, C. (ed.) *Treating Compassion Fatigue*. New York: Brunner-Routledge.

Georgeson, J. and Campbell-Barr, V. (2015) 'Attitudes and the early years workforce', in *Early Years*, 35(4), pp. 321–322.

Goldman, E. (1906) 'The child and its enemies', in *Mother Earth*, 1(2), pp. 7–14.

Goldman, E. (1911) 'Anarchism: What it really stands for', in *Anarchism and Other Essays*. New York: Mother Earth Publishing Association.

Goldman, E. (1979) 'Red Emma speaks', in Shuman, A. (ed.) *Red Emma Speaks: An Emma Goldman Reader*. London: Wildwood House.

Gottfried, A. (1990) 'Academic intrinsic motivation in young elementary school children', in *Journal of Educational Psychology*, 82, pp. 525–538.

Guay, F., Chanal, J., Ratelle, C., Marsh, H., Larose, S. and Boivin, M. (2010). 'Intrinsic, identified, and controlled types of motivation for school subject in young elementary school children', in *British Journal of Educational Psychology*, 80, pp. 711–735.

Guérin, D. (1970) *Anarchism: From Theory To Practice*. New York: Monthly Review Press.

Hart, K. and Sasso, T. (2011). 'Mapping the contours of contemporary positive psychology', in *Canadian Psychology*, 52(2), pp. 82–92.

Held, B. (2002) 'The tyranny of the positive attitude in America: Observation and speculation', in *Journal of Clinical Psychology*, 58, pp. 965–991.

Honderich, T. (ed.) (2005) *The Oxford Companion to Philosophy (New ed.)*. Oxford: Oxford University Press.

Joinson, C. (1992) 'Coping with compassion fatigue', in *Nursing*, 22(116), pp. 118–120.

Jung, C. (1964) *Man and His Symbols*. New York: Doubleday and Company, Inc.

Kinsella, E. (2009) 'Professional knowledge and the epistemology or reflective practice', *Nursing Philosophy*, 11, pp. 3–11.

Kolb, D. (1984) *Experiential Learning: Experience as the Source of Learning and Development*. Englewood Cliffs, NJ: Prentice Hall.

Kropotkin, P. (1972) *The Conquest of Bread*. (ed.) Paul Avrich. New York: New York University Press.

Kropotkin, P. (1972) *Mutual Aid: A Factor of Evolution*. London: Allen Lane.

Leontiev, D. (2006) 'Positive personality development: Approaching personal autonomy'. In Csikszentmihalyi, M. and Csikszentmihalyi, I. (eds.), *A Life Worth*

Living: Contributions to Positive Psychology. New York: Oxford University Press.

Linley, P., Joseph, S., Harrington, S. and Wood, A. (2006) 'Positive psychology: Past, present, and (possible) future', in *Journal of Positive Psychology*, 1(1), pp. 3–16.

McDonald, M. and O'Callaghan, J. (2008) 'Positive psychology: A Foucauldian critique', in *The Humanistic Psychologist*, 36, pp. 127–142.

Martin, R. (2006) 'The neuropsychology of sentence processing: Where do we stand?', in *Cognitive Neuropsychology*, 23(1), pp. 74–95.

Maslach, C. and Jackson, S. (1986) *MBI: Maslach Burnout Inventory: Manual Research Edition.* University of California, Consulting Psychologists Press, Palo Alto.

Maslow, A. (1954/1987) *Motivation and Personality 3e.* Chichester: John Wiley & Sons.

Merriman, J. (2015) 'Enhancing counsellor supervision through compassion fatigue education', in *Journal of Counselling & Development*, 93, pp. 370–377.

Miller, W. and Seligman, M. (1975) 'Depression and learned helplessness in man', in *Journal of Abnormal Psychology*, 84, pp. 228–238.

Moss, P. (2006) 'Early childhood institutions as loci of ethical and political practice', in *International Journal of Educational Policy, Research & Practice: Reconceptualizing Childhood Studies*, 7, pp. 127–136.

Mueller, J. (2012) 'Anarchism, the state and the role of education', in R. H. Haworth (ed.) (2012) *Anarchist Pedagogies: Collective Actions, Theories, and Critical Reflections on Education.* Oakland, CA: PM Press.

Nagel, T. (1987) *What Does it all Mean? A Very Short Introduction to Philosophy.* Oxford: Oxford University Press.

Pines, A. and Aronson, E. (1988) *Career Burnout: Causes and Cures.* New York: Free Press.

Rank, M. Zarparanick, T. and Gentry, J. (2009) 'Nonhuman-animal care compassion fatigue: Training as treatment', in *Best Practices in Mental Health*, 5, pp. 40–61.

Reio, T. (2007) 'Exploring the links between adult education and human resource development: Learning, risk-taking, and democratic discourse', in *New Horizons in Adult Education & Human Resource Development*, 21(1/2), pp. 5–12.

Seligman, M., Maier, S. and Greer, J. (1968) 'The alleviation of learned helplessness in dogs', in *Journal of Abnormal Psychology*, 73, pp. 256–262.

Seligman, M. and Csikszentmihalyi, M. (2000) 'Positive psychology: An introduction', in *American Psychologist*, 55, pp. 5–14.

Sheldon, K. & King, L. (2001). 'Why positive psychology is necessary' in *American Psychologist*, 56, 216–217.

Sprang, G., Clark, J. and Whitt-Woosley, A. (2007) 'Compassion fatigue, compassion satisfaction, and burnout: Factors impacting a professional's quality of life', in *Journal of Loss and Trauma*, 12, pp. 259–280.

Strangroom, J. (2006) *Little Book of Big Ideas: Philosophy.* London: A & C Black.

Sundararajan, L. (2005) 'Happiness donut: A Confucian critique of positive psychology', in *Journal of Theoretical and Philosophical Psychology*, 25(1), pp. 35–60.

Suissa, J. (2006) *Anarchism and Education.* Abingdon: Routledge.

Wain, K. (2006) 'Contingency, education, and the need for reassurance', in *Studies in Philosophy and Education*, 25, pp. 37–45.

Practices

5 Flourishing through Forest School

Bob Pilbeam

Introduction

If you go down to the woods today you probably won't be surprised to find them occupied by children and practitioners earnestly engaged in a host of fun, play activities: building dens, making mud pies, discovering insects and plants, climbing trees and lighting and cooking on fires under the close facilitative supervision of Forest School practitioners. Forest School is flourishing. But is this proper education and learning? Is all this play and 'mucking about' achieving anything useful in a child's learning?

This chapter describes, explains and critiques the growth of Forest School as an emergent concept, compares and contrasts with other experiential and outdoor learning (OL) approaches and the unique contributions of Forest School, its strengths and weaknesses, are discussed. A critical review of the existing research into evidence-based practice in Forest School is included together with a discussion of the relevance of wider research into the benefits of Outdoor Learning. The chapter explains the enthusiasm for a concept, which has struck a chord with those educating younger age groups, and those with concerns for the implications of increasingly protected and sedentary lifestyles at a time of environmental crisis.

Where does Forest School come from?

In the UK Forest School has a very clear, distinct origin. Bridgewater College (2015), in Somerset, created the concept in 1993, after a study trip to Denmark inspired staff to develop a similar ethos for children younger than had been the norm in outdoor education in the UK. Before this there has been a long tradition of outdoor learning in both the formal and informal sectors working with children that should not be forgotten. As Joyce states:

> each generation builds on the previous one, forgets it has done so and thus fails to understand itself and its times.
>
> (2012: 11)

The history of outdoor learning is a long one (Ogilvie 2013) and is a reflection of what children do outdoors to enhance learning, and the cultural, political, technological and environmental climate in which the activity takes place (Joyce 2012). A number of historical theorists or schools of thought provide strong evidence of a philosophical and academic rationale for outdoor learning. Cree and McCree (2012) refer to multiple influences: in the 1800s of American environmental thinkers Thoreau, Emerson and Muir, who challenged the impact of industrialisation on nature, developing a conservation and spiritual ethos to nature experiences; the English Romantics Wordsworth and Ruskin whose emphasis was on imagination, creativity and childhood innocence; and European childhood educational theorists Steiner, Froebel and Pestalozzi. Their contribution was to provide a focus on the outdoors and natural spaces as wonderful places to learn. In the early 1900s McMillan, Montessori and Isaacs contributed to both the philosophical and practical development of play-based, child-centred educational practices, particularly using the outdoors, which still influence early childhood education. All the above emerged at times of significant cultural change, have had a longstanding, continuing influence and remain relevant to Forest School practitioners today.

Over the same time period a number of movements emerged, many of which underpin practices today. Ogilvie (2013) categorises these in three ways: as public, private or voluntary sector initiatives. In the voluntary sector Baden-Powell's Scouts Association was formed with Royal Approval in 1908, followed shortly after by the Girl Guides in 1910, amidst social concerns for the fitness and health of young men and their preparedness to go to war. The Duke of Edinburgh's award was first established in 1956 with an emphasis on skills for life and more recently the John Muir Award (1983) was created to provide opportunities for young people to learn about and conserve wild places through participatory experiences. The Woodcraft Folk was formed in 1924, in reaction to the militaristic perception of the Scouts. It has links to and receives funding from the cooperative movement and shares values of equality, justice and peace achieved through the medium of living in the open air close to nature and, although much smaller in scale, still manages a few residential centres today.

In the public sector post the Second World War many local authority, school and National Outdoor centres were created, mostly in National Parks, to enable school children to have an outdoor education and residential experience in wild, outdoor places. Ogilvie (2013) argues these have always occupied a vulnerable and marginal position in education, despite attempts to rationalise and link to curricular subjects, partly because of their non-statutory status and because the predominant teaching methods, experiential education (Freire 1972; Athey 1990), were at odds with mainstream knowledge-based education.

In the private sector (including charities) The Outward Bound, a global adventure-based training organisation, created by Kurt Hahn, first opened its doors in 1946, with a focus on 'character building', which in other contexts was more acceptably labelled as personal and social education or PSE. There was a growing market for private commercial companies like PGL, named after its founder Peter Gordon Lawrence, formed in 1957, initially for adventure holidays and later for educational outdoor adventure programmes. Charities such as the YMCA were involved with the early development of Earth Education in the UK. Similarly, the Field Studies Council established a number of residential centres in the 1940s, which continue to grow in number, contributing to policy, practice and research on using the outdoor classroom to enable children to discover, explore and understand nature.

In the informal sector youth workers also have a tradition of using the outdoors significantly as a medium to achieve their objectives, in urban and rural settings, the aims of which broadly align with the Forest School ethos but are more frequently applied to an older age group. Within this domain the concept of adventure playgrounds helped to develop a child-centred ethos in play, initiated in post-war urban sites of dereliction where children were often found to be playing unsupervised. Knight (2009) points to more contemporary childhood education movements with similar philosophical approaches to Forest School. The Reggio Emilia work in Northern Italy is not an outdoor approach but echoes many of the principles of Forest School. Its focus is on adult facilitated, child-centred learning, with parental involvement, building a learning community with an emphasis on project work, and using a variety of creative ways to observe, record, reflect upon and evaluate work.

Te Whariki,[1] an approach that emerged from New Zealand government policy in early years education in 1996, has four central principles:

empowerment of children, appreciation of holistic learning, the importance of a community of learners in children's learning and reciprocal learning through people, places and things. This, again, is a very similar set of values to Forest School.

One influence that has not received as much recognition to date is Earth Education. Van Matre (1990) first developed this approach in USA in the 1970s and it quickly became popular in the UK, particularly with environmental educators in outdoor centres who saw it as different and innovative: Rhymer (2014). Designed for an older age group of children, with a focus on teaching ecological concepts, Earth Education includes many 'acclimatization' activities, which lend themselves to developing senses of, and feeling for, nature. Magic spots, swamp walks, tree hugging, micro hikes, feely boxes, Rhymer (2014), are all experiential activities that stimulate children's excitement and awareness of nature and are in evidence in Forest School programmes.

Outdoor learning has not been without its problems in perception and reality. In this same post Second World War era the need for a professionalisation of the outdoor learning workforce emerged, an impetus created by a number of major accidents, notably Cairngorm 1971 and Lyme Bay 1993, leading eventually to the creation of the Adventure Activities Licensing Authority (AALA) in 1996 and the Institute of Outdoor Learning (IOL) in 2001. The IOL continues to develop today and has been instrumental in the formation of the Forest School Association (FSA) in 2012.

This potted history of Outdoor Learning reveals a long standing, varied and constantly changing set of influences, some with very close associations with Forest School and others quite different. They have emerged in different places in the world, in different cultures and in response to the needs of children to learn and develop and mostly with a strong emphasis on using the outdoors as a medium of learning.

- Forest School in the UK began post 1993 and was introduced to the country by staff at Bridgewater College.
- Forest School is a specific concept, but learning in an outdoor environment was not new and there was a rich culture of this within the UK.
- Outdoor education can be linked to many of the pioneers of early childhood education including: Pestalozzi, Steiner, Froebel and MacMillan.

What is Forest School?

Forest School is based on the simple premise that children flourish in outdoor, woodland settings.

The Forest School Association (2015) provides this definition:

> Forest School is an inspirational process that offers all learners regular opportunities to achieve and develop confidence and self-esteem through hands-on learning experiences in a woodland or natural environment with trees. Forest School is a specialized learning approach that sits within and complements the wider context of outdoor and woodland education.

There are some bold claims made for the power of Forest School. McCree M. (2015) who has a PhD on leadership in Forest School, believes:

> Forest Schools is currently the fastest growing educational movement in the UK. Outdoor play and learning is exploding in popularity and interest in the UK and beyond, perhaps because it compensates for something temporarily lost in the pell-mell of our twenty-first century lives.

Forest Schools Education, part of the Archimedes Forest School provider, a leading commercial provider of Forest School training, claims that Forest School is:

> one of the most important educational developments in the world today. It is changing the way people think about education and about our connection to nature.
>
> (Forest Schools Education 2015: 1)

Knight (2009), a leading academic author on the subject, identifies eight key characteristics of Forest School:

> i) The setting is not the usual one.

Ideally this is a woodland setting, although natural areas in school or early years settings can be used to good effect. Immediately this makes for a different experience, outdoors, in a natural environment, which stimulates curiosity and excitement in participants, in contrast with the day to day indoor, unnatural and constrained, constructed experience of the conventional school day:

> What children find in the natural world rewards their initiatives and encourages their continuing engagement, for nature is particularly rich in responsive affordances. It provides all the conditions for events that hold children's attention.
>
> (Chawla 2007: 153)

ii) Forest School is made as safe as is reasonably possible in order to facilitate children's risk taking.

Gill (2007: 61) describes our risk-averse society, which displays:

> a collective failure of nerve about children's need to learn for themselves how to cope with many types of risk.

Forest School introduces risk incrementally by employing trained leaders, thorough risk assessment processes and positively encourages safe use of tools, climbing trees and lighting of fires as part of a long-term experience.

iii) Forest School happens over time.

In contrast with day trips or one-off experiences Forest School is designed to happen over the long term with frequent and repetitive sessions allowing participants to experience, remember, learn, repeat, experiment and reflect upon those experiences, creating the conditions for memorable and enduring learning.

iv) There is no such thing as bad weather, only bad clothing.

This is a long established adage in the outdoor world possibly of Scandinavian descent, explaining how, with aforethought, one can be quite comfortable in most weather conditions with the appropriate and relatively inexpensive clothing. Being exposed to the vagaries of the weather can add significantly to the pleasure of the experience or conversely to the challenges of being comfortable. In my work with undergraduate students I frequently encounter mature adults who have little knowledge or experience of the appropriate clothing to enable them to stay warm and dry in an outdoor classroom setting, and find this is a lesson quickly learnt for later sessions.

In the words of one of my undergraduate students:

> Forest School has significantly redirected my outlook on the outdoor environment. I no longer perceive it to be dangerous and unpredictable.
>
> (unpublished professional journal)

Appropriate clothing also becomes essential in role modeling when working with children and supporting building resilience in the outdoors and making it accessible.

   v) Trust is central.

Longitudinal experience fosters the development of a trusting relationship between children, leaders and other adult helpers. Using the Forest School training approach to boundaries, tool use and fire safety provides a consistency and familiarity over time, which allows for increasing trust in the use of these areas. The preferred leadership style is facilitative, observational leadership or as Cree describes it being 'on tap' rather than 'on top', in the learning process (Cree 2010: 1).

   vi) The learning is play based, child initiated and led.

This is a key distinctive quality of Forest School. The emphasis is on the process and not on any pre-determined, specific outcomes: it focuses on the holistic development of children, however that arises within the woodland setting, facilitated in a shared, democratic way. Learning arises from the inquisitive and exploratory nature of children's play expressing themes of self-determination and affiliation. Activities frequently involve working collaboratively with peers or with adult helpers; alternatively, children may choose to work autonomously.

> Early childhood education can play a significant part in creating flourishing lives and democratic societies.
>
> (Moss 2014: 35)

   vii) The sessions have beginnings and ends.

There is a subtle balance in the sessions between the structure and freedom. Practically this involves activities such as icebreakers at the beginnings of sessions and reflective times and spaces whenever relevant, for example, at the beginning of a session remembering what was done in a previous week (before), or at a moment when something significant has happened (during) or at the end of a session when either looking back or looking forward to next week (after). As Joyce (2012) suggests even though the emphasis should be about play and self-organised learning there should still be a strong structure to sessions.

viii) The staff are trained.

The Forest School Association (FSA 2015), formed in 2012, seeks to establish and maintain consistent standards and a regulatory framework. The Forest School Programme Leadership Level 3 award, currently accredited by a number of national awarding bodies, is the most appropriate qualification. Level 1 is an introduction to the Forest School ethos via the participant experience. The Level 2 qualification is designed to give the experience of assisting a Level 3 practitioner in the delivery of a programme. Evidence of prior learning and experience, say for existing teachers or outdoor practitioners, can be used to gain entry to this qualification process.

- The Forest School movement is making some bold claims about the value of such an approach to education.
- Forest School provides opportunities for children to be introduced to risk incrementally and to learn how to manage this risk.

What does research tell us about Forest School?

As the Forest School movement has gathered pace research has become more important for a number of reasons. Firstly, to prove that it works and to support the many claims made for its benefits and provide a strong rationale for its adoption; secondly, to improve theory and practice, by using thorough reflective and evaluative techniques; thirdly, for control purposes, to maintain standards and quality in delivery and safety; lastly to learn something new, to find out the unusual, the unexpected or the previously unknown (Easterby-Smith 1991).

> [E]ducators are often energised as they learn about recent research that forms the basis for the 'science of learning' or the 'art' of their work.
>
> (Wilson *et al.* 2013: viii)

The following examples demonstrate the kind of research approaches and agendas that are currently informing Forest School. They include research findings from the wider literature of the benefits of outdoor learning, then provide a progressive focus on the research that shows the potential benefits of Forest School, and finally focus on the research that has been carried out specifically in Forest School contexts.

Literature reviews of the generic field of outdoor learning, children and nature have proliferated in the first decade of the twenty-first century. Wooley *et al.* (2009) identify trends in children's play as being less outdoors, less close to home and more in designated and controlled places. In asking the question 'why don't children get out more?' they cite the familiar risk perception issues of traffic, stranger danger, litigation, media inspired fear mongering and add the idea of the perception of the 'unreliable child', not to be trusted to play unsupervised. Their research suggests the outdoors has to compete with ever more appealing indoor attractions, identifies a lack of volunteers, funding and inspired teaching and discovers the preferred constituents of children's play wish list as including homemade equipment, as in adventure playgrounds, trees, bushes, secret spaces and water. Forest School is a good fit to provide a solution to many of these issues. Charles and Loge (2012) provide an extensive review of US and UK academic literature (based on 77 articles) on the topic of the benefits to children of contact with the outdoors and nature. A consistent set of themes emerges. Proximity and easy access to nature and green environments improves human health and gives residents better attachment to an area, a greater sense of place. The design and safety of natural resources and careful management, also improve outcomes. Physical and mental health is improved by contact with nature, as is the potential for personal and social development. Taking breaks, doing something different and playing in nature lead to improved attention, learning and concentration. Professional leadership and a facilitative, democratic leadership style enhance the participant experience in the outdoors. Many of these findings reflect positively on Knight's eight characteristics of Forest School described earlier. Gill's (2014) literature review set out to test the claims made by Louv (2008), which are often cited as a starting point in discussing the fractured relationship between children and nature. Gill comments on the difficulties of researching the relationship between children and nature and points to the growing volume of empirical evidence, but also to the variable and incomplete qualities of the research thus far conducted. His study, which focused on 71 academic studies, nevertheless concludes that children should spend more time in nature, engaged in a style of learning with a strong emphasis on open ended, child directed playfulness. All three of the above research publications based on literature reviews give strong support to the Forest School approach and add credibility to the focus on child-centred play in Forest School experiences.

Another interesting source of research has emerged in the area of nature benefits, namely sponsored research by stakeholder agencies. For example, the RSPB, Forestry Commission and Natural England have conducted research either in-house or by commissioning and partnering with university departments. This research is intended to inform their own policy and is used in promoting their objectives and services. This is important to Forest School as these agencies are often land owners, with educational strategies, keen to work with educational partners, particularly those working with young children learning lessons for a positive future lifestyle and who have a strong influence on parental decision making.

An economic assessment of the value of learning outside the classroom based on the lifetime earnings associated with educational qualifications in relevant subjects is provided by Dillon and Dickie (2012), sponsored by Natural England. They put this figure at £2.1 billion for 2010. They also argue for more investment in schools and in teacher training, to increase confidence in using the outdoors for learning.

The Royal Society for the Protection of Birds (RSPB 2013) conducted research to describe children's connection with nature, identifying issues of concern as being a risk averse culture, time poor parents, reduced access to wild places, reduced environmental learning in the curriculum, an increase in screen time children, an increased commercialisation of play and thus a reduced level of informal play. Their research is explicitly described as intending to influence public policy and research conducted by O'Brien (2015) in her work for the Forestry Commission has identified the health benefits of forests as contributing to long-term physical health, emotional well-being, providing social contact and educational opportunities. In particular O'Brien's research points to that by Gill (2007), which confirms forests as ideal places for children to play including elements of nature, adventure, challenge and even a little danger.

Improved physical and emotional health is identified frequently as a benefit in the literature. Layard and Clark (2014) in their work on mental illness identify that only 1 in 4 children with mental health problems, depression, suicide, anxiety or ADHD, are in treatment. Half of all adult mental health starts in childhood and, emotional health as a child, is the best predictor of later adult life satisfaction. They argue that simple cognitive behavioural therapies are better long-term preventative solutions than drugs, recommend doing three things a day to improve mental health: take exercise, talk to someone and do something you like. They argue that social and emotional health facilitation should take place in schools.

These themes link closely to both the central concepts of flourishing (well-being, happiness, pleasure) and the overlapping concepts present in the practice of Forest School, such as concentration, involvement, self-esteem, working with others.

O'Brien and Murray (2006) completed some of the earliest evaluative research specifically on Forest School. This identified positive impacts for children's confidence, social skills, language and communication, motivation, concentration, physical skills, knowledge and understanding. Wider impacts were also discovered for practitioners who gained new perspectives on the children and on parents and families who benefitted from a 'ripple effect', when children took home an enthusiasm for their learning and getting outdoors. This latter finding is endorsed by more recent evaluative research by Ridgers and Sayers (2010) who found that families welcomed opportunities to participate with their children in natural play opportunities provided within the Forest School settings. Parents perceived their children as having fewer opportunities to engage in natural play, had concerns for their safety, particularly on the roads and had less time to play. Slade *et al.* (2013) have subsequently developed an evaluative toolkit, which can be used in their Forest School setting focusing on four key areas of: engagement, motivation, creative/critical thinking and personal/social development of participants, parents and leaders.

Knight's (2011) case study research identifies themes in practitioner experience. Forest School is found to be providing therapeutic and spiritual experiences, prompting lifestyle changes, development of creative skills and the more predictable outcomes of adventures, survival skills and education. She discovered an emphasis on the value of Forest School for boys and young men and in particular some interesting research on the links between neuroscience, and the impact of being outdoors on well-being. Although she does not make the links with Seligman's work explicitly, the similarities between positive psychology and the practical experience of young people in Forest School are worthy of comparison.

Pether (2012) sees the importance of the leadership role as the best way to embed outdoor learning into the primary curriculum. Providing vision and positive culture, opportunities for training, curriculum design and forward planning, involvement of community and partners and making use of research to inform and promote practice were all seen as strong drivers of achieving a greater emphasis on learning outdoors. This is consistent with Chawla's (2007) earlier research, which identified the importance of significant childhood experiences in the company of influential role models as an indicator of positive pro-nature attitudes in adulthood.

This review of the research literature shows both repetitive and distinctive themes emerging, which describe consistent potential benefits of participation in Forest School programmes. While, Gill (2014) summarises the research to date as being incomplete, variable in quality, predominantly short term and methodologically challenging, the empirical evidence is growing. He suggests the best evidence will come from large scale randomised controlled trials if such can be conducted.

- Research evidence demonstrates that both physical and mental health is improved with contact with nature, elements that are essential if children are to flourish.
- Forest School experiences appear to provide positive impacts for children's confidence, social skills, language and communication, motivation, concentration, physical skills, knowledge and understanding.

Why is Forest School flourishing in the UK now?

There seems little doubt that the Forest School movement is gaining in awareness and popularity. An analysis of the historical roots tells us both about strong positive influences and also identifies essential differences in provision. Social movements often emerge because of a combination of factors and influences coming together synergistically at a particular point in time generating new momentum.

Forest School is a response to the sometimes-conflicting political, social and cultural concerns of the safety, security and development of young children. It provides an antidote to the impact of an overly zealous culture of health and safety and of 'risk free' childhood, balancing the benefits and costs of risk taking in the child development process, by providing a rigorous and safety conscious approach to programme design and training. In addition, Forest School complements the grand narratives of the global environmental crisis, which call for an educational paradigm putting our relationship with the natural world at its centre. An education that facilitates an understanding of our dependence on nature and a respect for other living things is surely necessary at this time and at the earliest opportunity in a child's life.

Forest School is an approach to outdoor education and learning developed for children of a younger age group than traditionally considered appropriate. Bridgewater College's 'discovery' of alternative early years pedagogies in particular in Scandinavian countries has made many outdoor practitioners re-think the nature and relevance of their practice with all age ranges. As Knight (2011) demonstrates Forest School is now used with a wide variety of age groups and for many different purposes. At the same time the early years workforce has become increasingly professionalised, triggered by New Labour policy post 1997, evidenced in the growth of early years courses and degree level qualifications. Practitioners working with younger age groups are more highly qualified, and as a result one might hope more reflective, more challenging of the status quo and more aware of best and alternative pedagogical practice.

Forest School 're-localises' outdoor learning, making it more accessible to both children and settings. There has been a perception of outdoor learning that it takes place 'somewhere else' away from the immediate environment, at the end of a minibus journey, and needs large amounts of expensive equipment. Forest School is a means to encourage teachers and leaders to reconnect with the immediate outdoor environment, effectively and economically. EYFS policy statements make explicit the necessity of outdoor provision and Ofsted reports make reference to the quality of provision where appropriate. Forest School is designed to be a long term, enduring and integral part of the curriculum with holistic child-centred outcomes. Shifting away from the past where delivery of outdoor learning has been occasional, interruptive, poorly linked to curriculum concepts and costly it encourages research into local places and spaces where suitable environments can be found or created.[2]

There is now greater organisation among practitioners. The Forest School Association (FSA) was established in 2012 from a special interest group of the Institute of Outdoor Learning (IOL) after consultation with over 1,000 practitioners based in the UK, 74 per cent of whom supported the idea of a National Governing Body (NGB). The intended outcomes in summary were to:

- provide a professional voice
- create nationally agreed standards
- develop existing qualifications and become the awarding body
- facilitate continuing professional development for practitioners
- share best practice
- develop research

Practitioners are also getting qualified. The Forest School qualifications are relatively accessible and affordable, delivered flexibly in ways that meet the needs of busy practitioners and awarded by long established examining bodies. The FSA business plan (2012) identified that 7,000 people in the UK had qualifications in Forest School awarded by various exam boards (OCN, BTEC and NCFE) over 80 per cent of whom held the Level 3 FS Programme Leader Award, the most valuable qualification for practitioners to lead in settings. This figure was estimated to grow to over 10,000 by 2014 (Wellings 2012: 17). The number of training providers and available course is also growing, particularly at Level 3. More universities and colleges programmes include Forest School and Outdoor Learning modules. Student research at both undergraduate and postgraduate levels is increasing as are academic publications in books and journals.[3] Placements and work experience enable students to work toward the Level 2 Forest School award, having assisted in the delivery of a Forest School programme. The FSA has established a research group, including academic interest, to develop a research agenda. Early Years settings and schools are increasingly making reference to Forest School as part of their ethos and making reference to their staff holding Forest School FS qualifications. This adds credibility to provision and helps with practical issues such as insurance.

From a marketing perspective Forest School is a neatly packaged concept, which is easily reproduced, accessible and relatively inexpensive in comparison with other outdoor learning media. This makes it available for independent sole traders to set up a small business to provide for local need in early years settings or schools. Many practical guides on activities, planning and design are being published to support practitioners.[4]

As evidenced earlier in this chapter there is a flourishing literature in the theory and practice of the generic concepts of outdoor learning, of play and the specific interest in Forest School. At the same time the more recently emerging literature of reflective practice[5] in the early years increased the value of experiential learning dimension of Forest School by emphasising not just the experience leading to learning but the reflection on that experience, which makes the learning concrete and enduring, Kilvington and Wood (2010), Brock (2015). Similarly, practitioner research is demonstrating the particular relevance of Forest School to kinaesthetic learners, children lacking in confidence, children struggling to cope in the classroom and children with little contact with nature, Knight (2011). Parents want to participate. Early years settings require higher ratios than in primary, more so in using outdoor learning. Parent volunteers often welcome the chance to get involved in their child's development and learn more about their children and their learning in the process. Other stakeholders want to get involved. A number of nature-based agencies, such as the RSPB, Natural England, The Woodland Trust, The National Trust, are either facilitating the use of Forest School on their land or funding research to support their policy objectives. The Forestry Commission (the biggest owner of forests in the UK), has in the last 45 years changed their policy and public perception of forests from that of an industrial landscape for timber production, or indeed tax avoidance, to places of leisure, recreation and learning. My first job on leaving school in the early 1970s was to promote the newly built Forestry Commission woodland holiday cabins. Since then Forestry Commission forest centres have become places for art, sport, therapy, learning, conservation and increasingly a place for research, which proves the benefits of being in woodlands, O'Brien (2015). Indicative of these changed public perceptions was the outcry in 2010 when it was suggested national forests should be sold off. A YouGov poll[6] suggested 84 per cent of the public would be against such a plan.

These are the positive indicators of growth in the value and interest in Forest School, but what of the future of Forest School?

- The Forest School movement appears to be developing in the UK and part of the attraction appears to be that it specifically meets the needs of younger children.
- Forest School provides opportunities not simply for experiential learning, but for reflective learning too.

What does the future hold for those involved in Forest School in the UK?

Forest School is in the growth stage of its life cycle and there are often tensions between those in different sectors, private, public or voluntary and Forest School is no different. Similarly, natural conservatism among professionals can create what Illich (1971) calls social or cultural iatrogenesis, namely, a self-interested protectionism of disciplinary boundaries and resistance to innovation. Joyce (2012) argues there will always be tensions between practitioners and regulators. Nevertheless, a positive start has been made by the FSA in establishing its identity and maintaining a collective idea of what it is and what it is not.

From a critical perspective Leather (2015) makes a number of observations about Forest School. Firstly, that the claims for outcomes are not supported by evidence and that this is evidence of a poorly explored theoretical base. This is acknowledged to some extent (by Cree and McCree 2012; Knight 2011 and the FSA 2012) and identified as a priority area in a developing research agenda. The literature reviews discussed previously similarly propose further research to substantiate the validity and outcomes of the Forest School approach. Arguably Forest School is growing because of its accessibility to practitioners, who are themselves in a developing profession, and it is growing from the grass roots.

Second, Leather (2015) is critical of the commercial motive of some providers. Currently providers are mixed and varied in background and motive. Public, private and voluntary sector providers are all represented. The market is an open and accessible one, the FSA has been created to represent the interests of all involved and has positively encouraged this open market approach. As seen from the example of PGL in the Adventure Holiday and Education market there is no reason why commercial providers cannot play an important and longstanding role in the development and progression of Forest School without dominating or corrupting the principles and practices.

Third, Leather (2015) is concerned at the exportability of the concept to other countries and cultures. As Bridgewater College did in the UK, Forest School was developed by taking the most attractive ideas from a Scandinavian context and culture and making them appropriate and relevant to early years practitioners here. In mature democracies with well-established educational systems this should not pose a threat so much as an opportunity for change.

Forest School is not the only initiative that focuses on outdoor learning. For example, Growing Schools, Learning through Landscapes and Natural Connections are all on-going projects with an emphasis on re-localising children's experiences, be that through growing food, caring for their local environment or reconnecting with nearby nature. These are all complimentary rather than competitive schemes and demonstrate a wider desire to enable children to learn more outdoors. Forest School has contributed to a rethink of the way settings and schools use their grounds. Titman (1994) provided a critique of the use of outdoor spaces and suggestions for the reclamation and redesign of outdoor places and spaces, which have been neglected in many cases. Robertson (2015) and Pace (2014) provide up-to-date examples of how these ideas can be extended and linked to curriculum. O'Brien (2015) proposes the Forestry Commission could get more involved in providing woodlands nearer to places of learning.

Forest School may also offer a more balanced gender representation to children. In the past men have dominated the outdoor pursuits profession in particular. Providing positive female role models as facilitators in outdoor learning in the early years may do much to address this imbalance. Participation in the FSA national conference in 2015 was illustrative of this point in that 90 per cent of participants were women. The emphasis of Outdoor Education has traditionally been as an extension of physical education, using the outdoors as a gymnasium, competing against nature. Forest School places more emphasis on being in nature and being creative with natural materials.

- Forest School has positively contributed to a rethink of the way settings and schools use their grounds.
- Forest School offers a more gender-balanced approach to learning in the outdoor environment than is offered by other approaches. This may be part of the reason for its growing strength and may support its development in the future.

Conclusion

Reflecting on Seligman's (2011) five elements of the concept of Flourishing: positive emotion, engagement, meaning, positive relations, accomplishment; Forest School seems to tick all the boxes. Forest School sessions require physical, social and emotional engagement from the outset: the pedagogy is experiential, participatory and child led. From the evidence provided in this chapter children for the most part seem to love being in the outdoors, learning and development are positively affected and positive relationships are created between the children, their learning facilitators and parent helpers.

REFLECTIVE QUESTIONS

- How do the principles behind practice relate to early years learning and child development theories?
- What do young children and their adult facilitators gain from outdoor learning experiences?
- What questions does this raise for room or setting based learning?

Notes

1   www.education.govt.nz/early-childhood/teaching-and-learning/ece-curriculum/te-whariki/

2   See Robertson (2015) for some good examples.
3   For example, Danks and Schofield (2013), Pace (2014) and Robertson (2015).
4   For example, www.muddyfaces.co.uk/forest_schools.php; www.forestschools.com; www.educationscotland.gov.uk/Images/OutdoorLearning; www.wild-learning.net.
5   For example, Brock, A. (2015) *The Early Years Reflective Practice Handbook.* London: Routledge; Knight, S. (2011) *Risk and Adventure in the Early Years.* London: Sage; Waller, T. *et al.* (2010) 'The dynamics of early childhood spaces: opportunities for outdoor play?' *European Early Childhood Education Research Journal, 18(4), Special Issue: Outdoor play and learning.*
6   www.theguardian.com/environment/2011/jan/22/poll-england-forest-sell-off

References

Athey, C. (1990) *Extending Thought in Young Children: A Parent-Teacher Partnership.* London: Paul Chapman Publishing.

Bridgewater College, U.K. (2015) Forest School Adult Courses. [Online] Available from: www.bridgwater.ac.uk/subject.php?sector=2&subject=223 [accessed 09 April 2015].

Brock, A. (2015) *The Early Years Reflective Practice Handbook.* London: Routledge.

Brookfield, S. (1995) *Becoming a Critically Reflective Teacher.* San Francisco: Jossey-Bass.

Charles, C. and Loge, A. (2012) Health Benefits to Children from Contact with the Outdoors and Nature. [Online] Available from: www.childrenandnature.org/downloads/CNNHealthBenefits2012.pdf [accessed 13 April 2015].

Chawla, L. (2007) 'Childhood experiences associated with care for the natural world: A theoretical framework for empirical results', in *Children, Youth and Environments,* 17(4), pp. 144–170.

Constable, K. (2015) The Outdoor Classroom in Practice, Ages 3–7. Oxon: Routledge.

Cree, J. (2010) Forest School and the Learning Outside the Classroom Manifesto. [Online] Available from: www.essexfei.co.uk/Documents/Frontpage/Forest%20School%20and%20the%20Learning%20Outside%20the%20Classroom%20Manifesto.pdf [accessed 09 April 2015].

Cree, J. and McCree, M. (2012) 'A brief history of the roots of Forest School in the UK', in *Horizons,* 60, pp. 32–34.

Danks, F. and Schofield, J. (2013) *The Wild Weather Book.* London: Frances Lincoln.

Diamond, J. (2011) *Collapse.* London: Penguin.

Dillon, J. and Dickie, I. (2012) 'Learning in the Natural Environment: Review of social and economic benefits and barriers', UK: Natural England Commissioned Reports, Number 092.

Easterby-Smith, M. (1991) *Management Research.* London: Sage.

Forest School Association, F.S.A. (2015) What is Forest School. [Online] Available from: www.forestschoolassociation.org/what-is-forest-school/ [accessed 26 March 2015].

Forest Schools Education, Archimedes Ltd. (2015) Forest Schools Education. Course Material. [Online] Available from: www.forestschools.com/course-material/forest-schools-general/ [accessed 10 April 2015].

Forestry Commission, F.C. (2015) History of the Forestry Commission. [Online] Available from: www.forestry.gov.uk/forestry/CMON-4UUM6R [accessed 10 April 2015].

Friere, P. (1972) *Pedagogy of the Oppressed*. London: Penguin.

Gill, T. (2007) *No Fear, Growing Up in a Risk Averse Society*. London: Calouste Gulbenkian Foundation.

Gill, T. (2014) 'The benefits of children's engagement with nature: A systematic literature review', in *Children, Youth Environments*, 24(2), pp. 10–34.

Gore, A. (2006) *An Inconvenient Truth*. UK: Paramount. [Film].

Illich, I. (1975) *Medical Nemesis*. London: Marion Boyars.

Joyce, R. (2012) *Outdoor Learning Past and Present*. Berkshire: Oxford University Press.

Kilvington, J. and Wood, A. (2010) *Reflective Playwork*. London: Continuum.

Klein, N. (2014) *This Changes Everything*. UK: Penguin.

Knight, S. (2009) *Forest Schools and Outdoor Learning in the Early Years*. London: Sage.

Knight, S. (2011) *Forest School for All*. London: Sage.

Layard, R. and Clark, D. (2014) *Thrive*. London: Allen Lane.

Leather, M. (2015) 'Lost in translation: A critique of "Forest School" from a UK perspective' in *Pathways: The Ontario Journal of Outdoor Education*, 27(2), pp. 11–14.

Lindon, J. (2012) *Reflective Practice and Early Years Professionalism*. London: Hodder Education.

Louv, L. (2008) *Last Child in the Woods: Saving Our Children from Nature-Deficit Disorder* 2e. Chapel Hill: Algonquin Books.

McCree, M. (2015) Outdoor play & learning and Forest Schools. [Online] Available from: https://melmccree.wordpress.com/ [accessed 26 March 2015].

Moss, P. (2014) *Transformative Change and Real Utopias in Early Childhood Education*. Abingdon: Routledge.

O'Brien, E. A. and Murray, R. (2006) A marvellous opportunity for children to learn: a participatory evaluation of Forest School in England and Wales. [Online] Available from: www.forestry.gov.uk/pdf/fr0112forestschoolsreport.pdf/$FILE/fr0112forestschoolsreport.pdf [accessed 13 April 2015].

O'Brien, L. (2015) We Have Stopped Moving. [Online] Available from: www.forestry.gov.uk/pdf/Wehavestoppedmoving_FINAL1.pdf/$FILE/Wehavestoppedmoving_FINAL1.pdf [accessed 10 April 2015].

Ogilvie, K. (2013) *Roots and Wings*. Dorset: Russell House Publishing.

Pace, M. (2014) *I Love Forest School*. London: Bloomsbury.

Pether, T. (2012) Leadership for embedding outdoor learning within the primary curriculum. [Online] Available from: www.outdoor-learning.org/Portals/0/IOL%20Documents/Newsletters_Docs/leadership-for-embedding-outdoor-learning-within-the-primary-curriculum%20(3).pdf [accessed 10 April 2015].

Pike, E. and Beames, S. (2012) *Outdoor Adventure and Social Theory*. Abingdon: Routledge.

Rawles, K. (2012) *The Carbon Cycle: Crossing the Great Divide*. South Lewis: Two Ravens Press.

Rhymer, J. (2014) Earth Education and Forest School. An interview with Jon Cree. [Online] Available from: www.eartheducation.org.uk/programmes/Earth Education_v_ForestSchool.pdf [accessed 08 April 2015].

Rickinson, M., Dillon, J., Teamey, K., Morris, M., Choi, M., Sanders, D. and Benefied, P. (2004) A review of research on outdoor learning. [Online]

Available from: www.field-studies-council.org/media/268859/2004_a_review_of_research_on_outdoor_learning.pdf [accessed 22 April 2015].

Ridgers, N. and Sayers, J. (2010) Natural Play in the Forest; Forest School Evaluation. Parts 1 & 2. [Online] Available from: www.merseyforest.org.uk/our-work/forest-school/ [accessed 10 April 2015].

Robertson, J. (2015) *Dirty Teaching*. Carmarthen: Independant Thinking Press.

Ryder Richardson, G. (2014) *Creating a Space to Grow 2e*. Abingdon: Routledge.

Seligman, M. (2011) *Flourish*. London: Nicholas Brealey Publishing.

Slade, M., Lowery, C. and Bland, K. (2013) 'Evaluating the impact of Forest Schools: A collaboration between a university and a primary school', in *British Journal of Learning Support*, 28(2), pp. 66–72.

Te Whariki (Available online: www.education.govt.nz/early-childhood/teaching-and-learning/ece-curriculum/te-whariki/) [accessed April 2015].

Titman, W. (1994) *Special Places, Special People*. UK: WWF.

Van Matre, S. (1990) *Earth Education: A new beginning*. USA: Institute for Earth Education.

Waller, T., Sandseter, E., Wyver, S., Ärlemalm-Hagsér, E. and Maynard, T. (2010) 'The dynamics of early childhood spaces: Opportunities for outdoor play?' in *European Early Childhood Education Research Journal*, 18(4), pp. 437–443.

Watters, J. (2011) 'Edinburgh's Forest School Partnership Project: "Building Local Capacity"', in Knight, S. (ed.) (2011) *Forest School for All*. London: Sage.

Wellings, E. (2012) Forest School National Governing Body Business Plan. [Online] Available from: www.outdoor-learning.org/Portals/0/ForestSchool Association/FS%20NGB%20FINAL%20BP%202012%5B1%5D.pdf [accessed 10 April 2015].

Wild-Learning (available online) www.wild-learning.net/index.php/early-years-forest-school/ [accessed April 2016].

Wilson, D. and Conyers, M. (2013) *Flourishing in the First Five Years*. Maryland, USA: R & L Education.

Wooley, H., Pattacini, L. and Somerset-Ward, A. (2009) Children and the natural environment: experiences, influences and interventions-summary. [Online] Available from: http://publications.naturalengland.org.uk/publication/37005 [accessed 09 April 2015].

6 Parent partnership for flourishing in an age of austerity

Michael Gasper

Introduction

This chapter is in two parts. The first, *Parent Partnership for Flourishing* explores the nature and value of parent partnership and the concept of flourishing. The second considers Parent Partnership for Flourishing *in an Age of Austerity*, reflecting on the impact of government policy on the reality of parent partnership. Throughout, the word parent is used to include anyone in a parental capacity or undertaking parental responsibilities and functions, therefore it includes carers and anyone who, for the child, is a 'significant other', whether or not they have actual parental responsibility. Partnership refers to purposeful interaction and here will include any combination of parent–child interaction and parent–professional interaction. Seligman (2011, p239) proposes the following criteria for flourishing:

> being in the upper range of positive emotion, and engagement, and meaning and positive relationships and positive accomplishment.

This definition encompasses '*high self-esteem, optimism, resilience, vitality, self-determination and positive relationships*' (ibid. 2011, p. 238) plus accomplishment. Seligman's definition works for all human beings. It is applied here to parents and their children and the professionals who work with them. It is applied to each individually and their interaction, including with their immediate, local and national contexts. To flourish as individuals requires self-confidence and a secure grounding in who we are, awareness of and sensitivity towards others, a degree of flexibility in how we interact, but also a degree of assertiveness. This chapter proposes a match between the characteristics of personal flourishing (Seligman

2011) and organisational flourishing (Wenger *et al.* 2002) including at local and national governmental levels.

The stringent criteria for flourishing are underpinned and paralleled by the same characteristics and accomplishments required for positive child development. Positive influences take effect before birth with the foetus responding to the mother's internal and external rhythms, to sounds and movement. At birth babies have already acquired a relationship with their mother, a foundation on which to build. Therefore positive early interaction is important to establish optimum conditions for flourishing and early identification of parents who may struggle in their ability to engage with their child, together with open access to parents who are seeking help and guidance, are essential to allow the maximum time for restoring parents' confidence and improving conditions for flourishing.

Successful identification and appropriate, focused support depends on adequate resources being provided, enabling trusting and supportive relationships to develop between parents and professionals and between professionals themselves in coherent, multi-agency working. The second part of the chapter reflects on the effects of the reduction in resourcing at all levels since 2012 and the subsequent reduction in the frequency and quality of support, and beyond a certain point, its effective denial (Moss 2014). It is mentioned here because adequate resourcing and realistic expectations are critical to enabling trusting relationships to develop. The theory and practice of early intervention, including parents as equal partners, is not new. It became established as policy in the first decade of the new century, with models in the United Kingdom (Whalley *et al.* 2007; Siraj Blatchford *et al.* 2007; Anning and Ball 2008; Weinstein *et al.* 2007; Trodd and Chivers 2011; Gasper 2010) reflecting best practice from around the world and in particular, Te Whariki in New Zealand, Scandinavia, particularly Forest Schools, and Europe, notably Reggio Emilia in Italy.[1] In more recent times 'austerity' has become the watchword in the United Kingdom and significant reductions in funding have constrained the ability of agencies involved in ECEC to continue the range and frequency of support, or to keep pace with the identification of those who desire or need it.

This chapter re-asserts the value and nature of early intervention in building strong, effective partnerships with parents in order to enhance their confidence and improve their knowledge and understanding of the importance and value of interacting positively with their children, in order for those children to flourish (Seligman 2007; Gopnik *et al.* 2004, pp. 277–294). It recognises the challenges created by reduced resources and persistent re-organisation and the need to make best use of remaining resources, in particular by improving multi-agency working. It calls for a better understanding of the harmful reality of the effects of austerity on parents and their children.

Part 1 – Parent partnership for flourishing

Partnership with parents and children as agents

The bond between parent and child is critical to their mutual well-being. Attachment theory is well established and recognises the long-term effects of positive and negative attachment (Bowlby 1993). Bowlby also recognises attachment behaviours continuing to affect individuals into adolescence and adulthood particularly when under stress or threat, and that the intensity, quality and nature of the response is directly affected by their relationship with their parent or 'significant person':

> A feature of attachment behaviour of the greatest importance clinically, and present irrespective of the age of the individual concerned, is the intensity of the emotion that accompanies it, the kind of emotion aroused depending on how the relationship between the individual attached and the attachment figure is faring. If it goes well, there is joy and a sense of security. If it is threatened, there is jealousy, anxiety, and anger. If broken there is grief and depression. Finally, there is strong evidence that how attachment behaviour comes to be organized within an individual turns in high degree on the kind of experience he has in his family of origin, or, if he is unlucky, out of it.
>
> (Bowlby 1993, p. 4)

Attachment is therefore, critical to the well-being of children and their ability to flourish in childhood and beyond. It involves both parent and child interaction. The work of Colwyn Trevarthen[2] has captured the subtle 'dance' and musical interaction between mother and baby, which suggests that the child's instinctive role is far more active than passive. Gopnik *et al.* (2004) reaffirm the importance of early interaction and the importance of this continuing, recognising the mutual benefit to mother and baby and the active nature of their interaction, which provides a reward of joy for both. It therefore follows that the sooner any threat to secure attachment can be identified and appropriate support provided, the better. Focus on attachment has been an important part of ante and post-natal medical and social care for many years with professionals working with parents to help them achieve a secure relationship with their child. Positive attachment provides a secure foundation for flourishing.

The approaches used to support attachment reflect an equal partnership between professionals and parents. The partnership between parent and potentially their child and professionals begins before birth. The quality of this experience can be positive or negative from the parent's perspective of the nature and value of such interaction, therefore this first contact is critical. Over time the nature of the relationship will change as will the relationship between the parent and their child. While this may be stating the obvious, many parents, particularly mothers, are emotionally vulnerable during pregnancy and after the birth of their child. For the partnership to flourish requires sensitivity and awareness on the part of the professional. This principle of equal partnership with parents has shifted from an autocratic 'top down' perspective, with parents 'done to' by professionals who 'know best', towards a more democratic model where the parent is valued and nurtured, mentored by professionals as an equal partner. But what do we understand equal partnership and inclusion to mean?

- Attachment is essential if a child is to flourish and therefore there needs to be investment in these early relationships that support the child.
- The relationship with the mother begins prior to birth.

Independence and intervention: support for flourishing

Equality and inclusion are deceptive concepts. They are not absolutes. Their meaning depends on the interpreter's philosophical stance and the moral, political, social and cultural organisation of the context in which they are found. Within developed Western society and broadly democratic culture, their meaning and application seems obvious at first sight: we do not like to be excluded or treated unequally or as an inferior; we like to be included, valued and treated equally. Yet we also recognise we are all different: we need attention that is differentiated; the urgency of need varies, so requires differentiated time allocation; the degree of seriousness increases or decreases the immediacy of need. Friere and Shor (1987) refers to 'transformational dialogue', which is 'open and inclusive'; 'Dialogue is a permanent tension in the relationship between authority and liberty' (p. 102). We believe in the right to lead our own lives yet recognise that intervention by others can be helpful or essential to improve its quality and of those whose lives we touch or whose lives touch ours. Critical to this is who decides why, when, how and what kind of intervention will take place, how long it will continue or when it will be reviewed or cease once started. The apparent contradiction between independence and intervention in relationships is justified by intention and motivation: society recognises the need to protect children from varying degrees of intended or unintended harm. To some extent the same is true of parents: society recognises the right to intervene when a parent is deemed to be putting their child at risk, although achieving the same in reverse, a parent attempting to intervene when they believe society or officials representing society are putting their child at risk, is never as easy. There are varying degrees of need and risk and the professionals with different skills are the agents of society leading intervention. This kind of intervention is for the most extreme cases and occasions when professionals have to make the least bad choice and the parent has to abide by the decision. It is more usual for additional support to be provided for the parent to help restore stability and extremes can be avoided with earlier recognition of need and earlier intervention where trust can be built. Where there is trust, parents will actively seek support, or recognise and acknowledge they need it once asked (Gasper 2010). Establishing mutual trust is a critical factor in successful relationships between professionals, parents and children and in many ways successful relationships reflect the features of successful attachment, with the professional in the parallel role to the 'parent'. Parents respond positively when treated with respect. Quinton (2004, p. 81) notes: '*parents (want) services to treat them like adults and to see them as partners in solving their problems*'. This desire is echoed by Anning and Ball (2008).

The aim of professional early intervention is to support parents and children enabling them to regain control of their lives and to rebuild self-confidence. The value of multi-agency involvement is to bring diverse skills and perspectives to bear in identifying the needs of the child and the parent, identifying the issues involved, and with the parent and child arriving at strategies to move forward. Whittington, C. Chapter 2 in Weinstein *et al.* (2003, p. 56) underlines the importance of interaction to flexible strategic planning raised in the Audit Commission (2002a) report, paragraph 19, arguing: '*senior managers must engage directly with service users to enable them to shape the services*'. When the parent and child are included in consultation and decision making it shows they are valued, and that their skills and limitations are recognised; it potentially increases their self-esteem and encourages their ownership of their lives, and increases the chances of planned service provision matching their needs while retaining the flexibility to adapt and change with those needs. This process requires skill and time, gradually helping the child[3] and parent to progress by taking small steps and by building on success, sometimes beginning separately until they can do so jointly. The initial approach used will need to vary with each family and parent. Collette Tait (Whalley *et al.* 2007, p. 33) shares nine models of engagement used by the Pen Green team over a three-year research project. Cath Arnold (ibid., 2007, p. 65) highlights that: '*Parents are experts on the subject of their own children and can share their expertise with professionals*' and that '*It can be helpful if professionals share specialised language and concepts with parents*'. In taking account of parents' perspectives alongside professionals' skills there is a recognition of changing factors in the parent's and child's lives as well as those of professionals, which can affect the dynamic and improve or reduce interaction.

Price *et al.* (2012, p. 164) identify the following aspects of the relationship between parent and professional in the early years: '*Maintaining professional boundaries and relationships with the child and their parents/carers, whilst consulting with parents/carers on all aspects of the child's care in order to include them, respect their wishes and acknowledge them as the main carer of the child, is at the heart of this professional relationship*'.

Positive psychology is used extensively throughout the process on interaction at all levels. It is the foundation of establishing an initial relationship, building on it and developing it to enhance the parent's self-confidence, as well as being fundamental to improving their relationship with their child and the child's opportunities to flourish (Seligman 2011, p. 40; John 2008[4])

The emphasis on the positive is based in developmental psychology, which builds 'resilience', which is a necessary prerequisite for flourishing. Resilience is recognised as '*a dynamic of interaction between socio-cultural contexts and developing individuals*'. (Howard *et al.* 1999 in Edwards *et al.* 2009). Pascal and Bertram (2010) in their Accounting Early for Lifelong Learning (AcE) initial assessment programme recognise *resilience, independence, creativity and self-motivation* as four key attributes of '*attitudes and dispositions to learn*'. All four are underpinned by emotional well-being, which in turn grows from positive interaction. Restoring positive interaction is a fundamental aim of early intervention and often needs a key worker supported by a variety of professionals from different areas of knowledge and expertise.

- ■   Parents respond well when they are treated with respect and their expertise in relation to their own children is acknowledged.

- Creating mutual trust is an essential element in developing successful relationships between professionals, parents and children.
- Successful relationships can be considered to reflect the features of successful attachment.

Case studies

Case Study 1 is a Children's Centre evaluation report covering a 12-month period of an outreach programme. It illustrates what was achieved when a Children's Centre team used the AcE (Pascal and Bertram 2010) programme as an assessment tool to help them engage more proactively with parents. The programme includes the parents as equal partners and uses observations at home and at provided settings to assess childrens' starting points, to focus on areas of need and to develop early intervention to improve well-being and achievement[5] for children and their parents. The Case Study involved 24 parents and their children, with 19 used in the final analysis, who were partners in assessing children's readiness for school in four key areas of the AcE programme: A&D – Attitudes and Dispositions to learn; CLL – Communication, Language and Literacy development; SC&SC – Social Competence and Self Concept and EWB – Emotional Well Being. Figure 6.1 shows that at the start of the focused intervention programme: '*all the children were at risk of a significant delay in their Communication, Language and Literacy development and Social Competence and Self Concept. The vast majority were demonstrating significant delay in their Attitudes and Dispositions to learn and Emotional Well Being*'. Figure 6.2 shows a clear improvement, '*this delay was reduced in all four domains, with the biggest reduction made in Attitudes and dispositions to learn which suggests that the children who have experienced [AcE] will be better prepared as learners as a result*'. However, the commentary also recognises that: '*Although a good percentage of children have made gains within their Communication, Language and Literacy development, there still remain no children who are achieving at the expected level*'. This highlights the enormous challenge presented by developmental delay and how hard it is for children to regain the 'norms'. This was recognised and emphasised by Bronfenbrenner (1990). It does call into question the value of linear measurement, which sees achievement as a straight line from fixed point to fixed point and which takes no account of the individual effort made and progress achieved for those falling short of the fixed mark, nor the value and importance of emotional and social factors. The report acknowledges areas to develop in the process to achieve a more reliable assessment including allowing staff and parents more time for child observations and greater use of the parents' knowledge of their child.

Case Study 1

Key:
CLL – Communication, Language and Literacy development
A&D – Attitudes and Dispositions to learn
SC&SC – Social Competence and Self Concept
EWB – Emotional Well Being

Table 6.1 Initial assessment

	CLL	A&D	SC&SC	EWB
At risk of significant delay (25–49%)	100%	95%	100%	95%
At risk of delay (50–65%)				5%
At the level expected (66–75%)		5%		
Ahead (76% +)				

Table 6.2 Final assessment

	CLL	A&D	SC&SC	EWB
At risk of significant delay (25–49%)	68%	68%	95%	89%
At risk of delay (50–65%)	26%	16%		5%
At the level expected (66–75%)		10%		5%
Ahead (76% +)		5%	5%	

Please note: Some of the percentages may not add up to 100% because of the need to round figures up or down, but these figures are consistent with the data provided.

This example demonstrates the benefits of positive partnership at all levels. The children benefitted through the increased focus brought about by the partnership of their parents and the staff team, the increased opportunities to interact with their parents, which enabled closer bonding, increased use of language and a shift towards being attended to more closely. The parents benefitted through being valued by the team who took their opinions, feelings, ideas and efforts to increase interaction seriously and supported their ideas, and by experiencing the joy of seeing their children begin to achieve and progress. The team members benefitted from being brought together with a common focus, developing professional knowledge and skills, sharing their experiences and ideas and supporting each other to develop their reflective practice. The organisation benefitted through a shared sense of achievement and an increased sense of direction and purpose.

Case Study 2 illustrates what can be achieved in partnership with parents and partner agencies, in particular the importance of the relationship between the children's centre key worker and the parent, other centre staff and health visitors. The description covers a two-and-a-half-year period.

Case Study 2

Context

Two-parent family neither of whom are in work, three children – boy 3, girl 2, boy 6 months

Identified needs:

- Family eligible for two-year funding
- Eldest child's self-esteem very low

Additionally:

- Mum's lack of confidence resulting in children constantly staying in the flat as she does not like going out
- Mum has poor mental health
- Dad isolated and not able to find work due to mum's dependency on him

Aims:

- To carry out six [*name of support programme*] sessions with eldest child and family
- To improve child's self-esteem
- For child to express his emotions
- To support mum with choosing a nursery and ensuring a smooth transition for child

Partner agencies:

> Health Visitor
> Community Mental Health
> Job Centre Plus
> Adult Education

Narrative:

> *The family were referred on by the children's centre home learning team whose assessment was based on AcE. The home learning arose because of the mother's poor mental health. The initial visit to the family was done jointly with the Health Visitor. We spent this session exploring the needs of the family as well as the eldest child by completing AcE. The support worker initially worked with mum and the older child, who was very bright but had been affected by his mum's mood. Mum found it very difficult to manage her own self-esteem and found it difficult to leave the house without dad consequently the child also was very low in confidence to try new things. AcE clearly identified that the child was struggling with expressing himself, and that his self-esteem was very low. (Name 'A') became the child's key worker.*
>
> *'A' supported the family with their housing needs and they successfully moved and are now settled in more suitable accommodation.*
>
> *When the middle child was due to start nursery, 'A' did a piece of pre-school support with that child and mum, again to improve both their confidence around play and support their interactions and supported the family to look around schools for the older child.*
>
> *In the remaining five sessions with the middle child 'A' provided activities that would encourage the child to ask questions, thereby using his language and building his self-esteem. 'A' used the role model approach to encourage mum to do the same activities with him.*
>
> *This gave mum more confidence in knowing her child's self-esteem will develop. She felt it was her fault he did not have any self-esteem and confidence due to her own needs. A play diary was created by mum and dad.*
>
> *Two joint visits to different nurseries took place with 'A' and the family. A suitable setting was chosen and a Team Around the Child (TAC) meeting was held to share the play diary and to ensure a smooth transition. The nursery provided extra settling in sessions and invited the whole family in. This allowed him to gain confidence and get to know the staff.*
>
> *All seemed well, so the case was closed.*

The case was re-opened because the middle child (who was now in nursery) stopped talking (becoming selectively mute) and the nursery was concerned. 'A' held a TAC meeting to fully ascertain the middle child's needs. A lead professional was appointed and it was agreed that it was a series of difficult life events, which prompted her becoming selectively mute. These included:

- *Her older brother leaving the nursery setting to go to school*

- *A physical move in nursery as her group moved to another building*

- *Her close friend was diagnosed with leukaemia and was backwards and forwards to hospital, which she was kept informed about and seemed to understand the seriousness of what was happening.*

A worker was appointed to do some therapeutic play sessions with mum and the child in the home (Theraplay), but logistically this was difficult, so the nursery was supported to provide similar opportunities there for the little girl to help her regulate her emotions.

At the time of writing, dad has been able to return to work because of mum's much improved mental health and mum is now doing an Avon round and I am about to close the case as all the children seem to be thriving.

Child now attends nursery and is starting to talk to the other children, and playing alongside them, he has also made a best friend.

Mum says 'although he can still become shy, child is starting to use words and join in with others when they are out with friends'

He also sang a song in front of his peers at nursery.

Outcomes achieved:

Family: Mum has now started to go out of the flat with dad and the children, as a family.

Evidence:

'Going to the park which the children love but I still don't think I can do this on my own'.

Mum is now able to recognise child's interests and create activities that will challenge his abilities and stimulate him.

Adults: Knowing how to play and understand the child's needs.

Mum and child now spending one to one time.

Dad started applying for volunteering positions and has now gained employment.

Evidence:

'[Child] helps me with the cooking most days, and he is now also eating better, he also uses more language when cooking'.

Children: Have become more sociable with others and interact with other children. Expressing his emotions using language. Child's confidence has improved.

Evidence:

Child now attends nursery and is starting to talk to the other children, and playing alongside them, he has also made a best friend.

Mum says 'although he can still become shy, child is starting to use words and join in with others when they are out with friends.'

He also sang a song in front of his peers at nursery.

Remaining areas not yet achieved:

Mum's confidence has improved. She has started to leave the flat.

Sustained outcomes:

The child continues to attend nursery.

Mum attended CBT to improve her mental health.

Next steps:

Outreach support is now being provided for the family by the same worker. Mum has secured a volunteering position as an administrator at the Children's Centre to build her skills and confidence. She has also signed up for a free computer course. Outreach support is now being provided for the family by the same worker.

What can be seen clearly is the value and importance of the key worker role and the initial work carried out by the home and pre-school support programme, which identified needs for one child and led to support for the whole family. In this case the mother's need was limiting her ability to provide a stimulating home environment in which her family could thrive. Focus on the child alone was not enough without also supporting the mother to build her confidence and develop more secure well-being and to rebuild the positive bonding between herself and her children. The father also benefitted from the gradual improvement in the mother's confidence, as did the other children in the family. Little could have been achieved without developing trust with the mother, and this example also shows that this takes time to build. The relationship with the key worker is critical and through them relationships with other partners both within the children's centre team and beyond, ensuring appropriate specialist help is provided at critical times. The development of Team Around the Child[6] (TAC) meetings has enabled a range of professional involvement to identify and plan how best to meet the needs of the focus child and each family member.

The first two examples show what can be achieved when parents are included as partners, but also that progress takes time, is rarely smooth or linear and outcomes are seldom directly proportionate to the input. Case Study 3 illustrates the complexity of working holistically with families, including combining with partner agencies, and shows the uneven and unpredictable nature of the progress made but with the low points reducing in frequency and intensity and high points rising over time, showing gradual improvement. It is worth noting that the aim is to support parents in shifting towards regaining independence and control of their own and their childrens' lives and away from dependency on support.

Case Study 3

[Note: this is based on original material edited to retain key aspects]

Context:

This case study covers a two-year period from November [Year 1] to October [Year 3]. The family comprised: Father (Afro-Caribbean), Mother (White British), an older sibling aged 9 (White British) and the focus child aged 4 (White/Afro-Caribbean). The main additional agency involved was the Health Visitor, but in the course of the support the following other agencies were involved:

[Name] Pre-School (Until July [Year 3])

[Name] Nursery (Until September [Year 3])

[M] Primary (From September [Year 3])

Cochlear Implant Team

Sensory support service

Health Visitor (HV)

[Name] Children's Centre

Paediatrician

Speech and Language Therapist

Audiology

Issues:

The key issues identified in the initial assessment were:

- Younger child was born prematurely and is profoundly deaf.
- Mum has anxiety, depression and a history of agoraphobia. She felt isolated and unsupported by dad.
- Dad is out of work; felt that [Name] was a racist place to live.

In addition, the following aspects became focus areas:

- Mum's feeling of being isolated
- Mum and dad's relationship

Aims:

The aims of the intervention were:

- For the younger child to have more social opportunities to encourage his development, through attending [Name] nursery.
- Regular Team Around the Child (TAC) meetings.
- Mum to feel less isolated. Able to attend Child's appointments in [Name of City].
- Mum to be more confident in her ability to parent.

Narrative:

[OW Outreach Worker; HV Health Visitor]

November and December [Year 1] – initial meetings established contact with mother, linked with city pre-school support organisation. First TAC meeting – OW Lead Professional. Concerns over the parents' relationship – referral to a support service.

January and February [Year 2] mother missed appointments with OW, but attended Individual Education Plan (IEP) meeting and agreed to younger child having places at the Preschool Support programme and children's centre, to support his social development. Mother wanted to look at schools for younger child to see what was available.

*March TAC meeting – younger child started attending [Name M]
nursery – settling in, but not eating well. Family's irregular sleep patterns
noted – Mum, Dad and son attended sleep clinic, but mum didn't believe
recommendations would work for them, and didn't agree with advice given.
OW – application to a local charity for new carpets and sofa – Mum granted
support.*

*May – OW supported mum to look at [Name W] primary school
with hearing resource base, however, mum and dad's relationship not
supportive. OW supported mum to get younger son to nursery – attendance
hadn't been great. CAF completed with mum. Mum anxious about
schools – younger child due to start in September 2013. Mum looked at
[Name M] primary school. OW to support mum attending audiology
appointment but family ill so appointment cancelled.*

*June – OW supported mum to attend coffee morning at family centre
for deaf children. Mum made connections with the deaf community for the
family and internet links.*

*July TAC meeting – improved sleep patterns and mum making
application to learn BSL with OW support to get funding. OW using AcE
assessment and mum also using protocol for Deaf Children to monitor
progress. Decision made for younger child to attend [Name M] Nursery
four days a week, all year round. Mum concerned at giving up place at
Preschool Support so OW liaised with support centre and place kept open
until September.*

*OW noted – mum anxious and confused as different professionals
saying different things – arranged a professional meeting to discuss and make
sure that clear and consistent advice is given. Mum thinking, she should
support son to sign as speech not developed. Mum had chosen implants so
that he could speak. She attended fun day with OW. Funding achieved
for mum to learn BSL.*

*August – preschool support team provided sessions in the home – Mum
attended stay and play at [Name M] nursery. OW arranged professionals
meeting in readiness for school.*

*September – professionals meeting agreed: to ensure the younger child
accessed full nursery entitlement, to continue with joint placement, to change
nursery hours so days together rather than apart and to help consistency.
Continuing issues with sleep noted. Statement process to begin. Parents 50
minutes late picking up from nursery – contact numbers incorrect – family
had overslept. OW addressed this with parents – liaised with nursery. Mum
supported to attend college.*

*October – child engaging and turn-taking with OW, no longer hiding.
However, OW felt something happening for the family – not sure what
and she was due on annual leave. Mum confident to go into children's centre*

to ask for support as tax credits were stopped because of a false claim. Centre arranged for Food Bank items to be delivered to the family.

Mum decided on [Name M] primary school as was local, anxious about the distance to [Name W]. [Name M] is a familiar environment. OW supported mum to sort housing claims and tax credits. TAC/Early Years Action Plus meeting: identified strengths and needs for statement.

November, a year on from the initial meeting, OW supported mum to complete budget form. Mum prescribed [medication] to help sleep pattern but was unsure whether to use it. Dad applying for cleaning job at supermarket. The younger child continued engaging with OW, particularly with trains and cars. Education Welfare Officer (EWO) visit for older child, mum admitted attendance lacking due to family sleep pattern. OW liaised with EWO.

December − OW liaised with HV support for Mum's agoraphobia. [Medication] given. Dad has a job. TAC meeting recorded: Child more confident with professionals now. Mum's confidence grown through attending college. Dad working so mum able to put bedtime routines in place. Mum's decision for son to start school in September, [there is uncertainty] about his readiness for school − still at a two-year-old stage by the Deaf protocol.

January [Year 3] − attendance at both nurseries not good so OW gave mum visual timetable. During joint home visit with children's centre manager mum asked to be referred into freedom programme. Better sleep reported.

February − older son questioning dynamics of his family. OW liaised with Speech Therapist over visit, targets and activities to use.

March − OW recorded missed appointments with professionals and attendance not good at preschool support programme. TAC meeting − Mum requested 1:1 support for youngest at [M Primary]. Agreed to make an application, although attendance needed to improve. Referral to children's disability nurse by HV for support with behaviour at home. 'Only I can change things' (Mum). Meeting at older child's school around emotional well-being. Younger child asked to go in outreach worker's car − indicated and signed what he wanted.

April 2013 − Mum changed school she wants to [Y Primary]. Mum has contacted school and admissions, happy with decision. Younger child more vocal and expressive − can put two-piece puzzle together but mum and dad struggling to get son to wear implants constantly.

May − TAC meeting − both mum and dad − Theraplay referral for son and dad. Child wearing processors more, Mum keeping a diary of wearing processors. Mum not wanting [Y Primary] to know all her history. However, in June the place was refused as younger child not school ready

– they were unable to meet his needs. Mum upset about decision. Child to attend [M Primary]; OW supported mum through anxious time.

July – OW and mum made a joint visit with new Teacher of Deaf Children. Transition meeting at [M] primary. Attendance at nursery not good. Mum invited to attend summer trips. Dad working two jobs. Made Playdough with child who was unsure of texture, mum supported child to engage.

August – concerns about mum and dad's relationship noted – relationship not good. Mum wants to look at possible other diagnosis as well as deafness – sensory needs, obsession with trains and cars, limited speech even though processors have been worn more. Younger child little speech progress in a year. We know processors are working. Younger child started school at [M Primary] in September. Reviewed action plan. Implants not being worn at home, but being worn in school. OW liaised with Cochlear Implant team and Teacher of the Deaf.

October TAC meeting – younger child settled in at school, wearing processers all day at school. Signing less and vocalising more, gaining in confidence and is happy to be in school. Good attendance. Mum contacted brighter futures for behaviour management course and Makaton training. Sleep much better, mum finding what works around school. Mum happy and surprised with how well son has taken to school.

This example shows what can be achieved by joint working and the necessity of ensuring that agencies communicate with each other as well as the child, parent and family. It also shows that this is neither straightforward nor easy to achieve and requires constant adjustment. The importance of trust is again underlined: without trust between the outreach worker and the mother any progress would have been difficult; without trust and respect between the organisations much less would have been achieved. This particular case study also underlines how hard it is to obtain the child's perspective and contribution. The timescales are particularly significant and show the irregularity of progress that was achieved over time.

These three examples provide insights into the complexity of working with children and parents and engaging a range of support agencies to enable all to flourish. They are selective in order to show best practice and what can be achieved. Their veracity in relation to successes achieved by early intervention in the twenty-first century is supported by examples for the evaluation of the Early Excellence Centres[7] and Sure Start[8] programmes and by subsequent literature[9] and are matched by similar successes internationally. It is not possible to cover every aspect, however, themes arising from these three case studies form the basis of discussion points in the next section.

- Working with families is complex and the initially recognised need may be underpinned by other needs across the family.
- Gaining the child's voice can be difficult but for best outcomes to be achieved this is necessary.
- Positive partnerships are essential if progress is to be made and if the family and child are to flourish.

Part 2 Partnership for flourishing in an age of austerity

Social inclusion

Social inclusion is not a new principle, but became a stronger reality in England under New Labour from 1997 into the first decade of the new century, resources were made available to develop early intervention and establish local partnerships to improve the identification and support of parents and children in need. These built on Health and Education 'Action Zones', initiatives set up by the preceding Conservative administration, as well as relationships, which had developed independently in preceding decades between parents and children and Care, Health and Education agencies at the local level. The establishment of Sure Start in particular encouraged active partnership between agencies, including the private, voluntary and independent sectors, and at its best, provided an 'open door' for parents to access high quality support as well as encouraging multi-agency communication, cross-referrals and coordinated action. All these initiatives built on a partnership, which was grounded in an open, inclusive approach, and were making a difference to parents and families.

Following the 2010 General Election the Conservative–Liberal Democrat coalition coined 'austerity' as their watchword and all policy was justified by reference to austerity measures needed to bring the country back from the brink of economic disaster. While support for Children's Centres and Early Intervention was vocalised and remained a statutory obligation, the reality of policy shifts and legislative changes indirectly impacted negatively on all services involved. Unintended consequences of nationally imposed funding constraints included the undermining of established practice as 'silo' mentality destroyed the delicate balance enabling effective partnership working, and reductions in staffing meant the loss of the most experienced practitioners in Local

Authorities and partner agencies. Whether intended or not the reality of the impact on working with parents cannot be denied. Three examples serve to reinforce the negative impact: reductions in Local Authority funding, the 'Troubled Families'[10] initiative and the bedroom tax.[11]

- While not a new concept social inclusion certainly became a greater reality after the general election in 1997.
- The general election in 2010 saw a change as the watchword became 'austerity' and investment in social inclusion shrank.

Reductions in local authority funding

The reductions in funding, amounting to virtually a third, in reality meant wholesale re-organisation for many authorities, leading to amalgamations of departments, reductions in staffing and consequent increased portfolios for those remaining, particularly those in leadership roles. An early casualty was the removal of the 'ring fence' protecting the funding for Children's Centres, which instantly reduced it. The shifts and changes often caused connections to be lost and leaders to be unaware of the detail of departments included in their new responsibilities and unable to call on a knowledge and experience bank also lost through employee redundancies and changes at all levels. There were attempts at consultation with service users before changes were shaped, but plans to accommodate changes were often tied to and focused on strict timetables dominated by employment legislation, prohibiting more considered planning to maintain effective services. The effect on Local Authority services working with parents and children, particularly Children's Centres, was dramatic. Many Local Authorities closed sites, created much larger reach areas by grouping into 'localities' under a single centre leader, or closed all their centres completely. Many also contracted out service provision, which in turn created more uncertainty and disruption associated with change among centres and service providers. Children's Centres remain statutory and retain their statutory duties despite the reductions in funding:

> Improving outcomes for young children and their families, with a particular focus on the most disadvantaged families, in order to reduce inequalities in:
>
> - child development and school readiness;

Supported by improved:

- parenting aspirations, self-esteem and parenting skills;
- child and family health and life chances.[12]

Despite their determination to maintain centres and services, councils have found themselves having to focus on areas of greatest need to meet the Local Authority and revised Office for Standards in Education (OfSTED) national inspection targets. Many buildings, including those purpose built, have been closed. Many of the Children's Centre leaders in new 'locality' groups have not received any induction into their new and completely different role and have had to manage change while maintaining services. Delivering high quality services has proved difficult with reduced staffing, shorter, more sharply focused programmes of support, to a clientele with more complex needs. Working relationships at many levels have become more difficult, particularly with schools where the top down pressure by OfSTED for schools to demonstrate improvement in pupil achievement has changed the focus of early years, and is filtering down to pre-school. Parents have lost contact with key workers and are finding that while some services are being maintained by trained parent volunteers, they are taking time to establish, and other services are no longer available or their locations have changed. The main casualties of such change have been parents and children where continuity of provision has stuttered or been lost. The arguments justifying change of revised systems being more efficient by focusing on more specific groups of those in greatest need have ignored both the damage done to existing contacts with parents and the fact that 'greatest need' for individual families is not confined to statistical districts. It is debateable that the families in examples 2 and 3 in the previous section would now be helped.

- Many childrens' centres have become localities bringing a range of services together in an attempt to save money often in the process losing contact with the very people they were intended to support.
- Pressures that schools are subject to have changed their relationship with early years settings.

The 'Troubled Families' programme

The 'Troubled Families' initiative was one attempt to show support for those in greatest need. Government funding was made available for support over a fixed timescale for families with the most complex needs on a 'payments by results basis'. This seems reasonable, but there was a sting in the tail: families had to agree to work with multi-professional teams and had to adhere to the agreed plan and complete courses and programmes and failure to complete meant a withdrawal of benefits. The family in Case Study 3 would have been in such a position. Local authorities had to bid for the funding and those bidding were not necessarily those already involved with supporting families: at least one large metropolitan authority set up a new department, inviting many different agencies and professionals but not Children's Centres to contribute. The initiative itself seemed to ignore the excellent work, which had been established by partnership working often led by Children's Centres. The first report of the national evaluation of this programme in July 2014 gives no indication of effectiveness or of 'drop out' rate, and therefore no indication of how many families have lost benefits as a result. Instead it focuses on the type of issues and range of complexity faced by families, indicating within the sample data a peak of families with between four and 14 issues, with the greatest being those with 6, 8 and 10. While it remains to be seen how effective this programme is, it is not focused on the large group of people previously reached by Children's Centres whose needs were no less intense to the families involved and who, with support, were able to restore momentum towards more fulfilling lives. The reduction in funding and re-organ-isation has left many of these families beyond the current reach of centres and services. It also does nothing to address the increase in the need for food banks, often used by those who have achieved a return to work but who have consequently lost benefits, and those whose working wages are inconsistent and cannot be relied on to meet living needs. For a more detailed analysis see also Chapter 3, The ecology of flourishing.

- The troubled families' initiative did not necessarily mean that those who were familiar with the family would be the ones to work with them.
- Families needing support were usually facing multiple issues.

The bedroom tax

The shift to reduce benefits has disregarded the consequences of sudden change for those in greatest need. An example of changes creating an-xiety, stress and confusion has been the bedroom tax. Aimed at reducing

LIVERPOOL JOHN MOORES UNIVERSITY
LEARNING SERVICES

under-occupation of council and housing association properties by reducing occupiers housing benefit calculations as a charge for 'spare' rooms, the effect has been to push many families further into debt and to increase their needs. It is best illustrated by the following extract from SHELTER:

> For example, if you have one 'spare' bedroom and your rent is £100 per week, only £86 counts when your housing benefit is assessed. You have to pay at least £14 yourself. If you have two or more 'spare' bedrooms and your rent is £100 per week, only £75 counts when your housing benefit is assessed. You have to pay at least £25 yourself.[13]

The number of bedrooms that can be claimed for are as follows:

■ one bedroom for a couple

■ one bedroom for a person aged 16 or over

■ one bedroom for two children aged under 16 of the same sex

■ one bedroom for two children aged under 10 (boys and girls are expected to share a room)

■ one bedroom for any other child

■ one extra bedroom if you or your partner needs an overnight carer to stay[14]

There are exemptions, including for the elderly, but for many families in need this additional complexity has meant turmoil and increased stress. All the families in the case study examples have been affected.

These three examples are part of a larger picture, but serve to reinforce the negatives shown by Bowlby earlier, undermining parents' confidence and well-being.

Conclusion

A key responsibility of those who govern is to maintain and develop successful initiatives regardless of which political philosophy created them, as well as leading new initiatives. Governments and ministers who show a complete disregard for inherited structures and impose piecemeal changes abuse their privileged power and show a wilful disregard of their real responsibilities.

Previous administrations seemed genuinely to focus on parents and children whereas economics and austerity have become the new watchwords, dominating all else. While fiscal propriety is important the unintended consequences of political decisions have severely damaged much of the previous positive gains in professional partnerships with parents, children and each other.

The greatest concern is over the contradictory pressures affecting multi-agency working. There has been an emphasis on inter-agency cooperation[15] and professionals are endeavouring to maintain joint support for parents and children, but the unintended consequences of reduced funding and unrealistic targets and accountability are tending to break down the relationships that underpin successful multi-agency engagement.

Professionals working with parents and children have found systems and relationships, which have taken time to develop, destroyed by imposed changes even when these purported to be for the common good. Parents and children have been the first casualties where continuity of contact has been lost and service delivery has changed in focus, and location. While initial improvements can be achieved with short-term, focused programmes, maintaining those improvements and building on them requires longer-term support.

Change is inevitable and necessary but needs careful planning and time to be effective. Successful working with parents and their children is dependent on trust, which also takes time to build. The challenge for the future is to shift from short-term, austerity focused, imposed change to more considered, longer-term change based on what is already working well, if we are to maintain high quality multi-agency support of families and children to enable them to flourish.

REFLECTIVE QUESTIONS

- What ethical issues arise from the dilemma of a belief in autonomy and equal partnership with parents and the principle and practice of early intervention, which requires outside agencies imposing change?
- What principles should lead intervention in practice?
- What does the term 'agency' imply when applied to young children?
- What are the responsibilities of politicians in regard to developing the features that support flourishing for children and families, at local, regional and national levels?

Notes

1   See Gourd, J. Chapter 3 in Kingdon, Z. and Gourd, J. (eds) (2014) *Early Years Policy: The Impact on Practice*. London: Routledge.
2   www.psychologia.pl/lasc/Trevarthen2.pdf
3   Rutter, M. draws attention to the importance of '*the child's contribution to parent-child interaction*' and the intensity of the relationship.
4   Alfred Adler developed positive psychology. For more information go to the Adlerian Society UK: www.adleriansociety.co.uk/page3
5   For more information on AcE go to www.crec.co.uk/ or see www.earlyyears solutions.co.uk/ace_summary_23.html
6   For more information on the growth of multi-agency working see Siraj-Blatchford *et al*. (2007) *The Team Around the Child: Multi-agency Working in the Early Years*. Stoke on Trent: Trentham Books.
7   For Evalution of Early Excellence Centres see http://webarchive.national archives.gov.uk/20130401151715/www.education.gov.uk/publications/eOrderingDownload/RR259.pdf
8   For National Evaluation of Sure Start (NESS) see www.ness.bbk.ac.uk/
9   For example, Trodd and Chivers (2011).
10   Troubled Families Programme see: www.gov.uk/government/policies/helping-troubled-families-turn-their-lives-around and www.local.gov.uk/community-budgets/-/journal_content/56/10180/3691966/ARTICLE
11   The clearest information seems to be from independent agencies such as SHELTER: http://england.shelter.org.uk/get_advice/housing_benefit_and_local_housing_allowance/changes_to_housing_benefit/bedroom_tax?gclid=COSiperfmMUCFQoEwwodca8AyQ
12   www.foundationyears.org.uk/files/2011/10/Core_purpose_of_Sure_Start_Childrens_Centres.pdf
13   Source SHELTER (*op cit*).
14   Source SHELTER (*op cit*).
15   HM Government Working Together to Safeguard Children: A guide to inter-agency working to safeguard and promote the welfare of children March 2015, available at:www.gov.uk/government/uploads/system/uploads/attachment_data/file/419595/Working_Together_to_Safeguard_Children.pdf

References

Adlerian Society UK: www.adleriansociety.co.uk/page3 (accessed April 2015)
Anning, A. and Ball, M. (eds) (2008) *Improving Services for Children: From Sure Start to Children's Centres*. London: Sage.
Arnold, C. (2007) 'Chapter 4: Sharing ideas with parents about key child development concepts' in Whalley, M. and the Pen Green Team *Involving Parents in their Children's Learning 2e*. London: Paul Chapman Publishing.
Audit Commission (2002a) CPA Newsletter No. 7, London: Audit Commission, in Weinstein, J., Whittington, C. and Leiba, T. (eds) (2007) *Collaboration in Social Work Practice*. London: Jessica Kingsley Publishers.
Bowlby, J. (1993) *A Secure Base: Clinical Applications of Attachment Theory*. London: Routledge.

Bronfenbrenner, U. (1990) *The Ecology of Human Development*. London: Harvard University Press.

DFEE Research Report No 259 Pascal, C., Bertram, T., Gasper, M., Mould, C., Ramsden, F. and Saunders, M. (2001) *Research to Inform the Evaluation of the Early Excellence Centres Pilot Programme* http://webarchive.nationalarchives.gov.uk/20130401151715/www.education.gov.uk/publications/eOrdering Download/RR259.pdf (accessed April 2015)

Edwards, A., Daniels, H., Gallagher, T., Leadbetter, J. and Warmington, P. (2009) *Improving Inter-professional Collaborations: Multi-agency working for children's wellbeing*. London: Routledge.

Friere, P. and Shor, I. (1987) *A Pedagogy for Liberation: Dialogues on Transforming Education*. London: Bergin and Garvey.

Gasper (2010) *Multi-agency Working in the Early Years: Challenges and Opportunities*. London: Sage.

Gopnik, A., Melzoff, A. and Khul, P. (2004) *How Babies Think: The Science of Childhood*. London: Phoenix.

Gov.uk: Department for Education www.gov.uk/sure-start-childrens-centres-local-authorities-duties (accessed March 2015).

Harcourt, D., Perry, B. and Waller, T. (eds) (2011) *Researching Children's Perspectives: Debating Ethics and Dilemmas of Educational Research with Children*. London: Routledge.

HM Government (2015) 'Working together to safeguard children: A guide to inter-agency working to safeguard and promote the welfare of children', available at: www.gov.uk/government/uploads/system/uploads/attachment_data/file/419595/Working_Together_to_Safeguard_Children.pdf

House of Commons Education Committee. (2014) Oral evidence: Foundation Years: Sure Start Children's Centres: Government response, HC 144 Wednesday 18 June 2014 http://data.parliament.uk/writtenevidence/committeeevidence.svc/evidencedocument/education-committee/foundation-years-sure-start-childrens-centres-government-response/oral/10821.html (accessed March 2015)

Howard, S., Dryden, J. and Johnson, B. (1999) 'Childhood resilience: review and critique of the literature Oxford Review of Education', in Edwards, A., Daniels, H., Gallagher, T., Leadbetter, J. and Warmington, P. (2009) *Improving Inter-professional Collaborations: Multi-agency working for children's wellbeing*. London: Routledge.

James, A. and Prout, A. (1997) *Constructing and Reconstructing Childhood: Contemporary Issues in the Sociological Study of Childhood*. London: Falmer.

John, K. (2008) 'Sustaining the leaders of Children's Centres: the role of leadership mentoring', in *European Early Childhood Education Research Journal*, 16(1), pp. 53–66.

Kinchelo, J. and McLaren, P. (2002) 'Chapter 5: Re-thinking critical theory and qualitative research', in Zou, Y. and Treuba, E. (eds) *Ethnography and Schools: Qualitative Approaches to the Study of Education*. Lanham: Rowman and Littlefield Publishers Inc.

Mayall, B. (2002) *Towards a Sociology for Childhood: Thinking from Children's Lives*. Maidenhead: Open University Press.

Moss, P. (2014) *Transformative Change and Real Utopias in Early Childhood Education: A Story of Democracy, Experimentation and Potentiality*. London: Routledge.

Pascal, C. and Bertram, T. (2010) *Accounting Early for Lifelong Learning* Birmingham: Amber Publications and Training www.crec.co.uk/ (accessed April 2015)

Price, D., Wilkins, S. and Edmond, N. (2012) 'Chapter 9: Effective Communication and Engagement with Families, in Edmond, N. and Price, M. (eds) *Integrated Working with Children and Young People: Supporting Development from Birth to Nineteen*. London: Sage.

Quinton, D. (2004) *Supporting Parents: Messages from Research*. London: Jessica Kingsley.

Rutter, M. (1991) *Maternal Behaviour Re-assessed 2e*. London: Penguin.

Seligman, M. (2007) *The Optimistic Child: A Proven Programme to Safeguard Children Against Depression and Build Life-long Resilience*. New York: Houghton Mifflin Company.

Seligman, M. (2011) *Flourish: A New Understanding of Happiness and Well-being and How to Achieve Them*. London: Nicholas Brearley Publishing.

Siraj-Blatchford, I., Clarke, K. and Needham, M. (2007) *The Team Around the Child: Multi-agency Working in the Early Years*. Stoke on Trent: Trentham Books.

Trevarthen, C. (2010) 'What is it like to be a person who knows nothing? Defining the active intersubjective mind of a newborn human being', in *The Intersubjective Newborn, Infant and Child Development*, Special Issue, Edited by Emese Nagy available online at: www.psychologia.pl/lasc/Trevarthen2.pdf (accessed March 2015)

Tait, C. (2007) 'Chapter 3: Getting to know the families' in Whalley, M. and the Pen Green Team *Involving Parents in their Children's Learning 2e*. London: Paul Chapman Publishing.

Trodd, L. and Chivers, L. (eds) (2011) *Interprofessional Working in Practice: Learning and Working Together for Children and Families*. Maidenhead: McGraw Hill, Open University Press.

Weinstein, J., Whittington, C. and Leiba, T. (eds) (2003) *Collaboration in Social Work Practice*. London: Jessica Kingsley Publishers.

Wenger, E., McDermott, R. and Snyder, W. (2002) *Cultivating Communities of Practice*. Boston: Harvard University Press.

Whalley, M. and the Pen Green Team (2007) *Involving Parents in Their Children's Learning 2e*. London: Paul Chapman Publishing.

Additional website references:

Melhuish, E. National Evaluation of Sure Start (NESS) *NESS* www.ness.bbk.ac.uk/impact [accessed April 2015]

Troubled Families Programme:

www.gov.uk/government/policies/helping-troubled-families-turn-their-lives-around

www.local.gov.uk/community-budgets/-/journal_content/56/10180/3691966/ARTICLE [accessed April 2015]

National Evaluation of the Troubled Families Programme:

www.gov.uk/government/publications/national-evaluation-of-the-troubled-families-programme [accessed April 2015]

SHELTER website:

http://england.shelter.org.uk/get_advice/housing_benefit_and_local_housing_allowance/ changes_to_housing_benefit/bedroom_tax?gclid=COSiperfmMUCFQo Ewwodca8AyQ [accessed April 2015]

Children's Centres core purpose:

www.foundationyears.org.uk/files/2011/10/Core_purpose_of_Sure_Start_Childrens_ Centres.pdf [accessed April 2015]

7 The creative curriculum

Flourishing in the play environment

Zenna Kingdon

Introduction

This chapter explores how we need to provide an appropriate environment for young children, in which they are encouraged to: explore, to be curious and to develop the skills, knowledge and attitudes that will support their future development and their ability to flourish. In it I set out to answer a number of questions that are pertinent to considering a creative curriculum within the early childhood context and its relationship to the flourishing child. Firstly, I explore what constitutes a creative curriculum considering the ways in which creativity can support all aspects of the curriculum not simply those subjects that are historically associated with such an approach. I then ask the question as to whether or not play matters, drawing on current thinking as well as the work of Vygotsky who made some clear links between play and creativity for young children discussing the saliency of them in their lives. What constitutes a play environment is explored with a particular focus on: Reggio Emilia, Te Whariki, HighScope and Montessori, all of which comment specifically on the environment in their approach to an early childhood curriculum. Links between the environment and creativity are made. The use of a free-flow environment in which children are given opportunities to explore both inside and out is considered. Recent research has demonstrated how important it is that children are enabled to spend part of their time outdoors and are enabled to explore and experiment in the outdoor environment, something that has been demonstrated to support self-esteem, which in turn leads to flourishing. There are current proponents of a creative curriculum and these include: Sir Ken Robinson, Mick Waters and Michael Rosen, they appear to advocate a curriculum that is both creative and engaging in order that children feel enabled to make the best of themselves and to flourish. The impact on the children's ability to flourish of a creative curriculum in early childhood is discussed. The chapter concludes that in order for children in early childhood to be enabled to flourish there are a number of factors that need to be in place, these include: providing a creative curriculum, having a suitable environment that includes access to indoor and outdoor spaces, allowing children to explore their own interests, and providing open ended and engaging materials with which they can investigate and explore.

What is a creative curriculum?

A chapter such as this allows us to raise the question: does creativity matter and how does it impact long term on the lives of young children? Craft (2000, p. 3) argues that creativity is related to, 'possibility thinking such as being imaginative, asking questions and playing'. Play is usually seen as the way in which young children learn and develop. Though this is not without some challenges, the initial curriculum for the under-fives, Desirable Outcomes for Children's Learning on entering Compulsory Education (DLOs 1996) was considered by many to fail to recognise the centrality of play and creativity in children's learning and development with the consequential impact on self-esteem further impacting on other areas of development (David 1998). Subsequent curricula, including all three versions of the EYFS (2008, 2012 and 2014), appear to begin to recognise the importance of the children's self-esteem and their need to be creative.

Robson (2012) suggests that thinking is central to young children's ability to learn and understand. Without understanding it is not possible to apply knowledge. Robson (2012, p. 45) goes on to state that the, 'ways in which children see themselves as thinkers and learners is dependent upon their self-concept' The child's view of themselves is developed from their early relationships and whether or not they have been enabled to form effective attachment relationships (Bowlby 1988). Without these children are found to be unable to develop and learn effectively. He suggested that it was due to the existence of an internal psychological model with a number of specific features, which included replication models of the self and the attachment figure, attachment behaviour was made up of a number of instinctual responses that, 'mature at different times during the first year of life and develop at different rates; they serve the function of binding the child to mother and contribute to the reciprocal dynamic of binding mother to child (ibid., p. 351). Bowlby (1988) suggests that the patterns of attachment that are laid down in the first years of life tend to persist and influence their personality and interactions with others. Bowlby himself reviewed this idea and suggested that personality development was influenced by, 'the environment he meets with, especially the way his parents (or parent substitutes) treat him . . . (Bowlby 1988, p. 136). According to the statutory requirements of the EYFS (2012, p. 7), '1.11 Each child must be assigned a key person' The DfE (2012) states that the role of the key person is to provide appropriate learning and care for the child, to engage with the family and to encourage them in providing support for their child at home as well as where necessary supporting them to seek additional support for their child. Settings in England and Wales are organised in this fashion with all children allocated a key person given that it is a statutory requirement. The issue surrounding attachment remains central to discussions on the key person and its relationship with the attachment figure. More recent research suggests that the key person approach allows children to feel secure, enables them to participate in activities and make friends from as young as one and supports positive linguistic and cognitive behaviours (Elfer *et al.* 2012). In 1999 the National Advisory Committee on Creative and Cultural Education published its report, 'All our futures: creativity, culture and education'. In this notions of creativity across the curriculum were raised, suggesting that creativity, 'is possible in all areas of human activity, including the arts, sciences, at work, at play and all other areas of daily life' (ibid. p. 6). The report further suggests that we all have creative abilities but that we have them differently and that our ability to develop our skills and creativities are closely related to feelings of self-esteem (NACCE 1999).

Waters (2011, p. 4) states that the best place for children to learn, 'is in the real world'. So while early learning environments are not the real world, they can provide opportunities to make learning real. Wood (2013) argues that the links between literacy and play have become well established through research. She (ibid. 2013) suggests that practitioners should be planning literacy-rich environments in which children are able to access a range of print and technology based materials to support their play.

> When engaging in playful literacy, children are not just pretending to read and write; they are acting as readers and writers. This is a fundamental distinction which enables children to see the meaning and relevance of such activities.
>
> (Wood 2013, p. 83)

It is here where the difference between a creative curriculum and one in which children are taught didactically can begin to be unpacked. Wood (2013) goes on to argue that in Vygotskian (1978) terms the children are behaving beyond their actual stage of development but within a future one. Their playing at reading and writing demonstrates that they understand that print can be used to convey meaning in a range of different ways. While they may not be able to decode the exact print that is in front of them they are able to think creatively about what it may say or about the information that they may wish to convey. In a similar way Carruthers and Worthington (2011) and Boaler (2010) discuss mathematical graphicacy. They are concerned that if children are taught a narrow set of skills that are simply to be learnt and ticked off they will not develop the wider skills that are to be found when children are given opportunities to 'engage in the sort of dialogue that can scaffold their understanding about their graphical marks and symbols . . . (ibid. 2011, p. 5). They go on to argue that despite all the recognition of the importance of mathematics in our lives children face difficulties in learning the skills in the classroom. They (ibid. 2011) argue for a creative approach in which the children's, 'interest, motivation and enjoyment' are considered to be central to the process of learning and understanding mathematics, ensuring that they are supported to reach their potential. It would start to seem that creativity matters and that it underpins effective ways in which children can begin to learn about the world around them through play-based approaches that allow them to explore.

- Creative curricular support self-esteem, which is central to children's learning.
- Attachment relationships support children's ability to develop self-esteem.
- Children need opportunities to learn in real situations that make sense to them.

Does play matter?

We know that play has long been considered the core principle of early childhood education and care, with research evidence demonstrating that it is through play-based opportunities that young children learn and develop. Edwards and Cutter-Mackenzie (2013) suggest that open-ended play is viewed as being of particular significance within early childhood, however, without appropriate guidance the learning opportunities that are afforded by such play are lost. Likewise, Leong and Bodrova (2012) discuss what they refer to as mature play, which is a form of role-play that has been planned with adult assistance in order that the children are able to access both the language and an understanding of the roles so that they can develop meaningful play opportunities.

Howard (2010) suggests that during this century we have seen a renewed interest in play-based curricula in the UK. However, she suggests that this renewed emphasis is little more than a re-working of what we have previously seen. Howard (2010, p. 91) further suggests that despite, 'a legislative emphasis on play as an appropriate medium for learning has not necessarily guaranteed its successful implementation'. It is evident that learning rather than playing is what is considered by those in authority to be what is of central importance. Therefore, practitioners often seem to feel that play should be a secondary consideration rather that they should be teaching children, especially given the new focus on numeracy and literacy. Yet, despite this Pramling Samuelsson and Carlsson (2008) suggest that play is considered to be of the supreme significance in every early childhood curriculum the world over. They (ibid. 2008, p. 624) go on to suggest that from the perspective of young children, 'play and learning are not always separate in practices during early years'. Though they go on to suggest that 'when young children *act* they do not separate between play and learning, although they separate them in their talk' (ibid. p. 626). This suggests that while children are engaged in activities in their early childhood settings they are not aware of the dichotomy of play versus learning and learning versus development. Yet when researchers talk to children as young as three the children will discuss whether an activity that they have been engaged with is play or learning. It would seem that if the activity involves an adult and certainly if it occurred at a table then the children will perceive it as learning rather than play.

Whether you consider that development leads learning or learning leads development may well be determined by how you view the work of Piaget and Vygotsky. Hatch (2010, p. 263) argues that it is not possible to adopt an approach in which you accept both Vygotsky and Piaget's positions saying that we have been presented with a, 'classic "either/or" scenario (either Piaget or Vygotsky is right)' Hatch (2010, p. 259) demonstrates that he believes that Vygotsky's approach is key when he says that for Vygotsky learning is a social activity that occurs between children and more capable others acting as, 'the engine that moves cognitive development forward'. For Pramling Samuelsson and

Carlsson (2008, p. 623) 'Play as well as learning, are natural components of children's everyday lives'. However, they further argue that, 'education for children is, on the whole, organised to promote learning rather than play' (ibid. p. 623). In a more recent piece of research Pramling Samuelsson and Johansson (2009) look further into play and learning and consider that while the two are often considered different occurrences, in reality they share a number of similarities that describe them and they provide for similar experiences and challenges in children's lives. They (ibid. p. 78) go on to suggest that at, 'the foundation for both play and learning lies the creation of meaning'. It is this meaning making that is creative and an essential element of both play and learning. For Vygotsky (2004, p. 11) play was not simply repetition, a copying of something that the child had seen before, it was considerably more significant than that, demonstrating their ability to utilise their experiences in such a way that their play was, 'not simply a reproduction of what he has experienced, but a creative reworking of the impressions he has acquired'. He (ibid. 2004, p. 7) further argued that:

> Any human act that gives rise to something new is referred to as a creative act, regardless of whether what is created is a physical object or some mental or emotional construct that lives within the person who created it and is known only to him.
>
> (Vygotsky 2004, p. 7)

He believed that it was through a thorough understanding of these creative processes it was possible to recognise that creative processes are fully apparent in very young children and that through play activities children are able to further develop their knowledge and understanding, creatively fashioning new possibilities. This creative approach in which re-working and re-interpretation occur he referred to as combinatorial activity, which relates to the imagination (ibid. 2004). Therefore, the playing child is not simply engaging in activities that interest them and engage them, but through their re-creation of past experiences and their re-working of previous understandings they are demonstrating that they are creative individuals who are generating new possibilities and new knowledge, from which they are able to learn and develop. Edwards and Cutter-Mackenzie (2013) suggest that these creations are particularly important in early childhood education as they demonstrate what the child is learning about their lives and experiences, so through the combinatorial aspect of play there is evidence of creativity and learning occurring. Siraj-Blatchford (2009) draws on the work of Vygotsky in her conceptualising of a pedagogy of play that supports progression. She (ibid. 2009) makes links between theory of mind and meta-cognition, arguing that it is through this that children are able to develop their own concept of their own development. Play and play partners are considered to be key to this process as they interact, bringing their own experiences fashioned from their own perspectives. Vygotsky (2004, p. 11) suggests that one of the most significant aspects when considering child and educational psychology, 'is the issue of creativity in children, the development of this creativity and its significance to the child's general development and maturation'.

Given all those who are making links between creativity and play it would seem that play remains a significant if not central element of any creative curriculum. Its salience appears to be of greater significance in the early years where children are learning about themselves as well as the world around them.

- Play is an essential element of children's learning in the early years.
- Play provides creative opportunities for children to learn for themselves.

What is a play environment?

In order that children are enabled to reach their potential they need to be taught in an environment that meets their needs. Much has been written about specific approaches: High/Scope, Reggio Emilia, Montessori and Te Whariki all advocating specific approaches to the learning environment. The High/Scope approach to early years includes a daily plan-do-review cycle in which children are expected to plan in conjunction with their teachers what they will engage with, they are then expected to be able to find and select the materials needed themselves (Nutbrown 2011). Schweinhart and Weikart (1998) suggests that the activities should promote the development of social, intellectual and physical skills, further suggesting that a constructivist approach to learning is taken. High/scope is concerned with an active approach to learning in which the child is firmly based at the centre of the learning process with a degree of control over their learning environment. In Reggio Emilia the environment is referred to as the third teacher, thus demonstrating the centrality of its role in ensuring that young children are provided a suitable environment in which to develop and flourish (Gandini et al. 1998). Strong-Wilson and Ellis (2007, p. 40) discuss the way in which within the Reggio Emilia approach the environment appears to, 'take on a life of their own that contributes to the children's learning'. They further argue (ibid. 2007, p. 40) that as a result of the detailed thought that goes into the arrangement of the space that it becomes, 'a key source of educational provocation and insight'. The notion of provocation demonstrates the way in which the environment impacts on the children's curiosity and their engagement with learning and development. Montessori was the first to suggest that children should have furniture, resources and tools created for them that were size appropriate and light enough so that they could move them around if necessary and, also, that all the resources that they needed should be stored at a height that they could access (Giardiello 2014). She felt that the children should be able to select their own materials and work practically with them in order that they learn and develop a range of skills (Faryadi 2007).

In all of these approaches children are expected and enabled to develop and learn through a play-based curricular in an environment in which they can explore and investigate for themselves, but with the support of guiding adults sensitive to their developing needs. The EYFS (2008/12/14) all discuss the Enabling Environment suggesting that children need to be given an appropriate environment in which to develop their skills.

- The environment is an essential element in supporting children's flourishing.
- Particular approaches to early childhood view the environment as central in supporting young children to learn and develop.

Indoors and outdoors

Rose and Rogers (2012) comment that the outdoor environment often means another space that the practitioner is responsible for planning and the connection between the indoor and outdoor environment can be difficult to create. However, it would seem that children are often able to make the connections themselves, in some research that I recently conducted a child was working outside engaged in a painting activity when another child joined them there were insufficient paint brushes. The child demonstrated that she knew where to find an additional paintbrush. Not only did she find one for herself, but she later took a further child to find one as well. Tovey (2007) and Broadhead and

Burt (2012) suggest that play resources should be open-ended, supporting children's independence and ability to consider using resources in a range of different ways.

Much of the research that looks at provision in the outdoor environment (Tovey 2007; Broadhead and Burt 2012; Knight 2013) discusses the length of engagement with activities when they occur in an outdoor environment. It would seem that in settings where the practitioners take a pedagogical approach in which children are enabled to freely move their play from one space to another they will continue with a theme for an extended period of time, becoming immersed in their play. So, for example, the girls who were engaged in the painting activity above were engaged for approximately 45 minutes in the same play theme. The play ended not because they had lost interest but because the bell was rung for snack time. The time that they did spend engaged would seem to be longer than would normally be expected for four-year-olds to persevere with a given task (Piaget 1959; Canning 2007).

Maynard (2007, p. 321) suggests that while children are outside they are, 'able to find out about themselves and the world around them in a way that would not generally be tolerated within the classroom' Outdoors, children are given opportunities to build on a much larger scale and experiment with a range of materials and sounds without any apprehension of being reprimanded for leaving a mess or being too noisy (ibid.). In the outdoor environment children are able to engage in rough and tumble play opportunities, something that Jarvis (2007, p. 186) argues supports opportunities for, 'a vital socialising experience . . . complex physical and linguistic responses'. Storli and Hagen (2010) cite Kyttä who suggests that mobility supports cognitive development; it is through the ability to move that children find new information. Likewise, Jarvis (2007) suggests that much of what is seen as important in Western education policy is narrowly focused on cognitive skills rather than physical and social ones, yet these are equally important in order that children grow into healthy and competent adults. It would seem that movement could be argued to be supporting the children's abilities across a number of domains; they are being supported cognitively, socially and physically.

Maynard and Waters (2007), Tovey (2007), Moser and Martinsen (2010) all argue that the outdoor environment supports children's social and emotional development, leading to children being better able to manage disputes with peers. In settings where children are enabled to move their play from an indoor to the outdoor environment it would seem that they are better able to develop their play themes given that the opportunity afforded them by practitioners who utilise a playful pedagogy in which both the children's cognitive and emotional skills are developed (Rose and Rogers 2012; Moyles 2010; Rogers and Evans 2008). When children are enabled to choose to take a play theme from inside the setting to the outdoor environment; they are able to continue the theme rather than abandoning it hence they are able to make links between what has occurred indoors and what they are doing outside. In the outdoor environment the children are able to develop their play beyond the, 'normalising gaze' of the practitioner (Maynard 2007, p. 384). This is not to say that the adults are not present and watching when children are outdoors; however, there are generally fewer rules and greater freedom when play is taken outside. These opportunities for free-flow play in which the children move the play from one environment to another, inside or outside, as suits them, appears to support a flourishing agenda in which the child is enabled to make decisions for themselves.

- Recent research demonstrates that the outdoor environment is particularly important in supporting children in developing self-esteem.
- Children are usually afforded greater opportunities to make decisions for themselves outdoors.
- It would appear that there is a link between the outdoor environment and children's opportunities to flourish.

Current proponents of creative approaches: Robinson, Waters and Rosen

Robinson, Waters and Rosen have all had roles within the United Kingdom that demonstrate their interest in, concern for and knowledge of the education system. All three advocate a creative curriculum in which children's natural curiosity is nurtured and the children are enabled to develop skills and knowledge. Sir Ken Robinson is possibly best known for his inspirational TED Talk (www.ted.com/talks/ken_robinson_says_schools_kill_creativity). 'Do schools kill creativity?', which has now reached in excess of 38 million views on YouTube. In many respects it can be said that that was indeed what he concluded, that the school system was not fit for purpose. Robinson has worked as a professor of education in the UK and internationally as an advisor on education as well as being part of the National Advisory Committee on Creative and Cultural Education. In his most recent text Robinson (2015, p. ix) argues that education systems around the world are being reformed and the drivers behind the reforms are political and commercial rather than educational and as a result there is a standards culture, which, 'is harming students and schools'. Robinson suggests that there is a need to make education personal. He draws on international traditions from Locke through Pestallozzi, Rousseau, and Dewey to Piaget, Vygotsky and Chomsky. He argues that what these all do for education is to consider how the child learns and to place that at the centre of the process. He suggests that these approaches are often brought together to be seen as, "progressive education", which some critics imagine is the polar opposite of "traditional education". This is a damaging misconception that tends towards many false dichotomies' (Robinson 2015, p. 255). Child-centred approaches utilise creative curricula in which the child is set at the centre and their motivations are exploited as a way of supporting them to access a curriculum. Robinson (2015) further discusses the way in which education policies constantly swing between these opposing poles and that the standards agenda, which appears to currently be gripping education systems around the world, is one such swing. He (ibid. p. 255) goes on to suggest that, '[E]ffective education is always a balance between rigor and freedom, tradition and innovation, the individual and the group, theory and practice, the inner world and the outer world'. He also argues that there is a need to find a balance for both schools and students as the concerns move again. There will be no permanent solution, as education will always be concerned with attempting to create the best possible opportunities for, 'real people in real communities in a constantly changing world . . . The experience of education is always personal but the issues are increasingly global' (Robinson 2015, p. 256).

Like Robinson, Mick Waters has held both educational and academic roles. He is currently Professor of Education at the University of Wolverhampton and has previously been Chair of the Curriculum Foundation and Director of Curriculum at the Qualifications and Curriculum Authority. He argues that the curriculum, 'has always been a playground for some, a battleground for others and minefield for many children' (Waters 2013, p. 52). He concludes that often teachers or those who are delivering a particular curriculum are not involved in its design, which in turn makes it difficult for them to deliver and to see the bigger picture of the purpose of education. In another article Waters (2013, p. 8) suggests that the recent inspection regimes have focused rigorously on the minutiae of the ingredients of lessons, 'the objectives, the questions, the plenary, the "evidence" without properly considering whether what pupils are digesting is "learning"'. What has been missing through this is the notion of what equates to good teaching and learning opportunities. Waters (2013, p. 9) suggests that there are a number of essentials that few would dispute including: appropriate planning and preparation as well as 'authentic contexts, purpose, relationships and intrigue'. The notion of making learning real is a theme that he has returned to, having previously argued that children learn best, 'in the real world' (Waters 2011, p. 4). He goes on to suggest that children are usually, 'fascinated about how things work, why things are like they are and why some things differ from the pattern that they have learned to expect'. Waters advocates a creative curriculum, which allows children to learn for themselves to develop their knowledge rather than simply being given it and expected to inwardly digest it in a theoretical manner. He suggests that we are moving to a knowledge-based curriculum, which is not necessarily problematic, however, it is the way in which that knowledge is imparted to children that needs careful consideration. It is the difference between it being simply didactically reproduced or the children being given the opportunity to develop their own knowledge and ways of discovering new knowledge.

Similar to Waters, Rosen suggests that discovering new knowledge is fundamental if children are to develop and to become active learners. In an interview with the *Guardian* (06/09/14 accessed 03/08/15) Rosen discussed what his parents taught him, saying that, 'The explicit message was to be curious, all knowledge was worth it' Rosen published his first book of poetry for children in 1974, this was the start of a long publishing and performing career, which led to him becoming the children's laureate in 2007, a post that he held for two years. By then he had already not only published in excess of 150 books for children, but he had also spent years working closely with schools and teachers developing literacy skills and imbuing all those he met with a love of language and literature. Lambirth (2006) discusses his experiences of working in 1995 with a number of teachers and Rosen on an action research project for the Centre for Literacy in Primary education, stating that it was an experience that he would never forget and that it had supported him in both his development as a teacher of literature and in his ability to write. In recent years Rosen has been vocal in his opposition of the phonics strategy. In his inaugural professorial lecture at Goldsmiths in July 2014 Rosen focused on humour in children's literature, demonstrating how children are often exposed to very particular types of literature that have particular messages within them, which those in authority wish children to be exposed to:

if by chance you are a secretary of state for education you can make great play of how you are increasing the cultural capital of the nation with the compulsory input of great, classic texts.

(Rosen 2014, Accessed 04/08/15)

Towards the end of the lecture he drew some conclusions about the ways in which education makes claims about what it needs from school leavers and the difference between the rhetoric of seemingly wanting well qualified staff and the reality of what is wanted when it is often necessary to lay off thousands of staff as big businesses merges. The phonics strategy that only allows one way of teaching children to read using systematic synthetic phonics and exposes children in the early part of their education to texts that allow them to practice these strategies does not allow children to develop as independent and investigative readers.

Millions more pounds have been spent creating and running what they call the Phonics Screening Check given to children towards the end of Year 1. . . . There is no evidence in existence anywhere to suggest that any of this helps children to understand what they're reading or to help children write in more interesting or informative ways.

(Rosen 2014, Accessed 04/08/15)

He further suggests that if children are given access to a range of interesting, humorous, engaging texts that they wish to read and, which as a result they read regularly and for pleasure, the result will be that we will create young people who are informed and critical.

Robinson, Waters and Rosen all advocate approaches to education that are playful, critical and creative. They believe that the research evidence to which they have access demonstrates that when children are engaged in learning in ways in which they are enabled to discover for themselves, to work in collaborative ways with both their peers and their teachers, co-learning, that they are considerably more likely to engage more deeply and that the learning will be embedded and long term.

- Current proponents of creative approaches suggest that there is evidence that creative approaches support long-term learning.
- Placing the child at the centre of the educational process is essential if the child is to get the most from the experience.

The impact on flourishing

Flourishing is concerned with happiness, not at a superficial level, but with long-term happiness, which is developed through values and relationships, rather than by consumerism. Clear links between flourishing and creative curricula can be drawn. Children engaged with a creative curriculum will be able to follow their own interests, to develop their own natural curiosity and be enabled to achieve. Achievement is not necessarily about being able to decode text using systematic synthetic phonics, it may be about creating a picture using found items from the natural environment; it may be about being able to climb higher than some of their friends or actually being able to make friends. Cherkowski and Walker (2014) draw on a Canadian Institute of Well-being document in which schools are encouraged to consider not simply the academic curriculum, but also the elements of the curriculum that support the development of moral, social and emotional proficiencies. Flourishing is directly related to notions of self-esteem. Children who feel that they are able to achieve and, that their achievements are acknowledged, particularly by the adults around them, are likely to have greater self-worth than those who feel that they are being judged in particular ways and that they are failing to reach the standards expected. It is therefore essential that children are given opportunities to engage with curricula that meet their needs, allows them to be curious, to explore and investigate and to develop skills, knowledge and attitudes to learning that will support their development. Similarly, Narvaez (2015) suggests that resilience is about developing the skills to be able to return to a good enough experience of life while flourishing moves beyond that to consider whether experiences are the best that they can be. Children who experience opportunities to have their needs met; to explore, to be curious, to investigate and to develop skills in their early years settings and beyond will be enabled to flourish. If we want a society, which works effectively together, supports those who are facing challenges, then we need to ensure that we enable all participants to flourish.

- Flourishing is associated with long-term happiness, which is developed through both relationships and values.
- Flourishing is about experiences that are the best that they can be.
- Children who are supported to: be curious, to investigate and to develop skills will be enabled to flourish.

Conclusion

It would seem that if a curriculum is to be creative there are a number of factors that need to be in place. The children need to feel secure in the environment and therefore an appropriate system of support needs to be available to them. Equally they need to recognise the relationship between what they are doing and real life experiences in order that the learning makes sense (Waters 2011). Likewise, the environment needs to be rich in resources in order that the children are stimulated to explore (Wood 2013). In an early years environment, play needs to be central to children's experiences of the curriculum. Leong and Bodrova (2012), Siraj-Blatchford (2009), Edwards and Cutter-Mackenzie (2013) all argue that play is a central and creative element of any early childhood curriculum, however, the play opportunities that are offered should provide children with opportunities to extend their thinking and learning rather than to simply engage them in low-level repetitive activities. Children themselves tend not to recognise the play or learning dichotomy when they are engaged in tasks in their play environment, but they may begin to do so in talk and this can occur from the age of three onwards (Pramling, Samuelsson and Carlsson 2008). Robinson, Waters and Rosen advocate an approach that is creative in a way that children will not feel the need to articulate the difference between working or playing, because all that they are engaged with is just that – engaging, exciting, challenging and interesting. Within early childhood the environment is key and has been discussed by different proponents and through different approaches. Essentially though the environment in the early childhood sector needs to place the child at the centre and demonstrate an awareness of their innate curiosity enabling them to select tools and materials for themselves in order that they can follow their interests. In the last few years there has been a resurgence in interest in the outdoor environment and children are being encouraged to move between the two spaces. While Rose and Rogers (2012) have identified the issue that for some practitioners this is simply another area that they need to plan, they suggest that these practitioners are beginning to recognise the benefits that the children receive from being enabled to take their experiences into an outdoor environment. There is significant research evidence that demonstrates that experiences in the outdoor environment support social and emotional development as an essential aspect of early childhood (Maynard and Waters 2007; Tovey 2007; Moser and Martinsen 2010). A creative curriculum and early childhood experience in which children are enabled to explore and to investigate for themselves both indoors and outdoors, where they are supported by appropriately experienced practitioners will enable them to flourish.

REFLECTIVE QUESTIONS

■ Why do we need to be particularly mindful of the type of curriculum that is on offer to our youngest children?

■ How does an enabling environment support young children to flourish?

■ What is the relationship between a creative curriculum and young children's opportunities to flourish throughout their lives?

References

Boaler, J. (2009). *The Elephant in the Classroom. Helping Children Learn & Love Maths*. Souvenir Press: London.

Bowlby, J. (1988) *A Secure Base: Clinical Applications of Attachment Theory*. London: Tavistock/Routledge.

Broadhead, P. and Burt, A. (2012) *Understanding Young Children's Learning through Play: Building Playful Pedagogies*. London: Routledge.

Canning, N. (2007) Children's empowerment in play. *European Early Childhood Education Research Journal*, 15(2), pp. 227–236.

Carruthers, E. and Worthington, M. (2011) *Understanding Children's Mathematical Graphics: Beginnings in Play*. Maidenhead: Open University Press.

Cherkowski, S. and Walker, K. (2014) 'Flourishing communities: re-storying educational leadership using a positive research lens', in *International Journal of Leadership in Education*, 17(2), pp. 200–216.

Craft, A. (2000) *Creativity Across the Primary Curriculum Framing and Developing Practice*. London: Routledge.

David, T. (1998) Learning properly? Young children and desirable outcomes. *Early Years*, 18(2), pp. 61–66.

DCSF (2008) *Statutory Framework for the Early Years Foundation Stage*. Nottingham: DCSF Publications.

DfE (2012) *Statutory Framework for the Early Years Foundation Stage*. Runcorn: DfE.

DfE (2014) *Statutory Framework for the Early Years Foundation Stage*. London: DfE.

DfEE (1996) *Desirable Outcomes for Children's Learning on Entering Compulsory Education*. London: DfEE.

Edwards, S. and Cutter-Mackenzie, A. (2013) 'Pedagogical play types: What do they suggest for learning about sustainability in early childhood education?' in *International Journal of Early Childhood*, 45, pp. 327–346.

Elfer, P., Goldschmeid, E. and Selleck, D. (2012) *Key Persons in the Early Years 2nd ed.* London: Routledge.

Faryadi, Q. (2007) *The Montessori Paradigm of Learning: So What?* http://files.eric.ed. gov/fulltext/ED496081.pdf [Accessed 05/04/15]

Gandini, L. (1998) Educational and caring spaces. In Edwards, C., Gandini, L. and Foreman, G. (1998) *The Hundred Languages of Children: The Reggio Emilia Approach*. London: Ablex Publishing Corporation, pp. 161–178.

Giardiello, P. (2014) *Pioneers in Early Childhood Education: The roots and legacies of Rachel and Margaret McMillan, Maria Montessori and Susan Isaacs*. Abingdon: Routledge.

Hatch, J. (2010) 'Rethinking the relationship between learning and development: Teaching for learning in the early childhood classrooms', in *The Educational Forum*, 734(3), pp. 258–268.

Howard, J. (2010) 'Early years practitioner's perceptions of play: An exploration of theoretical understanding, planning and involvement, confidence and barriers to practice', in *Educational and Child Psychology*, 27(4), pp. 91–102.

Jarvis, P. (2007) 'Monsters, magic and Mr Psycho: a bio-cultural approach to rough and tumble play in the early years of primary school'. *Early Years: Journal of International Research and Development*, 27(2), pp. 171–188.

Knight, S. (2013) *Forest School and Outdoor Learning in the Early Years 2e*. London: Sage.

Lambirth, A. (2006) 'A ripple that ruffled feathers: An appreciation of 30 years of Michael Rosen's poetry for children', in *Changing English: Studies in Culture and Education*, 13(1), pp. 45–54.

Leong, D. and Bodrova, E. (2012) 'Assessing and scaffolding make-believe play', in *Young Children*, January 2012, 67(1), pp. 28–34.

Maynard, T. (2007) 'Forest Schools in Great Britain: an initial exploration'. *Contemporary Issues in Early Childhood*, 8(4), pp. 320–331.

Maynard, T. and Waters, J. (2007) 'Learning in the outdoor environment: a missed opportunity?' *Early Years*, 27(3), pp. 255–265.

Moser, T. and Martinsen, M. (2010) The outdoor environment in Norwegian kindergartens as pedagogical space for toddlers' play, learning and development. *European Early Childhood Education Research Journal*, 18(4), pp. 457–471.

Moyles, J. (2010) *Thinking About Play: Developing a Reflective Approach*. Maidenhead: McGraw-Hill.

National Advisory Committee on Creative and Cultural Education (1999) *All Our Futures: Creativity, Culture and Education*. London: DSEE.

Narvaez, D. (2015) 'Understanding flourishing: Evolutionary baselines and morality', in *Journal of Moral Education*, 44(3), pp. 253–262.

Nutbrown, C. (2011) *Threads of Thinking: Schemas and Young Children's Learning 4e*. London: Sage.

Piaget, J. (1959) *The Language and Thought of the Child*. London: Routledge Kegan Paul.

Pramling Samuelsson, I. and Carlsson, M. (2008) 'The playing learning child: Towards a pedagogy of early childhood', in *Scandinavian Journal of Educational Research*, 52(6), pp. 623–641.

Pramling Samuelsson, I. and Johansson, E. (2009) 'Why do children involve teachers in their play?' in *European Early Childhood Education Research Journal*, 17(1), pp. 77–94.

Robinson, K. (2004) Schools Kill Creativity, www.ted.com/talks/ken_robinson_says_schools_kill_creativity %5Baccessed December 2015

Robinson, K. and Aronica, L. (2015) *Creative Schools Revolutionising Education from the Ground Up*. London: Penguin.

Robson, S. (2012) *Developing Thinking and Understanding in Young Children: An Introduction for Students*. London: Routledge.

Rogers, S. and Evans, J. (2008) *Inside Role-Play in Early Childhood Education*. London: Routledge.

Rose, J. and Rogers, S. (2012) The Role of the Adult in Early Years Settings. Maidenhead: McGraw-Hill.

Rosen, M. (2014) My professorial inaugural lecture at Goldsmiths, University of London: Humour in children's books, http://michaelrosenblog.blogspot.co.uk/2014/07/my-professorial-inaugural-lecture-at.html [accessed 05/05/15]

Schweinhart, L. and Weikart, D. (1998) 'Why curriculum matters in early childhood education', in *Educational Leadership*, 55(6), pp. 57–60.

Siraj-Blatchford, I. (2009) Conceptualising progression in the pedagogy of play and sustained shared thinking in early childhood education: A Vygotskian Perspective. *Education and Child Psychology*, 26(2), pp. 77–89.

Storli, R. and Hagen, T. (2010) Affordances in outdoor environments and children's physically active play in pre-schools. *European Early Childhood Research Journal*, 18(4), pp. 445–456.

Strong-Wilson, T. and Ellis, J. (2007) 'Children and place: Reggio Emilia's environment as third teacher', in *Theory into Practice*, 46(1), pp. 40–47.

Tovey, H. (2007) *Playing Outdoors Spaces and Places Risks and Challenges*, Maidenhead: McGraw-Hill.

Vygotsky, L. (1978) *Mind in Society*. London: Harvard University Press.

Vygotsky, L. (2004) 'Imagination and creativity in early childhood', in *Journal of Russian and East European Psychology*, 42(1), pp. 7–97.

Waters, M. (2011) 'Does a National Curriculum matter?' In *Education Review*, 23(1), pp. 52–60.

Waters, M. (2013) *Thinking Allowed on Schooling*. Bancyfelin: Independent Thinking Press.

Wood, E. (2013) *Play Learning and the Early Childhood Curriculum 3e*. London: Sage.

8 Pedagogical documentation to support flourishing

Jan Gourd

This chapter considers how pedagogical documentation has the potential to encourage flourishing among early years practitioners and how that in turn can help to create optimal conditions for children's flourishing. The link is made between practitioner well-being and children's flourishing. The particular facets of flourishing that are considered are taken from Seligman's (2011), De Ruyter's (2007) and Ryff and Singer's (2000) work. These are summarised below.

De Ruyter (2007) considers the holding and developing of ideals and values to be an important factor for work satisfaction. This was discussed in Chapter 1 and is relevant here in the context of the production of pedagogical documentation. Ryff and Singer (2000) talk about the necessity of good interpersonal relationships for flourishing individuals, which clearly links to the co-construction of pedagogical documentation and Seligman's (2011) PERMA (Positive Emotion, Engagement, Relationships, Meaning and Accomplishment) continue to underpin the discussion over whether flourishing is 'buildable'.

There are many differing perspectives on pedagogical documentation. The embodiment of it can take many forms and fulfil many different purposes. I propose to look at what is meant by the term pedagogical documentation and how it is used within the UK context.

The roots of pedagogical documentation in the UK

The idea of learning from observing children dates back to the classical theorists, such as Rousseau (1712–1778), Pestalozzi (1746–1827) and Froebel (1782–1852) as demonstrated by Falk and Darling-Hammond (2010). These theorists felt that educators should be responsive to children's needs and build on what they already knew and could do. These child-centred practices fell out of favour among policy makers and therefore became an almost forgotten debate during the late 1980s onward as the neo-liberal agenda gained prominence (Ball 2013; Passy 2013). The drive for accountability and data generation took over at an ever accelerating pace and the debates around pedagogy became focused on delivering developmentally-based outcomes rather than understanding the deeper practices of teaching and learning. Indeed, it is this uncontested idea among many educators of developmental curricula that the debates around documentation seek to disrupt. Rinaldi (2006) suggests that documentation is a collaboration between educator and learner, a dialogue of shared experience and understanding that defines future curricula and potential learning rather than 'the next steps' in a pre-determined policy missive. It is the child and the educator who have the agency. This feeling of agency of collaborative engagement with learning is one of Seligman's (2011) necessary conditions of flourishing.

- Pedagogical documentation is a shared process between pedagogue and learner.
- Such documentation seeks to support dialogue and a consideration of future possibilities in terms of curricula and learning.

Documentation as assessment against developmental norms

The current unease with measuring attainment against pre-set standards and indeed neo-liberalism per se, plus the growing concerns about children's mental health and future adult flourishing has led to a growing activist position among educators who want to open the deep critical dialogue about practice that seems to have been stifled by the testing techniques and practices.

Ideal practice has been compromised to allow practitioners to survive the performativity agenda that has dominated the last 30 years (Ball 2013; Troman 2008). Documentation of learning has in many cases become synonymous with the assessment of learning. It has become a technical exercise to make summative judgements against developmental outcomes. Waters (2013) discusses this in relation to game theory, seeing education managers as the players in the policy maker's games. Waters (2013, p. 104) sees the games not only as a diminishing of professional identity but also as a 'compromise (of) their beliefs and practices in order to meet the perceived demands'. This compromising of beliefs and practices creates uncomfortable tensions for professionals (Cottle and Alexander 2012) and in my view restricts their flourishing as they in turn feel unable to fully engage with the children in their care in the way that they feel is right. Indeed, many practitioners see documentation as an assessment burden rather than a dialogic document for learning.

This game playing has also resulted in an uncontrollable proliferation of 'evidencing' quality. The desire to evidence all that goes on in a setting against pre-set developmental criteria has compromised not only practitioners' beliefs and understanding of young children, but has also taken them away from interacting with the children themselves in order to complete the 'paperwork'. This de-professionalisation, falsely labelled as up-skilling and professionalisation by policy makers has led to a lack of confidence among many practitioners who now feel that they are not true to themselves and their intuitive beliefs about young children (Cottle and Alexander 2012; Passy 2013). This agenda restricts the flourishing of those who are at the forefront of protecting children's development and well-being and they often see themselves as implementers of policy rather than educators of children.

Forman (2010) critiques the practice of recording against developmental norms around skill acquisition by suggesting that what should be adopted is a narrative approach to unique learning episodes. He argues for the use of indexed video clips for each child to record their unique and 'clever' representations of knowledge and skill acquisition. Forman doesn't feel that quality education can be reduced to scores on a page nor that learning can be measured against developmental norms as this does not allow for the cleverness and uniqueness of each child's individual response to be recorded. Despite the ever-increasing technological advances Garrick *et al.* (2010) notes reluctance on the part of practitioners to use these new technologies to document children's learning.

- Current English documentation processes are often narrow and set against pre-determined criteria.
- Such approaches can leave practitioners feeling de-professionalised.

How documentation can diminish interaction

Ryff and Singer (2000) suggest that human flourishing is predicated on the quality of interpersonal relationships that an individual makes. When practitioners' time is taken up with paperwork such as documenting what the child is doing, it distracts them and takes the time away from inter-actions with children and making the positive relationships that contribute so much to human flourishing. Indeed, Macmurray (1946) argued that schooling is not dependant on curriculum but on people. Waller (2015, p. 12) notes that when the researcher was involved in documenting a child's engagement with an activity 'opportunities for joint engagement and shared activity were more restricted'. Tizzard and Hughes (1984) in their study on home and school learning noted that children tended to learn more when in the home rather than the school environment due to the number of adult child conversations that took place.

These tensions and dilemmas often lead to stress on the part of the professional who in turn finds it increasingly difficult to be the nurturing educator that children need. Wilson and Conyers (2013) suggest that one of the most significant attributes that practitioners can model for children is optimism. They see this as being one of the keys to flourishing. In order to project positivism and optimism we need to create the right conditions for practitioners to be positive about their work themselves and it is this that is being undermined by the constant performativity measures (Osgood 2012).

Passy (2013) in her study found that student teachers were clear that they needed to be employed in schools that supported their values, where they could have agency and certain freedoms to employ their own pedagogy within the constraints of the defined curriculum. These young teachers, however, recognised that teaching might not be their lifelong career. Passy (2013, p. 1073) concludes:

> The irony of producing highly promising teachers, whose flexibility enables them to survive and flourish in a neoliberal environment but who may be contemplating another career as they complete their training, should not be lost.

Many researchers see pedagogical documentation as having validity as a tool for opening up the pedagogical space for critical debate about these important aspects once again (Moss 2013; Pacini-Ketchabal et al. 2015; Falk and Darling-Hammond 2010).

- Too often the completion of documentation removes opportunities for the practitioners to interact with children.
- The performativity agenda can be seen to be having a negative effect on the optimism of practitioners.

Pedagogical documentation as meaning making

Dahlberg, Moss and Pence (1999) were probably the first to debate the use of pedagogical documentation to develop meaning making within early years dialogue. They see documentation as a way of sharing meaning about early years services so that there is a language of evaluation that goes beyond the neo-liberal hijacking of the term 'Quality'. For them the debate is about participatory meaning making, co-construction of meaning between all those involved. They see that pedagogical documentation makes 'practice visible' (Dahlberg, Moss and Pence 1999, p. ix). In this they mean that photographs, videos, notes, planning, drawings and so forth can all contribute to the public portrayal of practice and therefore enhance the opportunities for debate about what we are doing. Implicit in this idea is that the artefacts provide opportunities for 'reflection, dialogue and argumentation, leading to a judgement of value, contextualised and provisional because it is always subject to contestation' (ibid. 1999, p. ix). The processes of engagement with the documentation will be different for the different audiences, for example, a parent reviewing the display of photographs and account of the school visit may well view the worthwhileness of the experience differently to the Ofsted Inspector seeking evidence of creativity within curriculum design. The words used will be different depending on the audience, but the dialogue might well share many similarities as a site for reflection and judgement. I would argue that documentation cannot fail to invoke a response that reflects and judges whether verbalised or in silent thought.

- Different audiences will engage with documentation in different ways, parents and Ofsted inspectors may view the same document very differently.

Staying close to the learning

According to Krechevsky *et al.* (2010, p. 66) 'Documentation helps teachers stay close to students' learning and interests and get to know the students in front of them as individuals and as a group'. Bath (2012) suggests that to be valuable documentation needs to be democratic. A process engaged in by both adult and child together in collaboration. This view is supported by Falk and Darling-Hammond (2010), who draw on the theories of effective teaching to argue that documentation is key to understanding where children are and to providing curricula that are authentic and meaningful to individual children. Unless this happens Bath (2012) argues then that the documentation is unlikely to be viewed very positively by the child and its usefulness in aiding flourishing through dialogue and connectiveness will be diminished.

The types of pedagogical documentation that a setting has may vary from wall displays, learning journeys, reports and case studies through to children's own documenting of their learning. Often the voice that narrates the experience will be the adults and so the meaning making has been 'translated' through adult eyes. Maybe this is fine so long as the critical capacity of the audience can negotiate this. As a site for transformative democratic practice, documentation has a lot to offer (Falk and Darling-Hammond 2010).

The Reggio influence

One of the most influential pedagogies on practice in this area of documentation has been Reggio Emilia. The ideals and values that are embodied within the work of the practitioners within this geographic area are well documented (Abbot and Nutbrown 2001; Brunton and Thornton 2009; Davies 2014). Reggio pedagogy foregrounds documentation as an important method of co-constructing meaning between all those who engage with it. The authenticity of co-construction seems to be prioritised within Reggio and fully understood by practitioners who are culturally immersed within the history of the development. As outsiders we can view Reggio documentation that is publically available, for example, at Reggio touring exhibitions and we can reflect and judge the artefacts, but we cannot as outsiders ever know the full meaning to the individuals who were involved. This is the duality of documentation. It has a life outside of its original context that is valuable as a site of reflection and as an agent in the development of public dialogue about the practice it portrays, but it also has a second and more profound purpose when shared among the participants, which validates practice and learning, engages, celebrates and creates memories of a personal nature. As practitioners we need to be aware of the dual roles that this documentation can fulfil and make judgements that honour the latter yet do justice to the former.

Within Reggio practice it is commonplace for the teachers to document the work of the children through the use of public display. This documentation is not seen as an end product, it is a 'tool for listening, observing and evaluating the nature of our experience' (Turner and Wilson 2010, p. 6) It is ongoing throughout the learning project, not a product of it. Malaguzzi in the above cited article suggests that practitioners are 'like archaeologists who come home in the evening with their finds and look over their sketches, notes and writings' (Ibid., p. 6). This is how documentation is viewed as a reflective tool for teachers as well as stimulating public dialogue. For the learner reflecting on the documentation it can also raise new questions about experiences and learning. In this way documentation is not seen as linear, rather it allows and encourages new inquiry, this fits well with the Deleuzian (1987) idea of 'lines of flight'. Davies (2014: 25) suggests that there is a danger that within Reggio practice the documentation can become merely 'the reproduction of institutional life' closing down rather than opening up the debate, maybe as depicted by Brown-Dupaul et al. (2012) who suggest a rather formulaic construction of documentation panels. Davies (2014) suggests that some teachers struggle with the concept of public display as a somewhat untidy work in progress and therefore close down the topic rather than offer potential for additions and extensions to it. Davies also warns of the danger of the exploitation of documentation whereby the work becomes the focus of books or of evidence of a teacher's excellence or of a school's value. Davies suggests that there can be value in all of these things but warns against it becoming the primary aim of the documentation. She (ibid., p. 27) also warns of how the documenting of everything the children do can take over and become the primary purpose of the activity. She (ibid., p. 27) asks 'who is the agent' in the activity of documentation?

Davies also cautions against documentation being exploitative of children. She argues that practitioners must question the real purpose of the documentation. She suggests that often the true motivation behind the documentation may be forgotten and that unintentionally the documentation becomes a technology in itself and the opportunities for documentation are privileged over the richness of the potential experience as a site of learning. She gives the example of a park visit, the children hear birds but cannot see them, this is clearly the object of their current interest but the teacher takes over as agent of the learning and asks 'what else can you find? The next photo in the teacher's documentation shows a child's finger pointing at a clover flower' (ibid. 2014, p. 27). The experience has moved from the auditory listening to bird song to a photo opportunity with a clover flower in one swift move. Davies asks us to consider who is the agent, the children, the teacher or indeed the camera?

Davies (2014) argues for recognition and acknowledgement by practitioners of moments of grace, when learning is in the ascent. These moments she describes as being when the child is in the flow of new discoveries. In terms of well-being and flourishing this could be seen as the child developing self-actualisation, being happy and absorbed in the new discoveries. She argues that practitioners need to learn how to recognise these moments and give back or leave the agency with the child. She again illustrates her point with an example from practice. She gives the example of a child in a sand pit who is absorbed by the malleability of the wet sand and the buildings that he can make with it. The teacher decides that it is now time for group work on construction with blocks and tells the boy to come out of the sandpit showing him how to dust the sand off his body. He comes to the group activity, but the sand draws him back and he drifts back into the sandpit, the teacher lets him be the agent of his own activity and allows him to continue even though it is not her plan for the curriculum for him for that day. The task that the child had set himself with the sand was not finished when he was called away; he had not come to a satisfactory conclusion. He was interrupted mid flow. On being allowed to continue he was then able to complete the task that he had set himself. Davies ends the episode with the words 'He is happy now' (Davies 2014, p. 30).

The task then is how do we recognise and document such exciting episodes of learning; the episodes that occur in the ascent? How do we create a curriculum and opportunities for ascents to dominate our documentation rather than using the ascents to confirm developmental milestones? How do we make documentation a tool rather than a technology that enables us to develop and demonstrate a child's flourishing?

This all within the UK context that does not have a tradition, except perhaps within the most extreme forms of the progressive tradition such as Summerhill of democratic education and child voice is the most problematic cultural obstacle to embracing the true essence of Reggio. Within the UK invariably the teacher is; the controller, the manager, the designer of the documentation although tacit regard is sometimes given to asking children if they mind their work being displayed publically (Thomson et al. 2007). Generally, it is assumed that children will be motivated by seeing their work displayed (Brighouse and Woods 1999). Many teacher education text books proliferate on the subject, for example, a whole series of books published by Belair (2015). Thomson et al. (2007) cite Alexander (2000: 185) who comments on the 'Englishness of display'. This Englishness of display is the 'cultural velcro' that means we can never truly appreciate the authentic Reggioness of Reggio practice. This has been an issue.

The tradition certainly within primary schools within the UK has been to use displays of children's work to celebrate and show off achievement (Alexander 2000) and the danger here is that readers of the Reggio pedagogy misunderstand the opening up of spaces, which are so central to the true meaning of practice that comes under the Reggio heading. To do justice to Reggio practice one must deeply understand the values, context and political ideologies of the social democracy that underpins it.

- Within Reggio Emilia pedagogical documentation is part of the process of co-constructing meaning.
- While the documentation can be displayed for others to view it will only be fully understood by those who participated in its construction.

Documentation within Te Whariki

The other often cited examples of pedagogical documentation come from New Zealand and sit within the Te Whariki curriculum mat. Within this curriculum the complexity of children's learning is documented through learning stories.

The term learning stories is primarily attributable to the work of Carr and Lee (2012). The learning stories within this context are used to recognise the potential of the children in early years settings and clearly link to the Te Whariki curriculum intentions. There is a synchronous relationship between curriculum intention and assessment practice that is not always found elsewhere.

Carr (2001) identifies four main purposes for learning stories. They are describing, deciding, discussing and documenting. These stories are written to enable the children to understand what they have engaged with and the learning that has occurred for them. They are encouraged to regularly re-visit them even years later (ibid. 2001).

How does English practice differ?

Indeed, in England the learning journeys, as they are named, attempt to chart children's progress but tend to be a very different concept. In the English context they are often viewed as a dossier on the child's daily activity and are kept with the neo-liberal idea of evidence of attainment and reaching developmental milestones in mind. Practitioners take care to keep these up to date, not necessarily because of their usefulness to the child, parent or to future planning, but often in case of an Ofsted visit. This need to keep evidence for Ofsted is overtaking the need to go beyond developmental goals and so is in danger of limiting quality time spent with young children. We are putting at risk the development of deep relational practice that encourages human flourishing in pursuit of the ultimate tick sheet score that takes up practitioner time with little further gain to the child. Pacini-Ketchabaw *et al.* (2015, p. 121) warn against 'a superficial, oversimplified approach to documenting children's learning – what Ritzer (1993) calls "MacDonaldization"'. To truly aid flourishing documentation needs to give the child agency and be seen as joint collaborative research between practitioner and child. Waller and Bitou (2011) is very clear to point out that this is not the norm in English settings.

One of the reasons why this is the case is because they are located within very different cultural policies and understandings. The Te Whariki approach is located within a culture of potentiality and complexity in early childhood practice rather than the developmental milestones to be achieved. The curricular policies come from very different ideological standpoints.

Pacini-Ketchabaw *et al.* (2015) suggest that this acceptance of a developmentally constructed view of early childhood practice needs to be challenged. From their post-structural standpoint, they are of the opinion that practices such as age-related expectations, which normalise a child need to be viewed as only one lens through which to see a child and that practitioners need to recognise that there are multiple lenses that need to form a compound lens or an insect eye, which can assimilate multiple views into one vision. Cannella (2005) cited in Sellers (2013, p. 36) suggests that 'privileging cognitive development theory privileges the construct of the individual over collective orientations, and privileges stereotypically male, deterministic assumptions that presume to know the mind of the child'.

- Pedagogical documentation in the English system is about evidence of attainment rather than the co-construction of knowledge.
- The English system appears not to recognise the potentiality of the child, which is seen in other systems such as Reggio Emilia and Te Whariki.

Who is documentation for?

Garrick *et al.* (2010) found that children had little part to play in creating documentation in the English early years context. Although often called 'My Learning Journey' Garrick found that children had played a very minor part in selecting materials for the records, indeed she concludes that the records were primarily kept for Ofsted and parents and often included a lot of writing, only sometimes including reports on the child. The children in her study did not readily re-engage with the books to develop their learning further, they were not really part of a learning journey, more of a history of achievement against developmental norms (Bath 2012).

Indeed, Greishaber and McArdle (2010) in an Australian context relate a father's annoyance at the surveillance of his son by the practitioners as his pre-school. The Australian Early Years Curriculum published in 2009 emphasises being, belonging and becoming, but is firmly set within a 'homo-economicus' stance (Moss 2014) and over half the full curriculum document is given over to 'outcomes'. Assessment plays a large part in the Australian government's policy intentions so that children who are not making acceptable progress can be identified and the specific hindrances to that attainment analysed. Thus, the curriculum foregrounds deficit children, in terms of specific outcomes, as needing specific and special attention. Greishaber and McArdle (2010, p. 96) also point out that although play is a stated pedagogical tool for the practitioners 'there are almost no references to play as fun . . . the closest to fun is that children show enthusiasm for participating in physical play'. If we see fun as an essential ingredient for human flourishing and happiness then this demonstrates the absolute dismissal of this aspect of flourishing within the policy document and therefore it is easy to see why documentation by practitioners could be considered 'surveillance'.

The situation in England is very similar; the EYFS (Early Years Foundation Stage) 2012 has 17 learning outcomes against which evidence must be gathered. The children are also subject to a two-year-old progress test. Forman (2010) demonstrates the diverse problems with a standards-based evaluation of children's learning. Forman (2010: 30), describing the system of reporting within the Head Start Program, uses a vignette of two children Ben and Jensen and demonstrates that although they have both attained a particular standard – in this instance: *the child uses one or more of the senses to observe and learn about objects, organisms and phenomena for a purpose*, the general nature of the standard makes it difficult to exclude any actions that come close. So the two children both attain the standard even though one is 24-months-old and the other is aged 5 and they demonstrate deeply unequal levels of complexity of thinking. Forman asks how this approach to documenting learning tells us anything that is useful either about the quality of the setting or the achievement of the child. The approach that Forman argues for is an approach based on a digital portfolio of the child so that the uniqueness and context of each 'story' of learning can be shared. Forman (2010: 33) points out that this approach to validating learning does not generate data, he says that 'we do not know how to include story as data' and therein lies the problem for our regulatory systems. Numbers says Forman (2010, p. 33) are 'merely a substitute for not being there'. The parent who knows that their child has achieved a set of numerical grades is less guilty about not being there because they are assured that their child is doing well. Maybe this theme of parental guilt is something that pervades our obsession with measureable outcomes in which case the re-education and shared publishing of practice through pedagogical documentation, which engages parents, is even more important to enable children to flourish. Gasper in Chapter 6 of this book discusses how holistic engagement with parents, through dialogue, contributes to the flourishing of the child. Indeed, the involvement of the family and the community underpins Reggio practice. The flourishing of the child is viewed as a collective responsibility.

So we need to look at what is recorded in a learning journey or learning stories and ask how they help practitioners and parents to support the very essence of children's flourishing and move beyond surveillance. How can learning journeys help practitioners and parents to critically engage with the learning? Can they have the potential to allow all parties to question their interactions with individual children and assess how those interactions can inform their future work with the child to develop the critical aspects that engender children's flourishing in the specific setting?

Given *et al.* suggest that in their study one of the major advantages of documentation was that:

> Documenting, reflecting upon, and sharing practice with colleagues empowered teachers to identify themselves as experts in both their classrooms and within their communities of practice.
>
> (2010, p. 43)

The practitioners here flourished as they were able to self-actualise and engage in transformational practice as suggested as a constituent of human flourishing by Titchen and McCormack (2010).

- It would seem that in both the English and Australian systems the pedagogical documentation contributes to an outcomes-based agenda and is used to determine progression in numerical terms.
- Such pedagogical documentation appears to have little to do with flourishing.

Pedagogical narration and pedagogical documentation

Pedagogical narration is seen as being a tool for early childhood educators to share stories and critical reflection of their work with children. The use of narration or story telling as a way of making meaning from experience is a common activity within reflective and critical reflective practice (Beard and Wilson 2013; MacNaughton 2005). Berger (2015) suggests that pedagogical narration allows educators to orientate themselves towards complexity and this is also the stance of (Beard and Wilson 2013), who suggest that we are moving away from our constructivist model of the understanding of learning into a post-modern ecological model, which recognises former theoretical standpoints, but presents them in a holistic way that recognises complexity as identifiable as a space.

Beard *et al.*'s (2007) work looking at the place of the situated experiential and emotional journey within learning (albeit with first-year undergraduate students) gives a potential theoretical framework to exploring the processes behind pedagogical narration as a learning tool. The dominance of females within early childhood education has led to feminist discourses around professionalism as emotional labour (Osgood 2012). This recognition within the literature of the 'emotional' as a key component in making sense of experience is helpful in moving into the holistic theorisation of the complexity of the practice of Early Childhood Education (ECE).

Pedagogical narration as seen by Berger (2015) opens up new spaces to create new knowledge of the practice of early childhood education, spaces that are not controlled by routine or Foucault's (1975) notion of the regimes of truth, but are based on experiential learning, the experience of being an Early Childhood Educator.

Falk and Darling-Hammond suggest that:

> By interweaving the learning processes of students with the learning processes of adults, documentation improves the quality of

communication and interaction for both, making possible a process of reciprocal learning.

(2010, p. 79)

Interaction is the key here. Documentation alone by the adult as a solitary activity will not in my view promote the flourishing of the practitioner or the child. The discussion is vital as it is the connectedness that develops well-being and opens the space for affirmation.

Pedagogical narration is seen as a space to offer resistance and to disrupt the dominance of certain ideas surrounding early childhood practice (Pacini-Ketchabaw *et al.* 2015). Narratives are shared with the aim of engaging others in critical dialogue. The aim is for the space for the critical dialogue to be opened up, to be made public.

The notion of resistance is not new, indeed within the ECE field politics, resistance and agency are key themes within the work of Dahlberg and Moss (2005), Moss (2013, 2014) MacNaughton (2005), Olsson (2009) and Taguchi (2009) and Davies (2014). Indeed, the agency demonstrated by early years educators is generally far more considered and developed within this sector than within the compulsory education phase (Cunningham 2012; Moss 2014).

Pedagogical narration's aim is to work with other practitioners in discovering the complexity of the everyday, taken for granted work of the early childhood setting, to be transformative in the practitioner learning journey (Beard and Wilson 2013). This is where pedagogical narration and pedagogical documentation are essentially different in that pedagogical narration seeks to develop the practice of the practitioner whereas that is not always the starting point for pedagogical documentation.

Pedagogical narration can be seen as a personal and practice development tool and draws heavily on the work of MacNaughton (2005). In creating vignettes or stories of practice and the development of these into pedagogical narration MacNaughton (2005) demonstrates the power of the narration to challenge personal and workplace 'regimes of truth'.

This is where we begin to see pedagogical narration as having a place within a new conceptualisation of leadership within early years practice as suggested by Burger (2015).

Burger (2015) considers pedagogical narration in the context of activism within leadership in the early years settings. He further contests some notions of early years leadership that are seen as feminine and suggests that pedagogical narration can be used to give leaders a new sense of agency within their settings. It is this unlocking or uncovering of the space through narration that for Burger makes the idea powerful. This sense of accomplishment and having control over one's practice gives the practitioner a sense of purpose, can be linked back to their ideals and hopefully promote optimism.

- Pedagogical narration is different from pedagogical documentation because it is about practitioners critically reflecting on their roles and engagements.
- Pedagogical narration can provide opportunities for practitioners to flourish within their roles.

Conclusion

In order for pedagogical documentation to support flourishing then it has to be useful and worth the time that it took to compile. Krechevsky *et al.* (2010, p. 70) suggest that these questions are asked about any documentation produced to help us consider its usefulness:

- In what ways does the documentation focus on learning, not just something we did?
- How does the documentation make visible the learning process as well as product?
- Does the documentation promote conversation or deepen understanding about some aspect of learning?
- Is there evidence to support the interpretations made in the documentation?
- Is there other information the viewer needs in order to follow the account of learning represented in the documentation?

To these I think that I would further add:

- Does the documentation engage the child?

If the child who is the subject of the documentation is able to revisit the artefacts with pride, joy, positive memories and talk about and extend the narrative then I would suggest that the process has been supportive of that child's flourishing.

REFLECTIVE QUESTIONS

- How does the pedagogical documentation seen in Reggio Emilia and Te Whariki differ from that offered within the English system?
- Why might the co-construction of knowledge be considered as more appropriate than the measurements against milestones?
- In what ways can pedagogical documentation be considered to support the flourishing of the child and the practitioner?

References

Abbot, L. and Nutbrown, C. (2001) *Experiencing Reggio Emilia: Implications for Pre-school Provision.* Milton Keynes: Open University Press.

Ball, S. (2013) *The Education Debate 2nd edn* Bristol: Policy Press.

Bath, C. (2012) '"I can't read it; I don't know": young children's participation in the pedagogical documentation of English early childhood education and care settings', in *International Journal of Early Years Education*, 20(2), pp. 190–201.

Beard, C. and Wilson, J. (2013) *Experiential Learning: A Handbook for Training, Educating, and Coaching.* London: Kogan Page.

Beard, C., Clegg, S. and Smith, K. (2007) 'Acknowledging the affective in higher education' in *British Educational Research Journal*, 33 (2) (2007), pp. 253–271.

Belair publisher (2015) series of books at www.collins.co.uk/product/97800 07489398/Belair+On+Display+-+Hands+on+a+School+Year last accessed 9/4/2015:17:25

Berger, I. (2015) 'Educational Leadership with an Ethics of Plurality and Natality' in *Studies in Philosophy and Education*, September 2015, 34(5), pp 475–487.

Brighouse, T. and Woods, D. (1999) *How to Improve your School.* London: Routledge.

Brown-Dupaul, J., Keyes,T. and Segatti, L. (2012) 'Using documentation panels to communicate with families', in *Childhood Education*, 77(4), pp. 209–213.

Brunton, P. and Thornton, L. (2009) *Understanding the Reggio Approach.* London: Routledge.

Carr, M. (2001) *Assessment in Early Childhood Settings: Learning stories.* London: Sage.

Carr, M. and Lee, W. (2012) *Learning Stories: Constructing Learner Identities in Early Education.* London: Sage.

Cottle, M. and Alexander, E. (2012) 'Quality in early years settings: government, research and practitioners' perspectives', in *British Educational Research Journal*, 38(4), pp. 635–654.

Cunningham, P. (2012) *Politics and the Primary Teacher (Understanding Primary Education Series).* London: Routledge.

Dahlberg, G., Moss, P. and Pence, A. (1999) *Beyond Quality in Early Childhood Education and Care: Languages of Evaluation.* London: Routledge.

Dahlberg, G. and Moss, P. (2005). *Ethics and politics in early childhood education.* Abingdon: RoutledgeFalmer.

Davies, B. (2014) *Listening to Children: Being and Becoming.* Abingdon: Routledge.

De Ruyter, D. (2007) 'Ideals, Education, and Happy Flourishing', in *Educational Theory*, 57(1), pp. 23–35.

Deleuze, G. and Guattari, F. (1987) *A Thousand Plateaus*. Minneapolis: University of Minnesota Press.

DfE (Department for Education)(2012) *Statutory Framework for the Early Years Foundation Stage*. www.education.gov.uk/aboutdfe/statutory/g00213120/eyfs-statutory-framework.

Falk, B. and Darling-Hammond, L. (2010) 'Documentation and democratic education' in *Theory into Practice*, 49, pp. 72–81.

Forman, G. (2010) 'Documentation and accountability: The shift from numbers to indexed narratives' in *Theory into Practice*, 49, pp. 29–35.

Foucault, M. (1975) *Discipline and Punish: The Birth of the Prison*. Translated by Alan Sheridan, London: Allen Lane, Penguin. First published in French as Surveiller et punir, Gallimard, Paris, 1975.

Garrick, R., Bath, C., Dunn, K., Maconochie, H., Willis, B. and Wolstenholme, C. (2010) *Children's Experiences of the Foundation Stage. Report RR071*. London: DfE.

Given, H., Kuh, L., Keenan, D., Mardell, B., Redditt, S. and Twombly, S. (2010) 'Changing school culture: using documentation to support collaborative inquiry', in *Theory into Practice*, 49, pp. 36–46.

Greishaber, S. and McArdle, F. (2010) *The Trouble with Play*. Maidenhead: Open University Press.

Krechevsky, M., Rivard, M. and Burton, F. (2010) 'Accountability in three realms: Making learning visible inside and outside the classroom', in *Theory into Practice*, 49, pp. 64–71.

Macmurray, J. (1946) 'The integrity of the personal', in *Joseph Payne Memorial Lectures*. King's College: London.

MacNaughton, G. (2005) *Doing Foucault in early childhood studies: Applying poststructural ideas*. London: Routledge.

Moss, P. (ed.) (2013) *Early Childhood and Compulsory Education*. Abingdon: Routledge.

Moss, P. (2014) *Transformative Change and Real Utopias in Early Childhood Education*. Abingdon: Routledge.

Olsson, M. (2009) *Movement and experimentation in young children's learning: Deleuze and Guattari in early childhood education*. London: Routledge.

Osgood, J. (2006) 'Deconstructing professionalism in early childhood education: resisting the regulatory gaze', in *Contemporary Issues in Early Childhood*, 7(1), pp. 5–14.

Osgood, J. (2012) *Narratives from the Nursery: Negotiating Professional Identities in Early Childhood*. London: Routledge.

Pacini-Ketchabaw, V., Nxumalo, N., Kocher, L., Elliot, E. and Sanchez, A. (2015) *Journeys: Reconceptualising Early Childhood Practices through Pedagogical Narration*. Toronto: University of Toronto Press.

Passy, R. (2013) 'Surviving and flourishing in a neoliberal world: primary trainees talking', in *British Educational Research Journal*, 39(6), pp. 1060–1075.

Rinaldi, C. (2006) *In Dialogue with Reggio Emilia*. Abingdon: Routledge.

Ritzer, G. (1993) *The Macdonaldization of Society*. Thousand Oaks, CA: Pine Forge Press.

Ryan, R. and Deci, E. (2001) 'On happiness and human potentials: A review of research on hedonic and eudaimonic well-being', in *Annual Review of Psychology*, 52, p. 146.

Ryff, C. and Singer, B. (2000) 'InterpersonalAflourishing: a positive health agenda for the new millennium', in *Personality and Social Psychology Review*, 4(1), pp. 30–44.

Seligman, M. (2011) *Flourish*. London: Nicholas Brealey Publishing.

Sellers, M. (2013) *Young Children Becoming Curriculum*. London: Routledge.

Taguchi, L. (2009) *Going Beyond the Theory/Practice Divide in Early Childhood Education: Introducing an Intra-Active Pedagogy*. London: Routledge.

Thomson, P., Hall, C. and Russell, L. (2007) 'If these walls could speak: reading displays of primary children's work', in *Ethnography and Education*, 2(3), pp. 381–400.

Titchen, A. and McCormack, B. (2010) 'Dancing with stones: critical creativity as methodology for human flourishing', in *Educational Action Research*, 18(4), pp. 531–554.

Tizard, B. and Hughes, M. (1984) *Young Children Learning; Talking and Thinking at Home and at School*. London: Fontana.

Troman, G. (2008) 'Primary teacher identity, commitment and career in performative school cultures', in *British Educational Research Journal*, 34(5), pp. 619–633.

Turner, T. and Wilson, D. (2010) 'Reflections of documentation: Discussions with thought leaders from Reggio Emilia', in *Theory into Practice*, 49, pp. 5–13.

Waller, T. and Bitou, A. (2011) 'Research with children: three challenges for participatory research in early childhood', in *European Early Childhood Education Research Journal*, 19(1), pp. 5–20.

Waters, M. (2013) *Thinking Allowed on Schooling*. Carmarthen: Independent Thinking Press.

Wilson, D. and Conyers, M. (2013) *Flourishing in the First Five Years*. Lanham, MD: R & L Education.

Futures

9 Equality for flourishing in the early years

Sue Lea

Introduction

In recent times statistical information has become a substitute for exploring the profound and complex reasons why some children fail while others thrive in an unequal society. The education system continues to be enmeshed in the allocation of life chances and we measure and count in order to maintain the illusion that we live in a society that cares about equality of opportunity for all children. Truths about in/equality are relegated to media 'sound bites' in a political, economic and social system, which actively promotes competition and 'survival of the fittest', based on modernist ideas of scientific understanding and progress. Discussion emerging from data collection is often focused on understanding how to 'improve' early years workers, families, communities and the individual child, while politics and economics remain the 'absent' presence in educational debates.

In order to begin to explore the challenge of equality and inclusive practice one is challenged by a mass of complex literature. The research literature often explores the generally stable patterns of inequalities of the past rather than promote the practice of inclusion to meet the challenges of the unstable future that children currently in their early years will have to learn to negotiate. Evidence clearly shows that children face unequal life chances based on the circumstances of their birth, and it would seem that these inequalities are persistent across generations (Save the Children 2013; EHRC 2008; Cabinet Office 2007). Quite simply, if your parents were educationally disadvantaged you are also likely to be disadvantaged and this disadvantage will persist throughout the whole of your life. If you have children this legacy is likely to continue into their life too.

This chapter therefore proposes that a commitment to equality starts when practitioners develop a critically reflective understanding of inequalities: one that locates their understanding within a social, economic and political system that rests on ideas and practices that are inherently unfair to many children. This goes way beyond meeting the legal minimum standards of practice, which are readily available within written policy documents and easily accessible on government, and other websites.

An important starting point here is to seek to unearth and make explicit some of the values, paradigmatic assumptions and power relations that are always present in our own minds and that we carry through into our practice and our educational relationships. The chapter is therefore designed to prompt self-reflection in order to clarify the personal values and hidden assumptions that inform our practice, and to offer ideas that might help the reader to critically negotiate the various literatures, unearth these assumptions and to identify previously unrecognised connections between global paradigms, the educational ecosystem of the child and how this impacts on each of us in our local practice (Lea 2010).

Ecological systems and equality

The often unquestioned and complex ecological system into which we are all born generates particular values about human being and becoming; for example, our focus on memory testing at the expense of creativity or emotional intelligence. Success here privileges and values the acquisition and understanding of certain types of information and particular ways of thinking at the expense of others. Robinson (2011, p. xiv) argues for vision, imagination creativity and transgression in education, as 'we will not succeed in navigating the complex environment of the future by peering relentlessly into a rear-view mirror'. So it is with these inequalities in education that there is now a recognition that we need to ask different questions and to reinvent an educational language to respond to current challenges (Biesta 2006). As a society, and specifically as educators, we will need to equip children to be able to make interpretive choices between competing ideas and help them to make sense of the challenges of the democratisation of knowledge via the World Wide Web. Now that we are experiencing the radicalisation of young people via the web and where incitement to terrorism via the web has become a chargeable offence, we will need to find new ways to equip children to negotiate the knowledge claims that are made beyond the pre-school, the classroom and the university. Perhaps more importantly, we will need to understand the impact of this change in access to different forms of knowledge and ways of knowing. This impact is already being felt epistemologically, but it is in the psychological, spiritual, emotional, cognitive and concretely lived, experiences of children coming into presence in a complex global environment that the real changes will impact. The way we conceive the emergence of the global child in all her and his diversity will inevitably lead to new understandings of how we can enable all children to flourish within and through their educational experiences and relationships.

- Where we are born will influence whether we like it or not and impact on our life experiences.
- As practitioners we need to support children as a global child who is able to operate and flourish.

Equality and power

The notion of equality remains a dangerous word because it is used so unproblematically and because it threatens existing power relations. It means different things to different people based on their own interpretative lens (see Brighouse, Tooley and Howe 2010). People will often limit their understanding of inequality to their own experience and even when they have experienced a particular oppression will fail to consider its source and may view it merely as an inter-personal process rather than a systematic experience, which emerges repeatedly through the choices made that frame our experience. There is often limited understanding of the ways in which inequalities are linked vertically to broader structural issues and horizontally to other oppressions. For example, a wealthy 'white' able-bodied feminist might argue for the equality of women without understanding that women of colour or of class, for example, experience their lives differently in terms of oppression(s). To develop a genuine understanding of equality is challenging both personally and professionally as we are forced to examine both our own experience and confront our own prejudices and taken-for-granted assumptions about our self and others. 'One of the hardest things teachers have to learn is that the sincerity of their intentions does not guarantee the purity of their practice' (Brookfield 1995, p. 1). To develop a genuine understanding of what it means to practice for human flourishing involves critically reflective questioning of our own value judgements. This is challenging as we recognise our own unwitting ignorance about the lives of children, families and communities that are both unfamiliar to us, and those that appear familiar to us but exist just beyond our experience. Not all welfare recipients conform to the discourse created by reality television programmes!

One of the challenges we face is that the complexities of inequality are often segregated into the simplified categories of social class, sexuality, religion, disability, race and gender and see differences rather than commonalities in oppressive practices. The literature then is diverse but bounded. If your interest is in special educational needs then many of the broader issues of objectification, socially constructed exclusions, lack of funding and support will apply to other equality domains. Children with English as an additional language (EAL) will share similar challenges to any child with a communication issue.

The issue of equalities language is one that often engenders fear in the minds of most professionals, as language is the practical expression of our consciousness. Implicitly then *we know* that there are different ways of speaking about and understanding plurality and difference just as there are different ways of expressing our humanity and diversity. In order to try to make sense of why some children flourish while others languish at the margins of an unequal education system we need to reintegrate our understanding of the overlapping nature of oppression/s and understand education's vital role in an unequal world (see Save the Children 2013). Questions about why some children are enabled to participate, benefit and flourish in the human society into which they were born are both broad and deep philosophical questions and inform the type of social, economic and political questions we ask. For early years educators these questions are also questions about our own responsibilities as the translators and interpreters of educational policy into educational practice (Lea 2014). In thinking about these questions we need to deal with the complex realities of how we, our ways of thinking and our practice, are nested in those broader contextual fields and informed by them. The challenge then is our ability to fully and intelligently reflect on whether we are part of the problem or part of the solution in challenging inequality and recognising its relationship with power.

- Being critically reflective and questioning one's own value judgements is essential in supporting human flourishing.
- In order to understand why some flourish while others do not it is essential to understand what can constitute oppression.

The context in which educational inequality is nested

Global events since the 9/11 attack on the twin towers in New York on 11 September 2001 have demonstrated the failures and partialities of modernity, and highlighted differences in ways of understanding and living in the twenty-first century as competing beliefs have become manifest in the global context. In economic terms the global financial crises of 2007/2008 further calls into question the sustainability of neo-liberal economics, which are practiced within the global capitalist system and demonstrably favour 1 per cent of the population (Weeks 2014). In political terms there has also been a loss of faith in democracy itself as global corporations have operated beyond the control of democratically elected governments (Beck 2000). These issues impact on equality and human flourishing and demonstrate the plurality and difference that will challenge human being in the future.

The causes of inequality are not simple. In the 'West', modernity broadly marked a shift from feudal society to industrial capitalism.

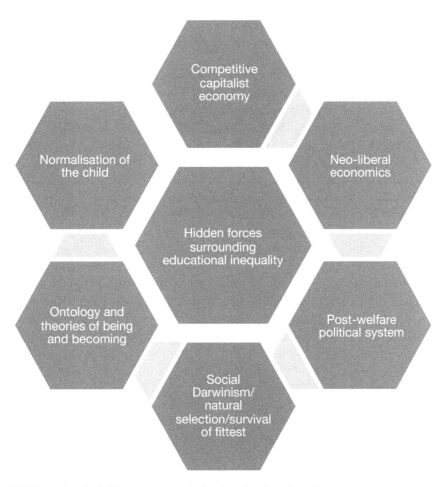

FIGURE 7.1 A contextual framework for understanding educational inequality

This shift also marked a philosophical change whereby science superseded religion as the primary vehicle for human progress and flourishing. Very broadly speaking, before the Enlightenment and the rise of scientific thought, one's role in life was allocated at birth by an all-knowing God. Although religious thought and authority were challenged during this period, most of the population were illiterate and inequality remained a given. People generally maintained the position they were born to. The rise of science favoured rationality and human directed activity as the solution to all-important questions, and social 'science' was born to address political, economic and social questions. Science and rationality were seen as the vehicle by which the future direction of humanity would be determined (Habermass in MacNaughton 2005). Philosophers and social scientists have struggled with the status of scientific enquiry ever since, in particular the idea that a science of society is possible, that statistics can 'speak for themselves' or that knowledge can ever be free from power and particular interests. It is this concern with the nature of knowledge that links *all education*, especially early years education, to equality of opportunity for human being, becoming and flourishing.

Echoes of past thinking are always present in current ideas. One of the implicit ideas that discriminates against and oppresses certain groups is the idea that every child born is not of equal value. This thinking was explicit during the mid-1800s when Charles Darwin, a naturalist, proposed a Theory of Evolution. His theories of 'natural selection' and 'survival of the fittest' allocated different values to different groups of people. Concerned with evolutionary progress he believed that white skinned people were a higher form of life than black skinned people and theories of white supremacy followed. He theorised that men were genetically superior to women. He saw the support or nurture of physically or mentally ill people as being flawed, and death as 'nature's way' of dealing with 'poor human stock'. His theories were taken up by Galton who was knighted for proposing a theory of eugenics; that is, the idea that humanity can be enhanced by selective breeding programmes similar to those used in farming. It is notable that these theories were developed and proposed by 'white' able-bodied men who benefitted from them (Fevre and Bancroft 2010).

Darwinism embeds the idea of the superiority of the 'white', able-bodied, heterosexual male in Western thought and this thinking remains implicit in society and in far-right politics today. It is the screening of the foetus for 'abnormalities' and abortion, in a new focus on 'corrective surgery', and in psychological and chemical (drug) interventions to normalise people who find it difficult to 'fit in' or 'behave' (Lafarge *et al.* 2013). We label people who are different as autistic or having

ADHD, we correct minor speech impediments and in so doing we medicalise human diversity. Girls are still subject to female genital mutilation, and one-child policies in China saw one hundred million missing girls as extensive infanticide and left them to die in favour of boy children (Ebenstein 2010). These are just some of the dangers of failing to take the pernicious context of inequality seriously, as are the dead babies and Syrian refugees being washed up on the shores of Europe in 2015. Emotionally intelligent reflection and action are essential if we are to bring a genuine equality of opportunity for human flourishing into the pre-school and wider society.

Policy and legislation are often seen as the solution to inequality. While they are an important part of the solution they cannot solve problems in isolation from intelligent and loving action. Despite policy and legislative change 'hate' crime continues to demonstrate violent attacks against gay men, black men and differently-abled/disabled people. Domestic violence and rape continue to oppress women. Notions of supremacy and human hierarchy continue to prevail in both scientific and religious thought and these have operated implicitly or explicitly in social, political and economic thinking and inform the rise of right-wing political parties. There remains ample evidence of differences in performance between children based on class, ethnicity, gender and diverse educational needs (Fusarelli 2015). Reflecting on the contribution that practitioners can offer in the creation of diverse communities in educational settings is part of the important and contested nature/nurture debate that is likely to continue with the advancements in genetics.

Marxism, feminism and post-structuralism are all, in effect, philosophical responses to, and critiques of, the Modernist project. Each has strands that question the notion that 'objective' truth is possible for all people, for all time. Marx first theorised the inevitable problems associated with capitalism and the inequalities of economic class; early feminists the political, social and economic inequalities faced by women; and post-structuralists, although more eclectic in scope, expose how power systematically operates to normalise people (Wrigley 2012). Foucault has been particularly focused on understanding the relationship between power and knowledge and how particular truths are produced through normalising discourses (MacNaughton 2005). Here, surveillance, observation, measuring and counting define normality, which is then used to create discourses that define particular sets of truths about children, which become accepted as 'normal' patterns of child development. Reflection about this process is particularly relevant for early years workers whose methods of observation and recording children's development is not value-free. It does have an impact of developing interventions, which may inadvertently lead us away from diverse, resilient childhoods towards disciplined and anxious childhoods, as some children are produced as docile units of human capital designed to meet the needs of employers and markets.

■   The causes of inequalities are not simple and can be considered to be embedded in past thinking that influences current practices.

■   Emotionally intelligent thinking needs to occur if we as practitioners are to develop opportunities for equality and flourishing for all.

The impact of our autobiographies

No early years educator should be afraid to recognise that each of us are inscribed with the culture of the society into which we were born because as Biesta (2006, p. 53) reminds us 'coming into presence is not something one can do by oneself'. That holds for every child in our setting. Our norms and values might be culturally ascribed, but that does not mean we should not aspire to be open to new ways of seeing and understanding the world in our educational relationships.

Reflecting on and understanding how our autobiographies impact on our taken-for-granted worldview is challenging and it is important to understand the influences we carry forward into our practice. Would an older, Christian, married, white, working-class woman with mobility issues approach early years education in the same way as a Buddhist, young, single, mixed-heritage, middle class, physically active woman? Would an experienced early years worker with 25 years' experience approach work in the same way as a newly qualified EYTs graduate? This diversity should not be a problem, but recognising and working with it often is. It is not a question of superiority and hierarchy, but of cooperation and collaboration. Diversity in staff teams is an essential pre-requisite for a diverse and inclusive education. Some of the ways in which our autobiographies will impact on our approach to equality are set out below for reflection so that we can explore our practice through multiple lenses.

An example of a fixed and narrow autobiographical lens is the student who informed me that she worked in a setting where children came from 'nice families with no problems'. She was surprised to be asked how she could know that. When asked to reflect on whether or not long hours in pre-school, hot-housing children and colonising their time with activities, parental stress, debt, gambling, domestic violence, alcoholism,

FIGURE 7.2 An autobiographical context for understanding educational inequality

drug-use and or abuse and child abuse were absent in her community she was genuinely shocked. When asked to think about the norms being modelled and assimilated in her setting and to consider whether children had a clear understanding of the difference and diversity that existed beyond their village she realised that she had never considered these issues. On reflection she admitted that it had simply never occurred to her that these issues might affect the flourishing of the children in her charge. Her positive judgement about the benefits of the nuclear family and her belief that visible economic success was all a child required to flourish had limited her imaginative capacity for initiatives to prepare children for the diverse society into which they would emerge. Perhaps this group of children would better flourish in the freedom, fun and physical environment of outdoors education? Perhaps genuine opportunity for 'messy' play or the joy of unstructured time that might not otherwise be available to them would benefit them? An understanding of difference and equality is particularly important for children living in the rural idyll where some children have never met children who come from different cultural heritages.

How we negotiate the complex journey through practice is challenging, but negotiation of the diverse equality literatures is even more challenging. It is likely that our reading will depend on our autobiography as we start to read literatures on disability, feminism, anti-racism and so forth. There is an important starting point that precedes the literature, however. It may be the most important reflective question we ask ourselves: '*Do I genuinely believe that every child born is without question or exception of equal value?*' If one can claim a genuine belief in this simple truth then we can seek to learn to practice with a profound commitment to equality of opportunity and it will be this commitment, supplemented by the literature that will offer opportunities for the child to flourish. This means moving beyond the basics required by policy in order to understand how to best support every child encountered in the pre-school to fully come into presence as a unique child.

A genuine commitment to ensure that children flourish does not rest on measurements and judgements or pre-existing templates. It is not about normalising judgements to meet the often arbitrary standards of the past that are set out in policy. It is about a quality of relationships in a pre-school community where communication, collaboration and cooperation are valued and children are listened to as they 'come into presence' (Biesta 2006, p. 84). Quite simply it is about 'love', where love is a kind and passionate commitment to nurture the creativity in all children and to value their own expression of their inner being as it comes into presence (Elfer 2015). It cannot be faked or forced or counted or measured, it is part of rapid cognition or intuition, which exists fleetingly when something is both known and felt. Children intuitively recognise this, trust it and feel either insecure and unsafe, or secure and free to truly become themselves. While this might sound Utopian, it is important that all education offers children opportunities to dream and to see beyond the immediately obvious (see Robinson 2011). This is only possible when practitioners commit to doing the hard work needed to ensure diversity in their approach to practice.

■   Reflecting on our own autobiographies is challenging, however it supports us in understanding how we view the world.

■   In order to enable children to flourish there needs to be positive
relationships within the early childhood setting and these are not
achieved without commitment from the practitioners.

Educational relationships and equality

For many, the study of knowledge and belief itself has demonstrated the
epistemological flaws in both our faith in science and in markets, to
enhance human being and becoming, to serve the majority population
and to increase human flourishing. These concerns have been translated
into educational contexts by writers like Apple (2013) and Giroux
(2011) and specifically for the early years by Moss (2014, Dahlberg and
Moss (2005) and MacNaughton (2005). It has now been acknowledged
by the European Commission that 'educational policies alone cannot
address educational disadvantage' (in Moss 2014, p. 37).

The politics of knowledge is therefore important for early years educators because we now have access to understandings that demonstrate
that inequality is produced socially and economically by power relations
that operate in favour of the interests of some children at the expense of
others. The masking of the power contained in the systems, which
approve particular ways of thinking, being and becoming are always
present. As demonstrated earlier, power relations are implicit in our
understanding of what it means to be an early years professional worker
and they infuse our ideas of what constitutes a 'normal' child and childhood. This type of thinking has the power to devalue difference and to
allocate privilege to some children, based on pre-determined notions of
linear patterns of child development that are often behaviourally based
and socially constructed. Standards of child development, after Foucault,
demonstrate the links between knowledge and power and their relation
to the creation of particular discourses about childhood based on
surveillance and normalisation (MacNaughton 2005). An unequivocal
acceptance and understanding of equality is essential in order to combat
educational relationships based on oppressive practice. If the notion
of children's ability to flourish is divorced from the concept of equality
and diversity, then power will operate to further normalise children to
a cognitive, spiritual, social and economic model of early childhood,
which continues to be Eurocentric, racist, classist, ableist, patriarchal and
heterosexist. Bronfenbrenner's Ecological Model (2005) can be a helpful
tool for mapping and understanding the contexts an early years practitioner needs to think about in order to fully consider the complex
systems that impact on the developing child and the possibilities of them

flourishing. Exploring the links between the various systems that affect the development of the child and mapping context in this way might seem complex and unnecessary, but it grounds our practice in critically reflective thought and enables us to become reflective practitioners. Thompson's Personal, Structural and Cultural (PCS) Model (1997) also offers us a useful insight into understanding how anti-discriminatory practice needs to consider the personal, cultural and structural domains. To some extent Thompson (1997) and Bronfenbrenner (2005) are complementary and overlapping ways of mapping oppression in order to decide our most effective interventions. I argue here that our commitment to understanding inequality is fundamental to performing our role effectively and that as educators we have a special duty to develop our professional knowledge for the benefit and inclusion of all of the children we work with and the families and communities who trust us with their futures. Without this commitment it will be impossible to ensure that we offer genuine equality of opportunity to the children whose care and education are entrusted to us. These broader contextual understandings, which operate as a context for our educational relationships, are of vital importance to ensure we understand how to avoid inadvertent harm to children in their educational journeys and in particular to their ways of thinking, speaking, being and becoming.

Educational relationships in the early years often rely on relationships beyond the early years setting. Families and communities *are* important as parents *are* the primary educator of the pre-school child (DfEE 2000). The relationship between home and school is crucial, but often this link is limited to very brief spoken and written exchanges, which act as proxy for a genuine relationship. In practice the educational relationships with parents in many early years settings involve minimum wage/low-paid early years workers in brief contact with minimum wage/low-paid working mothers. Here, child 'care' rather than 'education' is located in a political, social and economic system; designed to warehouse children and ensure women are 'off welfare and into work'. As such this raises much broader feminist and economic class questions around the role of women's equality and the issues they face around the poverty, which is often associated with parenthood (Osgood 2012).

- A clear understanding of equality is essential in order to combat educational relationships that are based on and propagate oppressive practice.
- Effective educational relationships in the early years extend beyond the setting into the wider aspects of a child's life.

FIGURE 7.3 A context for understanding relationship and educational inequality

Poverty and its impact on equality

In spite of our understanding of the ways in which sexism and poverty affect women with children, there are still organised bodies of knowledge that judge and negatively classify parents and families, particularly mothers, for educational inequality and 'under-achievement'. These often view the home environment as failing to meet the needs of children and blame struggling families for their own poverty. Save the Children (2013, p. 12) found that a quarter of all parents had less money than five years ago although many of them were working longer hours.

This meant parents had less time to spend with their children and less money to spend on providing them with essential extra-curricular activities. It also meant that children were more likely to be out of school while their parents were at work. Logically then, it is difficult to see all parents as the primary educators of children. Policies based on market ideology rather than welfare echo Darwinian survival theories and conflict directly with the rhetoric of equality for many children in 2016. Despite evidence of increasing child poverty, in 2015 the commitment of the government is to reduce Child Tax Credits to working families, which will exacerbate the obvious multiple disadvantages and the more subtle disadvantages faced by the children of low-income parents.

While the government and media continue to penalise and blame parents for the poor performance of their children in education, the conditions that actively create inequality continue to be politically, economically and socially constructed. Here the struggle over the truth about poverty is subsumed by the discourse of parents and educators who fail to properly meet the needs of their children. The truths about poverty, and in particular the impacts of insecure and or temporary work and housing are neglected, as parents are blamed for their own dis-advantage. If their children are denied an equality of opportunity to flourish in and through education, we must reflect on the broader contextual issues outlined above and this raises questions about the sort of society we wish to create for future generations.

We need to consider how the expansion of early years provision offers several advantages to neo-liberal governments. Evidentially there is little concern for equality or the flourishing of children when they and their families are being deliberately driven into poverty. In England the original driver of policy was two-fold. Firstly, to get mothers off welfare and into work and secondly, to ensure that 'Every Child Matters'. New Labours Every Child Matters (ECM) (2004) policies involved a range of measures to reduce child poverty and 1.1 million children were taken out of poverty prior to the financial crash of 2008. Since the general election of 2010 progress on child poverty has reversed and there has been *an increase* of 5 million children living in poverty in the UK. Nearly one in three children in the UK now live in poverty (Child Poverty Action Group cpag.org.uk 31/10/15). CPAG (2015) also found that when childcare costs were put into the mix, thousands more children were moved into poverty. The number of families in work and living below the official basic minimum living wage has increased year on year.

In addition to getting mothers off welfare and into work ECM (2004) also contained provisions for the professionalisation of the early years workforce and the development of an early years curriculum. This marked an explicit shift in pre-school provision from care to education. While evidence shows that the early years education affects the life chances of children positively there are still questions about the type of curriculum, and the ethos of the setting as a site for normalising children to create the human capital required by a voracious and competitive global economy.

As practitioners we need to reflect on why we believe what we believe and to ask ourselves in whose name and whose interests do we practice and what is it we are calling into presence with the children we work with. This is important because one's habits of thinking and taken-for-granted assumptions are always present in the subliminal messages we communicate through our body language, spoken language and in our customs, habits, dress and even food preferences. If we fail to take into account the diversity of the families and communities of origin of the children we work with this will be communicated to both family members and to children. Given the extent to which media discourses blame the poor, displace and impoverish them and revile refugee and asylum seekers and migrant workers from the EU, we need to reflect on whether or not our thinking and our practice are being polluted with disdain for those we work with.

- Despite the government's clear recognition of the relationship between poverty and educational underachievement, children and their families in poverty are often negatively judged for their difficulties.
- It would seem that the conditions that actively create inequality continue to be politically, economically and socially constructed.

Conclusion

There are many sources that indicate the formal building blocks on which equality rests but fewer that offer the type of alternative thinking required in order to achieve equality in practice. Many of the advisory texts are involved in setting out the requirements of law and commitments of policy and can be accessed readily online and in settings. Perhaps now is the time to consider alternative ways of thinking about the education and care of our children because despite policy commitments to equality and inclusion education continues to fail certain groups of children. How many more policy commitments like the United Nations Rights of the Child (1989), or New Labour's Every Child Matters (2004) are needed to ensure that a child's rights to equality are fulfilled? How much more data do we need to assert that education fails to meet the needs of children because the broader economic, political and social systems into which children are born are fundamentally unequal by design?

In thinking about how best to enable children to flourish we must first acknowledge that our education system is likely to continue to advantage certain children at the expense of others, and to allocate life chances based on a disregard for talent in favour of purchase power in the educational marketplace. Quite simply, we continue to look in Robinson's (2011) rear-view mirror because that continues to serve current interests. It is perhaps for this reason that Dahlberg and Moss (2005, p. viii) seek 'to help us to open up to new possibilities and new hope' in their Contesting Early Childhood Series. To open up hope and possibility is both simple in theory, but profoundly challenging in practice, as we grapple with complex philosophical, anthropological, psychological, sociological, cognitive and policy literatures. In seeking to find a different way of opening new possibilities and hope, this chapter has sought to find different lenses through which to view the challenge. It has done so by starting to map out some of the elements, which inform but are not always obviously present in inclusive and non-judgemental educational relationships.

Firstly, it has mapped some of the hidden forces, which inform the context in which we might understand and make sense of the both our way of thinking about education, and the design and delivery of educational policies, provisions and opportunities. Having made the claim that these ideas are both implicitly and explicitly woven into our ways of thinking and our concretely led lives, it has mapped some of the dimensions by which we might consider our ideas and experiences and the impact this has on our relationships with others. Finally, it has mapped a context where the broader picture, which is not always obviously present in our practice, meets the autobiographical self and informs our approach to equality and inclusion and impacts directly on children.

So how do we learn to question our taken-for-granted assumptions about how best to prepare children for a future that has yet to come into being? In seeking answers to these questions this chapter has claimed that we need to see ourselves in global contexts and then question what we actually believe in order to clarify the values on which our work rests. Once we better understand our self and our own beliefs we will be in a position to make informed judgements about the competing ideas about what it is to flourish. Without a values base to aid our understanding of the complex systems that inform early years education, it is unlikely that we can do anything other than repeat the mistakes of the past. That is, we will continue to harm some children and limit their opportunities and perpetuate inequalities. Hope and possibilities are therefore the key where:

> The gift of being human is that we have deep creative resources and from these we can continuously transform our lives if we choose. Whether you aim to change the whole world or the world within you, the limits are set as much by your imagination as by your current circumstances. This has been true for all people since the beginnings of human history.
>
> (Robinson and Aronica 2013, p. 237)

REFLECTIVE QUESTIONS

■ Why do practitioners need to be reflective and consider their own values in order to ensure equality and flourishing for the children with whom they work?

■ How can practitioners support the life chances of children, particularly those who have been born into poverty or another aspect social exclusion?

■ In what ways can practitioners equip children to be able to make interpretive choices between competing ideas and help them to make sense of the challenges that they face?

References

Apple, M. (2013) *Can Education Change Society?* Abingdon: Routledge.

Beck, U. (2000) *What is Globalization?* Cambridge: Polity Press.

Biesta, G. (2006) *Beyond Learning: Democratic education for a human future.* Boulder: Paradigm Publishers.

Brighouse, H., Tooley, J. and Howe, K. (2010) *Educational Equality.* London: Continuum.

Bronfenbrenner, U. (2005) *Making Human Beings Human: Bioecological Perspectives on Human Development.* London: Sage.

Brookfield, S. (1995) *Becoming a Critically Reflective Teacher.* San Francisco: Jossey-Bass.

Cabinet Office (2007) Fairness and Freedom: The Final Report of the Equalities Review. Norwich: HMSO.

Child Poverty Action Group cpag.org.uk (31/10/15) www.cpag.org.uk/child-poverty-facts-and-figures [accessed November 2015].

Dahlberg, G. and Moss, P. (2005) *Ethics and Politics in Early Childhood Education.* London: RoutledgeFalmer.

DfEE (2000) *Curriculum Guidance for the Foundation Stage*. London: QCA.

DfES (2004) *Every Child Matters: Change for Children*. Nottingham: DfES Publications.

Ebenstein, A. (2010) 'The "Missing Girls" of China and the unintended consequences of the one child policy', in *Journal of Human Resources*, 45(1), pp. 87–115.

EHRC (2008) Sixth Periodic Report of the United Kingdom to the United Nations Committee on the Elimination of all forms of Discrimination Against Women (CEDAW) http://tbinternet.ohchr.org/Treaties/CEDAW/Shared %20Documents/GBR/INT_CEDAW_NGO_GBR_41_8810_E.pdf [accessed November 2015].

Elfer, P. (2015) 'Emotional aspects of nursery policy and practice – progress and prospect', in *European Early Childhood Education Research Journal*, 23(4), pp. 497–511.

Fevre and Bancroft (2010) *Dead White Men and Other Important People: Sociology's Big Ideas*. London: Palgrave.

Fusarelli, D. (2015) 'Child welfare, education, inequality, and social policy in comparative perspective', in *Peabody Journal of Education*, 90(5), pp. 677–690.

Giroux, H. (2011) *On Critical Pedagogy*. New York: Continuum.

Lafarge, C., Mitchell, K. and Fox, P. (2013) 'Women's experiences of coping with pregnancy termination for fetal abnormality' in *Qualitative Health Research*, 23(7), pp. 924–936.

Lea, S. (2010) 'Educational relationships, reflexivity and values in a time of global economic fundamentalism', in *Critical and Reflective Practice in Education*, 2, pp. 80–91.

Lea, S. (2014) 'Early years work, professionalism and the translation of policy into practice', in Kingdon, Z. and Gourd, J. (2014) *Early Years Policy: The impact on practice*. London: Routledge.

MacNaughton, G. (2005) *Doing Foucault in Early Childhood Studies: Applying poststructural ideas*. London: Routledge.

Moss, P. (2014) *Transformative Change and Real Utopias in Early Childhood Education: A story of democracy, experimentation and potentiality*. London: Routledge.

Osgood, J. (2012) *Narratives from the nursery: negotiating professional identities in early childhood*. London: Routledge.

Robinson, K. (2011) *Out of our Minds: Learning to be Creative*. Chichester: Capstone.

Robinson, K. and Aronica, L. (2013) *Finding your Element*. London: Penguin.

Save the Children (2013) Annual Review: www.savethechildren.org/atf/cf/ %7B9def2ebe-10ae-432c-9bd0-df91d2eba74a%7D/SC_2013_ANNUAL REPORT.PDF [accessed November 2015].

Thompson, N. (1997) *Anti-discriminatory Practice 2E*. Basingstoke: Macmillan.

UNCRC (1989) *Convention on the Rights of the Child Adopted* and opened for signature, ratification and accession by General Assembly resolution 44/25 of 20 November 1989 entry into force 2 September 1990, in accordance with article 49, www.ohchr.org/en/professionalinterest/pages/crc.aspx [Accessed November 2015].

Weeks, J. (2014) *Economics of the 1% How Mainstream Economics Serves the Rich, Obscures Reality and Distorts Policy*. London: Anthem Press.

Wrigley, T. (2012) Class and culture: sources of confusion in educational sociology, in *Journal for Critical Education Policy Studies*, 10(3), pp. 144–183.

10 Flourishing and quality

Jan Gourd and Zenna Kingdon

Introduction

This chapter seeks to redefine quality within early years settings to engender flourishing for the child. We consider which aspects of provision are essential to promote flourishing and which fit synchronously with regulatory audits of quality within the UK and which are not suitably valued.

The current policy context of austerity, value for money and the education of pre-school children have now woven together notions of quality with techno-rational conceptions of professionalism within a performativity agenda (Moss 2014). This chapter will deconstruct these concepts, and question the particular way in which policy has come to define what counts as quality in early years provision. It will then go on to explore alternative conceptions of quality from the different perspectives of the child, the practitioner and the parent. This exploration will be located within the broader debates about the meaning and purpose of early years educational provision and will argue that a different discourse on quality offers an altered perspective of the importance of quality and its relationship to the flourishing of the pre-school child. The chapter will also explore practitioners who are framed and enabled or constrained in relation to the purpose of pre-school education and the flourishing of the child. It will conclude that 'quality' re-framed can be used as an important conceptual tool to re-capture the elusive concept of educational excellence within the complex early years environment.

Deconstructing the quality debate

Successive government drives for quality within the early years sector have been linked with an up-skilling agenda. Over the last two decades there has been a significant interest in the practitioners themselves, their qualifications and the pedagogical approaches that they undertake. The early years workforce has historically been poorly paid and poorly qualified (Roberts-Holmes 2012). While practitioner's pay has not been addressed, their qualifications have been; though this has not been without challenge as both Tickell (2011) and Nutbrown (2012) in their respective reviews of the EYFS (2008) and practitioner qualifications demonstrate.

Dahlberg, Moss and Pence began the quality discussion in relation to early childhood services in 1999. Taking a post-structuralist approach they contested how quality was conceptualised within dominant neo-liberal agendas. They sought to problematise the notion of quality itself and to promote discussion about the differences between quality itself and meaning making from quality. The former relying on checks and balances and the latter on shared understandings. It could almost be argued that one de-professionalises and the latter professionalises the sector, this in itself presents a challenge to control.

In relation to England the advent of Ofsted regulation and inspection of early years settings from 2001 has promoted the narrative of quality that is set within techno-rationale outcomes driven tick box cultures or situational templates (Dahlberg, Moss and Pence 1999). The willingness to comply with this agenda has been bought with the promise of additional funding for services once compliance has been shown. Previously unregulated and creative provision that arguably nurtured a quality agenda has been brought down to the sector minimum using a fixed mind-set of quality, whereas those settings that did not meet standards have been given a lifeline of meeting measureable minimum outcomes that could barely be considered quality in terms of the flourishing of the child (Dweck 2012).

The concept of quality in early childhood education and care has been a driving factor in many of the changes that have occurred over the last decade or more (Cottle and Alexander 2012; Dahlberg *et al.* 2007; Tanner *et al.* 2006). However, such discussions are not new and concepts of quality are contested and dependent on perspective and the stakeholder. Katz (1993) discussed the notion that quality is informed differently from an insider's or an outsider's view point and that children may well consider something to be high quality because they enjoy being there, while the local authority or inspectorate view it as a lower quality setting. Dahlberg *et al.* (2007, p. 87) suggest that the word quality is not impartial but that it is, 'a socially constructed concept'. They continue to suggest that the associated discourse is about quantification and objectification in order that judgements can be made that are not personal (ibid. 2007). However, Tanner *et al.* (2006) argue that while quality is regularly referred to and discussed in policy and documentation, there are no clear definitions of quality on which these discourses are predicated.

The Every Child Matters document (DfES 2003) was one of the first within the new era of regulation to consider quality. This document did little to define what was meant by the term and considered there to be an intuition as to the conceptualisation of quality among those engaged in the sector. This official conceptualisation of quality is according to Cottle and Alexander (2012) based entirely on developmental outcomes as defined in statutory requirements (DCSF 2007b). This they point out is contradictory to the non-statutory guidance (DCSF 2007c), which highlights how the early years curriculum should be play based and child led. The latter advice contributes, it would seem, to flourishing as defined earlier in this book, but does not enter the statutory document only the non-statutory advice.

In their research Cottle and Alexander (2012) found that the quality terminology promoted through policy documents and the inspection regime had become the main indicator of quality in some settings, but that others emphasised emotional development as a key indicator of quality. Where there was resistance to Ofsted's conceptualisation of quality this was often indicated by practitioners who talked about their personal values and 'ethics of care' Osgood (2006).

Cottle and Alexander (2012, p. 637) go on to suggest that quality has achieved a, 'generic, "common-sense" status and as such is promoted through national goals, standards, targets and various quality assurance procedures'. However, they (ibid. 2012), Ho *et al.* (20101), Dahlberg *et al.* (2007), Tanner *et al.* (2006) would all agree that there is a growing body of research evidence that demonstrates that the early years have a significant long-term impact on children's lives. Dahlberg *et al.* (2007), drawing on earlier studies, suggest that early childhood settings are often analysed using input, process and outcome criteria. They acknowledge that young children's lives, however, are often complex and they do not only attend one setting during the early years and therefore assessing the outcome of individual settings becomes complex (ibid. 2007).

Mathers *et al.* (2014, p. 55) suggest that process is, 'a dynamic concept relating to children's actual experiences'. They (ibid. 2014) go on to advocate that it is the quality of process experiences that is the strongest predictor of outcomes for the child long term. Dahlberg *et al.* (2007) suggest that a number of studies, mostly American, have informed the discourse of quality and have led to the development of ECERS (Early Childhood Environmental Rating Scale). Initially developed in America by Harms and Clifford it was adopted and adapted as part of the Effective Provision of Pre-school Education research (Dahlberg *et al.* 2005).

The EPPE research was initially commissioned by John Major in 1997 as a longitudinal study to consider the impact of early years education. It was later taken up by New Labour and extended as it appeared to demonstrate high-quality early years provision could mitigate for social disadvantage. As part of the research three environmental rating scales were subsequently created, ECERS –R, the revised edition of the original; ECERS – E designed by Sylva *et al.* (2003) to assess curricular provision of early years settings and ITERS-R, which was designed by Harms *et al.* (2003, cited in Mathers *et al.* 2014) to assess the provision for the youngest children from birth to approximately 30 months. While the early years regulator in England, Ofsted, suggests that settings should measure quality in this way and include the data on their Self Evaluation Forms (Sef), they do not include such assessments as part of their own inspection processes (Ofsted 2013).

Ikegami and Agbenyega (2014) considered how quality and happiness in early childhood were related. Their study was set within a group of settings, which adopted a Buddhist philosophy within their work. The settings in Japan were subject to governmental standards of quality, but predicated their provision on happiness. Ikegami and Agbenyega argue that:

> by framing the quality of early childhood education in happiness, educators and children can engage deeply with learning that has the potential to influence the whole child and their full participation in society.
>
> (2014: 46)

Such an approach can be seen to link directly with notions of flourishing in which happiness is at the centre of what is important for the child.

> The finding of this study reiterates the need for happiness to be placed ahead of rigid early childhood programs that focus exclusively on achieving optimum reading and numeracy standards.
>
> (Ikegami and Agbenyega 2014: 52)

These early childhood centres appear to focus on what is needed in order that the child can develop a sense of self-esteem an essential ingredient in flourishing. Noddings (2003: 260) suggests that 'the best schools should resemble the best homes' by this she specifies that both the best homes and schools are happy places that nurture children who seize educational opportunities and 'contribute to the happiness of others'. Ikegami and Agbenyega (2014: 53) continued to suggest that one finding stood out above any of the others and that this was that, 'happiness is a strong relational concept which can make a significant contribution to the quality of early childhood education when it is used to drive program planning and implementation'.

It would seem that from much of the research that has been conducted into flourishing children's happiness and well-being plays a central role. In order for children to flourish they need to have a good sense of self-esteem. Quality as set out in the neo-liberal agenda does not appear to have ways to measure such approaches.

- Quality is complex. There is not one single definitive meaning; it is a socially constructed notion that means different things to different people.
- Neo-liberalism seeks to measure and judge quality in order to justify investment. This is an industrial model where quality means that value is added to the child as they work their way through the setting. A measure of that quality is then applied in this model to measure 'outcomes'.
- Approaches to measuring quality that rely on pre-determined outcomes cannot easily measure the qualitative relational aspects of practice that encourage flourishing.

A quality curriculum

In 2008 Curriculum Guidance for the Foundation Stage (2000), Birth to Three Matters (2002) and the 14 National Standards for Day Care and Childminding (2001) were largely amalgamated into the Early Years Foundation Stage (2008). The curriculum was broadly welcomed by the early years community. The curricula Birth to Three Matters (2002), which had been aimed at the youngest children, adopted an approach that stressed the importance of relationships (Duffy 2010). This curriculum was felt by many to have adopted approaches that a number of early childhood researchers, Goldschmied, Jackson and Elfer had argued for, for many years (Baldock *et al.* 2005). These approaches had been adopted in the best settings and were a demonstration of high quality practice. Birth to Three Matters (2002) had been a clear recognition, sanctioned by government that the needs of the youngest children and the ways in which they learn were different from the learning styles and needs of older children. The EYFS (2008) created a distinctive phase for children that was considered to be developmentally appropriate, advocating a play-based curriculum that also merged notions of education and care (Roberts-Holmes 2012). The EYFS (2008) was referred to as a principled approach and was arranged around four broad themes: A Unique Child, Positive Relationships, Enabling Environments and Learning and Development.

The EYFS (2008) was predicated on a socio-cultural theoretical approach in which children are seen as effective co-constructors of knowledge (Roberts-Holmes 2012). There was a clear expectation that the curriculum would be delivered through a play-based experiential approach. It drew on the work of both Vygotsky (1986, 1978) and Bruner (1976, 1987 and 1990) in its co-constructed approach in which play could be seen as a central element. All of which could be considered to be a quality curriculum for children in their earliest years.

The approach to play within the EYFS (2008) was not without challenge; Wood (2010, p. 16) suggests that the EYFS (2008) draws on the EPPE (2004) and locates play within a, 'discourse of effectiveness'. This suggests that the play that was encouraged within the EYFS (2008) was a form of play that was in some way measurable. This would seem to be at odds with notions of playful pedagogies and approaches to early childhood in which children were expected to enjoy a qualitative experience through a play-based curriculum (Broadhead et al 2010, Moyles 2010, Rogers and Evans 2008) in which play, playful learning and playful teaching are underpinned by a pedagogical approach that is creative, imaginative and open-ended led by the children's interests rather than by pre-determined learning outcomes, notions that cannot be measured or quantified in ways that would be recognised via EPPE (2004). Howard (2010) further argues that while the EYFS (2008/12/14) advocated planned and purposeful play, this could be open to interpretation. The threat being that play could be misinterpreted in practice and lead to adult planning being privileged over children's planning (Wood 2010). Brooker (2011) discusses the fact that both EPPE (2004) and REPEY (Research into Effective Pedagogy in Early Years) (2002) have had a significant impact on both policy development and practitioner understanding. The result appears to be that practitioners and policy makers feel that they can comment with some assurance on what works for young children.

Brooker (2011) argues that play pedagogy appears to bring together two disparate approaches to early childhood, on the one hand, there is the eighteenth century Romantics notion of play as a natural part of childhood and on the other, the twentieth century developmentalists' approach that suggested that play was the most effective way for young children to learn. The EPPE (2004) and REPEY (2002) reports supported this through their research in which they discovered that children in high quality settings were offered appropriate opportunities to engage in a play-based curriculum and had their learning supported by the practitioners through episodes of Sustained Shared Thinking. These seemingly contradictory approaches to play have come together within the EYFS (2008/12/14). Brooker (2011, p. 142) states that within the statutory advice:

> there is the affirmation of play as the expression of children's natural inclinations . . . there is the view, supported by research that play is the means to achieve curricular learning outcomes.

Research evidence appears to suggest that in order that children are enabled to flourish they need to be offered a curriculum, which meets their needs and, which recognises that they do best when they are interested and engaged and that they are supported to develop their own areas of interest and to follow their natural curiosity.

- Very prescriptive curricula will not encourage a child to take agency in their own learning. A feeling of agency having control over one's own life is an important aspect of flourishing.
- Limiting curricula will not encourage practitioners to explore the range of possibilities that may be out there for the child to explore.
- Curricula by their very nature are of the past, they have been arrived at over a period of time that has past and therefore cannot be guaranteed to be relevant in the future.

Quality from the child's perspective

Play is usually considered to be the central element of early childhood provision through which any curricula is delivered. Yet it would seem that little prominence has been placed on discussing children's perceptions of play; recognising that much of the focus is on adult definitions

(Howard *et al.* 2006). Equally the majority of the literature is concerned with play from an adult's perspective and from observations of children at play. In their research Howard *et al.* (2006) recognise that much of the developmental potential of play comes from children recognising it as a play activity, rather than perceiving it as adult directed and therefore learning. They (ibid. 2006) explain that children define play using three different factors: behavioural, environmental and social contexts. In order for children to define an activity as play it is likely to include the following: it is enjoyable, it is likely to take place in a space other than at a table, it will not include adults but will include peers. Children who are in settings that are judged to be of a lower quality provision spent more time unoccupied or in solitary play (Sylva *et al.* 2007). It would seem that children were more likely to perceive parallel and cooperative activities as play, while they were less likely to categorise solitary activities as play (Howard *et al.* 2006). The EPPE research (Sylva *et al.* 2007) demonstrated that children in settings that were deemed to be of good quality spent greater periods of time participating in adult-initiated play-based activities that support cognitive development than in adequate settings (Siraj-Blatchford 2012). Interestingly in those same settings children spent more time playing in small groups and in creative or pure play, than children in adequate settings did (Moyles 2010; EPPE 2004). The EPPE research (Sylva *et al.* 2007) appears to demonstrate that in what they deemed to be good quality settings adults used open-ended questions and engaged children in Sustained Shared Thinking, children had a balance of freely chosen and adult-supported play opportunities and staff recognised the complementary nature of social and cognitive development.

- Play is recognised as a central element of young children's learning, yet little research has been conducted considering play from the child's perspective.
- It would seem that children themselves define play from three perspectives: behavioural, environmental and social.

Quality and parent perspectives

Sylva *et al.* (2010) argue that high quality settings within the EPPE research were effective in sharing their curriculum with parents and carers and that this resulted in more positive outcomes for children. They further suggest that research evidence demonstrates that children make better progress where families and settings work in tandem. This approach to creating and facilitating the curriculum allows children to develop their full potential (Rose and Rogers 2012).

Quality and practitioner perspectives

After almost a decade focused on up-skilling the early years workforce Cathy Nutbrown was asked to undertake a review of the qualifications of practitioners working in the sector. The Nutbrown review (2012) was broadly welcomed by the early years sector. However, for some the recommendations did not go far enough and those with Early Years Professional Status were left feeling that they were no longer valued as they had been previously told that they would be. The Nutbrown review (2012) suggested that the Level 3 qualification itself should be full and relevant and include study of both child development and play; the criteria for the new Early Years Educator (EYE) (2014) appears to have included these elements. Equally Nutbrown (2012) called for the government to consider how they could maintain and increase graduate pedagogical leadership in the sector. New Labour had committed to a graduate in every full day care setting by 2015; the coalition referred to this as an aspiration rather than a commitment. Since the election in May 2015 the aspiration appears to be less apparent though there remains a focus on the sector as the government seeks to increase free provision from 15 to 30 hours for all three and four-year-olds whose parents are working. Nutbrown (2012) further advocated that anyone with Early Years Professional Status should be given an opportunity to access routes to QTS as a priority. The government took only aspects of the review, diluting what had been recommended and appearing to cause further confusion over qualifications and statuses (Nutbrown 2013). New national standards for Early Years' Teacher (DfE 2014) and the EYE standards (2014) include reference to Sustained Shared Thinking.

The EPPE report (2004) identified that the qualification level of practitioners working with children impacted on the quality of Sustained Shared Thinking. Those who had the highest level of qualification, particularly those who were qualified teachers, engaged in both the highest frequencies of direct teaching and the highest frequencies of Sustained Shared Thinking. The evidence that they recorded demonstrated that those with higher qualifications were able to sensitively enter play opportunities extending children's ideas and thought processes while allowing the child the opportunity to remain in control of the play (Siraj-Blatchford *et al.* 2010). Those practitioners who had lower level qualifications, below a Level 5, were considered to demonstrate significantly better pedagogical practices when they were supported by qualified teachers (Siraj-Blatchford *et al.* 2010). The EPPE research (2004), which underpins governmental drivers towards having graduates in early years settings, clearly demonstrates that for children to engage in SST, which supports effective cognitive development, appropriately qualified and experienced practitioners are essential.

Standard 16 of the original EYPS standards for professional practice was, 'Engage in Sustained Shared Thinking with children' (2010, p. 41). In the new standards Early Years Teachers must demonstrate an ability to:

> 2.4 Lead and model effective strategies to develop and extend children's learning and thinking, including sustained shared thinking.
> (NCTL (a) 2013, p. 2)

Likewise, the new early years educator should:

> 2.5 Engage in effective strategies to develop and extend children's learning and thinking, including sustained shared thinking.
> (NCTL (b) 2013, p. 5)

This continued emphasis on SST as being part of a professional standard both at graduate and undergraduate levels clearly demonstrates the value that is placed on Sustained Shared Thinking by the government's validating bodies. Throughout agenda there has been little opportunity for the workforce themselves to engage in conversations about how they feel about the expectations that are being made of them. For many they are having to engage in Higher Education as mature adults, which is leading them to question who they are and what are their values (Gourd 2014).

- Some stakeholder voices are privileged in the debate on quality and some silenced. We need to find ways to listen to everyone's views.
- Up-skilling the workforce has been a major political driver in the quality debate.

Alternative ways of measuring quality

The Leuven Scales of Well-being and Involvement are concerned with children's involvement with their learning and their relationships with those around them and represent an alternative way in which quality can be measured (Laevers 2004). The Leuven Scales of Well-being and Involvement were developed out of work that was initiated in 1976 when a number of Flemish pre-school teachers working with two advisory teachers began to investigate and critically reflect on their practice. The concepts drew on the work of Czikszentmihyli's notions of flow, a state in which the participant is deeply involved and engaged in an activity. The initial research led to the development of the EXE-theory, Experiential Education, which was an approach that suggested that the most economic and effective method to assess the quality of a setting was to focus on two areas, 'the degree of "emotional well-being" and the level of "involvement"' (Laevers 1994 cited in Laevers 2004, p. 5). Both the scales operate on a five-point system,

> from level 1 (no activity) through level 3 (child is engaged in an activity, but is functioning at a routine level) to level 5 (continuous, intense activity of the child, with purpose and pleasure).
>
> (Leavers 2004, p. 6)

Laevers goes on to explain that the scales have been used with high levels of reliability and validity throughout the world, but places particular emphasis on the Effective Early Learning project that was conducted in the UK by Pascal and Bertram. Pascal and Bertram (2000) explain that they adopted the Leuven scales as part of the project because they felt that they were effective and focused on the processes of learning while being appropriately theoretically underpinned. The Leuven scales were intended to support the development of quality in terms of content and outcomes (Laevers 2011). In terms of early years education and care they support a pedagogical approach that values play as an effective method of engaging children and supporting their learning and development. The Leuven scales are concerned with undertaking a playful approach in which the child demonstrates spontaneity and self-confidence. What the Leuven scales fail to do is to provide a way in which the children are enabled to comment on their engagement. The Leuven scales consider play from the adult perspective, there is little opportunity for children to comment on their experiences, which could be considered to be inappropriate when considering flourishing. However, these issues are complex and for those looking for alternative

LIVERPOOL JOHN MOORES UNIVERSITY,
LEARNING SERVICES

and creative approaches such an approach may be useful in informing the practitioner's thinking.

- The Leuven scales offer an alternative way in which quality can be measured.
- However, even these do not provide opportunities for children to comment on their engagement in their play and learning activities.

Quality and complexity

As we have seen the issue of flourishing is a complex matter. There is not a set of quantifiable criteria that can legislate for a flourishing setting, although there are many politicians who like to pretend that this is the case. An Ofsted rating can ensure the relative safety of a setting, but it cannot hope to determine the level of the conditions for flourishing as each facet is in itself complex.

In order to provide and maximise the necessary conditions for flourishing we have seen that the whole community surrounding the child, the practitioners, parents and local community need to be able to flourish too. This utopian image of the flourishing community is where our aspiration must lie. In many ways the pictures painted of Reggio Emilia come a long way in helping us picture what this might look like and this is why the practice of Reggio Emilia has been held up as an aspiration in so many early years communities.

How then can we start to piece together the picture of the quality early years setting? Brighouse (2006) suggests that in order to thrive schools need to have all the pieces of the jigsaw in place. He uses the analogy of the jigsaw to demonstrate the complexity and interdependence of one piece in relation to all the others. The big picture is only complete when each piece of the jigsaw is in place. Although written in the context of statutory schooling Brighouse's (2006) ideas equally apply to the early years setting. Regardless of size the principles of creating a successful setting are the same.

For Brighouse (2006) each jigsaw has corner pieces, the cornerstones keeping the structure secure. The corner pieces include the following italicised quotes (ibid. 2006, p. 3).

We share values, a vision of the future and we enjoy telling stories.

Brighouse (2006) places great emphasis on the need for practitioners to talk together, to share stories from practice, they critically reflect. We know from the previous chapters that sharing practice engages a sense of well-being among practitioners. Sharing tensions and dilemmas, successes and celebrating achievement all adds to our sense of well-being. The constant purposeful talk builds a joint vision.

Our language makes the school.

He (ibid. 2006) is clear to point out that the language that is used in documents and in everyday exchanges should reflect the values of the setting. He suggests that practitioners speak as one voice using the pronoun 'we' rather than 'I' when representing the setting. He also suggests that we are careful about demonstrating inclusive practice and that we challenge each other when the discourse suggests that values are not embedded in the everyday conversations that are embodied in practice.

The school is a beautiful place.

The setting environment is an essential consideration. Previous chapters have suggested that 'enabling environments' need to be just that, they need to be cared for, carefully structured and embody beauty to engender well-being. An uncared for environment adds stressors to the users of the environment and can be an obstruction to flow. Again Reggio Emilia practice has much to offer here.

We try to do things right in our school. – taking a stand on detail.

The details that Brighouse (2006) mentions here could mainly be seen as administrational. He talks about job descriptions, the necessity to publish accurate information in advance, the calendar and public documents. The emphasis here is on avoiding potential confusion and therefore minimising the stressors such as date clashes and allowing parents to plan time off, for example, for special events. This attention to detail enables the whole community to understand and work together more easily.

In our school we sing from the same song sheet. – the elusive quest for consistency.

Consistency for Brighouse (2006) is essential for quality. The joint discussion around parameters, the agreement of all staff on how we do things and adherence to those democratic decisions helps to ensure flow. Brighouse (2006) does not suggest that 'regimes of truth' (Foucault 1975) established through discussion are never re-visited and challenged. Indeed his prioritising of staff development and reflective discussion suggest that the song words might constantly change, but that when it does everyone knows about it and sings it. This emphasis on democracy and agency is an essential ingredient to the flourishing setting.

Our teaching, learning and assessment.

The focus here for Brighouse is the dialogue between practitioners that goes on, the critical reflective practice whereby practitioners talk about their work, observe each other, learn from each other and constantly challenge the quality of the practice.

You will note that there are six corner pieces so the analogy is a little lost but the message is strong. Brighouse (2006) then goes on to indicate how the straightsided pieces:

'We develop all our staff'

'We listen and involve our pupils'

'Are we data rich and information poor?'

'We understand and welcome change, because change is learning and that's our business'

'We practise learning walks'

'We are fussy about appointments – it's a privilege to work here'

And the wiggly pieces:

'We value and involve our parents and the community'

'We make our school personal. Every child and adult matters here'

fit together to make the big picture.

The only reference to neo-liberal quantifiable data comes in the form of a question. 'Are we data rich and information poor?' Certainly if a setting managed to fit all the pieces of the jigsaw together successfully then this is not a criticism that could be levelled against it. What Brighouse (2006) presents us with is an image of all the complex pieces that have to be in place and synchronise with one another to ensure quality and promote flourishing. His analysis is not new. An analysis of leadership and management literature will come up with similar concepts, but he uses his extensive knowledge of education to simplify and present what are in fact common sense principles.

The last piece of the jigsaw for Brighouse (2006, p. 3) is 'the piece that dropped on the floor'. This piece introduces creativity to the picture.

He (ibid. 2006, p. 41) also here argues for a culture of 'appreciative enquiry', he suggests that when such a culture is attained then 'a boost of energy and self-belief' dominates.

Another tool such as the jigsaw that is useful in the development of the quest for meaningful quality for flourishing is the Needs Analysis Tool. This tool developed by Abbott (1998) allows collaborative and democratic analysis of a setting's perceived strengths and weaknesses. The practitioners decide upon the priorities for development based on their own knowledge and experience of the setting, thus the development builds upon known qualitative evaluation, which is arrived at through consensus and knowledge of the 'big picture'. Needs Analysis can help settings to develop practice within individual pieces of the jigsaw and extend practitioners 'notions of quality' (Gourd 2014).

- Performativity and monitoring agendas can stifle quality debates, that is once a setting has achieved its badge it might become complacent.
- Stakeholders need to debate and develop quality at a local level for their unique community.
- Not all facets of quality can or should be measured.

Conclusion

We opened this chapter by trying to question what constitutes quality and the relationship between quality and flourishing. What appears to be constituted as quality within the neo-liberal agenda does not appear to match with qualitative approaches that are concerned with flourishing. In order for children to flourish they need to be happy and to have high self-esteem. In this sense quality is not measurable and certainly does not fit an agenda of meeting targets within a particular approach. We recognise that it is necessary for children to engage with a quality curriculum in which they are placed at the centre where their needs are met and they are encouraged to explore and investigate and follow their natural curiosity. It is only when children follow such a curriculum that they are likely to flourish. It would seem that within the early childhood sector in England there had been high hopes of the Early Years Foundation Stage (2008/12/14) following as it did from Birth to Three Matters (2003). The latter curriculum appeared to recognise the need for positive relationships between the children and their carers and advocated a clearly play-based approach. While the EYFS (2008/12/14) appears to advocate such an approach Wood (2010) suggests that what is actually being sought is a particular form of play in which outcomes are specific and measurable rather than driven by the children. A quality curriculum needs to allow the children to flourish. It is clear that what constitutes quality will not necessarily be perceived as such by all those who are considering it. Katz (1993) discussed the notion of insiders and outsiders in respect of quality. She suggested that for children a quality setting would be one that they enjoyed attending, where they felt that they could have fun and where they had opportunities to play with their friends. While this is not necessarily incompatible with a setting that is considered by an inspectorate to be of high quality, they are not necessarily one and the same. The EPPE Research (2004) argues that high quality settings share with the parents and carers the curriculum and what happens in the setting for the child. Reggio Emilia settings see this as essential in order to enable them to form effective relationships with both the child and the family.

Quality in early childhood in England has been on the government agenda now for nearly two decades, yet in all of that time there has been little focus on the view of the practitioners. It seems that they are simply expected to deliver what has been decided while also up-skilling themselves. Practitioners need opportunities to flourish if they are to ensure that the children with whom they are working are also flourishing. Alternative ways of measuring quality do exist and have been used successfully in England. While the Leuven scales (Laevers 2011) do not engage the child in the process of measuring well-being, they do focus on the process of well-being and enable the practitioners to consider the individual child's level of engagement and well-being. All of these issues are complex and it would seem that quality and complexity are interrelated. There is not a set of quantifiable data that can be used to measure quality and flourishing, instead approaches need to be considered and embraced that allow settings to develop practice that supports the flourishing of the child, the parents and carers, the practitioners and the wider community.

REFLECTIVE QUESTIONS

■ How would you describe your own understanding of quality practice in the early years?

■ In what ways are prescribed professional standards in danger of limiting quality practice?

■ How does quality contribute to flourishing both overtly and subtly within the work of the early years setting?

References

Abbott, L. and Pugh, G. (1998) *Training to Work in the Early Years: Developing the Climbing Frame*. Maidenhead: Open University Press.

Baldock, P., Fitzgerald, D. and Kay, J. (2005) *Understanding Early Years Policy*. London: Paul Chapman.

Brighouse, H. (2006) *On Education*. London: Routledge.

Brighouse, T. (2006) *Essential Pieces: The Jigsaw of the Successful School* at www.rtuni. org/userfiles/TimBrighouseBook.pdf last accessed 22/02/2016:15:26

Broadhead, P., Howard, P. and Wood, E. (2010) *Play and Learning in the Early Years*. London: Sage.

Brooker, L. (2011) 'Taking children seriously: an alternative agenda for research'. *Journal of Early Childhood Research*, 9(2), pp. 137–149.

Bruner, J. (1990) *Acts of Meaning*. London: Harvard University Press.

Bruner, J. (1987) *Making Sense: The Child's Construction of the World*. London: Routledge.

Bruner, J. (1976) *Play its Role in Development and Evolution*. Harmondsworth: Penguin.

Cottle, M. and Alexander, E. (2012) 'Quality in early years settings: government, research and practitioners' perspectives', in *British Educational Research Journal*, 38(4), pp. 635–654.

CWDC (2010) *On the Right Track: Guidance to the Standards for the award of Early Years Professional Status*. Leeds: CWDC.

Dahlberg, G. and Moss, P. (2005) *Ethics and politics in early childhood education*. Abingdon: RoutledgeFalmer.

Dahlberg, G., Moss, P. and Pence, A. (1999) *Beyond Quality in Early Childhood Education and Care: Languages of evaluation*. London: Routledge.

Dahlberg, G., Moss, P. and Pence, A. (2007) *Beyond Quality in Early Childhood Education and Care*. London: Routledge.

DCSF (2008) *Statutory Framework for the Early Years Foundation Stage*. London: DCSF.

Department for Education and Skills (DfES) (2003) *Every Child Matters*. Cm 5860. London: DfES.

Department for Children, Schools and Families (DCSF) (2007a) 'Statutory framework for the early years foundation stage: setting the standards for learning, development and care for children from birth to five', in: *Department for Children Schools and Families (ed.) Every Child Matters, Change for Children*. Nottingham: DCSF.

Department for Children, Schools and Families (DCSF) (2007b) 'Practice guidance for the early years foundation stage: setting the standards for learning, development and care for children from birth to five', in: Department for Children Schools and Families (ed.) *Every Child Matters, Change for Children*. Nottingham: DCSF.

DfE (2014) Teacher Standards Early Years, available from: www.gov.uk/government/uploads/system/uploads/attachment_data/file/211646/Early_Years_Teachers__Standards.pdf

Duffy, B. (2010) 'Art in the early years'. In Moyles, J. (2010) *The Excellence of Play* 3rd edn, Maidenhead: Open University Press, pp. 123–128.

Dweck, C. (2012) *Mindset: How you can fulfil your potential*. London: Little Brown Book Group.

Gourd, J. (2014) 'Up-skilling the workforce: managing change in practice', in Kingdon, Z. and Gourd, J. (2014) *Early Years Policy: The impact on practice*. London: Routledge.

Ho, D., Campbell-Barr, V. and Leeson, C. (2010) Quality improvements in early years settings in Hong Kong and England. *International Journal of Early Years Education*, 18(3), pp. 243–258.

Howard, J. (2010) 'Early years practitioners' perceptions of play: An exploration of theoretical understanding, planning and involvement, confidence and barriers to practice'. *Education & Child Psychology*, 27(4), pp. 91–102.

Howard, J., Jenvey, V. and Hill, C. (2006) 'Children's categorisation of play and learning based on social context', in *Early Child Development and Care*, 176(3–4), pp. 379–393.

Ikegami, K. and Agbenyega, J. (2014) 'How does learning through "happiness" promote quality early childhood education?' in *Australasian Journal of Early Childhood*, 39(3) pp. 46–55.

Katz, L. (1993) 'Multiple perspectives on the quality of early childhood programmes'. *European Early Childhood Research Journal*, 1(2), pp. 5–9.

Laevers, F. (2004) *Starting Strong Curricula and Pedagogies in Early Childhood Education and Care*. OECD.

Laevers, F. (2011) *Experiential Education: Making care and education more effective through well-being and involvement*. Leuven: CEECD.

Mathers, S., Roberts, F. and Sylva, K. (2014) 'Quality in early childhood education', in Pugh, G. and Duffy, B. (2014) *Contemporary Issues in the Early Years 6e*. London: Sage.

Moss, P. (2014) *Transformative Change and Real Utopias in Early Childhood Education: A story of democracy, experimentation and potentiality*. London: Routledge.

Moyles, J. (2010) *Thinking about Play: Developing a reflective approach*. Maidenhead: McGraw Hill.

NCTL (2013a) Teachers' Standards (Early Years) available from: www.gov.uk/government/uploads/system/uploads/attachment_data/file/211646/Early_Years_Teachers__Standards.pdf

NCTL (2013b) Guidance to the Standards for Early Years Educator, available from: www.gov.uk/government/uploads/system/uploads/attachment_data/file/211644/Early_Years_Educator_Criteria.pdf

Noddings, N. (2003) *Happiness and Education*. Cambridge: Cambridge University Press.

Noddings, N. (2012) 'The language of care ethics', in *Knowledge Quest Caring is Essential*, 40(4), pp. 52–56.

Nutbrown, C. (2012) *Foundations for Quality*. Runcorn: DfE.

Nutbrown, C. (2013) *Shaking the Foundations of Quality. Why childcare policy must not lead to poor-quality early education and care*. Sheffield: Sheffield University.

Ofsted (2013) *Conducting Early Years Inspections*. London: Ofsted.

Osgood, J. (2006) 'Deconstructing professionalism in early childhood education: Resisting the regulatory gaze', in *Contemporary Issues in Early Childhood*, 7(1), pp. 5–14.

Pascal, C. and Bertram, T. (2000) *Further Memorandum from the Effective Early Learning Project (EY 81)* [online] Available from: www.publications.parliament.uk/pa/cm199900/cmselect/cmeduemp/386/0061406.htm [accessed] 16/06/14.

Robert-Holmes, G. (2012) 'It's the bread and butter of our practice': experiencing the Early Years Foundation Stage. *International Journal of Early Years Education*, 20(1), pp. 30–42.

Rogers, S. and Evans, J. (2008) *Inside Role-Play in Early Childhood Education.* London: Routledge.

Rose, J. and Rogers, S. (2012) *The Role of the Adult in Early Years Settings.* Maidenhead: McGraw-Hill.

Siraj-Blatchford, I. (2012) 'Curriculum, pedagogy and progression in sustained shared thinking'. *Every Child*, 18(3), 34–35.

Siraj-Blatchford, I., Sylva, K., Muttock, S., Gilden, R. and Bell, D. (2002) *Researching Effective Pedagogy in the Early Years.* Research Report No. 356, Norwich: DfES.

Siraj-Blatchford, I., Taggart, B., Sylva, K., Sammons, P. and Melhuish, E. (2010) 'Towards the transformation of practice in early childhood education: The effective provision of pre-school education (EPPE) project', in *Cambridge Journal of Education*, 38(1), pp. 23–36.

Sylva, K., Melhuish, E., Sammons, P., Siraj-Blatchford, I. and Taggart, B. (2004) *The Effective Provision of Pre-school Education (EPPE) Project: Final Report.* Nottingham: DfES.

Sylva, K., Taggart, B., Siraj-Blatchford, I., Totsika, V., Ereky-Stevens, K., Gilden, R. and Bell, D. (2007) 'Curricular quality and day-to-day learning activities in pre-school', in *International Journal of Early Years Education*, 15, pp. 49–65.

Sylva, K., Melhuish, E., Sammons, P., Siraj-Blatchford, I. and Taggart, B. (2010) *Early Childhood Matters Evidence from the Effective Pre-school and Primary Education Project.* London: Routledge.

Tanner, E., Welsh, E. and Lewis, J. (2006) 'The quality defining process in early years services: A case study'. *Children and Society*, 20(1), pp. 4–16.

Tickell, C. (2011) *The Early Years: Foundations for life, health and learning.* [online] Available from: http://media.education.gov.uk/MediaFiles/B/1/5/%7BB15 EFF0D-A4DF-4294–93A1–1E1B88C13F68%7DTickell%20review.pdf [accessed 26/01/15].

Vygotsky, L. (1986) *Thought and Language.* London: The MIT Press.

Vygotsky, L. (1978) *Mind in Society.* London: Harvard University Press.

Wood, E. (2010) 'Developing integrated pedagogical approaches to play and learning', in Broadhead, P., Howard, J. and Wood, E. (2010) *Play and Learning in the Early Years.* London: Sage.

Conclusion

Jan Gourd and Zenna Kingdon

Throughout this book we have explored what flourishing means from a variety of perspectives. We have considered the many nuances and shades of meaning that the word implies. We have looked at psychological and philosophical understandings. The importance of flourishing for all those involved in early years provision has been discussed in relation to our three key themes.

Contexts

Initially in Chapter 1 we set out to look at the ways in which flourishing can be considered to be a concept with a rich heritage, not simply a term recently coined by Seligman (2011). In order to do this, we consider the work of the Ancient Greek philosopher Aristotle and the work of Margaret MacMillan who can be considered to be an early childhood pioneer. Here we established a baseline from which to further consider the implications for practice.

In the second chapter Reynolds reminds us that a person can only be considered to be flourishing if they believe it themselves. How that is articulated and the means through which it is articulated will be different for each individual and thus the complexity of the concept engages us in further mental debate.

Gasper and Mathias in Chapter 3 considered how services provided by Government could help to further the desire of policy makers to create conditions for all children to experience quality early years provision. The services they describe have noble aspirations, but the neo-liberal agenda of 'value for money' and accountability technologies have disrupted their original purpose and created systems that struggle to fulfil the holistic nature of their work.

In Chapter 4 we were warned about the dangers of 'compassion fatigue' and it is clear that in our discussion we have to make sure that we prioritise the flourishing of all those involved in the early years community. Children will not flourish and be happy if the adults around them are constantly stressed and fatigued. There has to be a balance between resilience and nurturing that practitioners have to grapple with, resilience against the externally imposed pressures and the authentic nurturing practice that ethically rest easy with the practitioner. The internal struggles against accountability agendas on the one hand and intuitive ethical practice on the other can often be too burdensome to allow practitioners to flourish. Buckler therefore suggests that we embrace self-determination theory in order to take back agency in our own lives.

These chapters then set the scene for us to theoretically have a shared understanding of the context of flourishing in the early years.

Practices

In Chapter 5 Pilbeam discussed a curriculum approach that has gained popularity in recent years, the pedagogy now commonly known as 'Forest School'. He shows us how this innovative approach to education within the early years can develop a sense of awe, wonder and peace. All of these attributes facilitate the development of flourishing. In this pedagogical approach children develop agency to determine their creativity in a way that satisfies them and develops an awareness of sustainability and the need to take ownership of the planet on which we all live. This understanding and the development of important social skills and ability to take and manage risk all contribute to the sense of well-being that the child gains.

Gasper, in Chapter 6, highlighted the challenges to flourishing in an age of austerity. He showed how the progress made in the previous New Labour administration has been challenged and in some cases reversed by recent policy initiatives such as the bedroom tax. The case studies clearly show how given time multi-agency working can have a positive impact on the lives of many young families, but political landscapes are constantly changing and the lack of stability within policy means that rather than consolidation we have fragmentation of services. This agenda is not only within the family or multi-agency setting, but is also the agenda within health services and the current debates on the forced academisation of schools. It appears that the neo-liberal obsession with markets and value for money is still gathering pace with detrimental consequences for flourishing.

Kingdon continues the debate in Chapter 7 and focuses on the creative curriculum. She makes suggestions as to how play can forward children's development as flourishing individuals, how it can develop the necessary pre-requisites of socialisation, agency, curiosity and enjoyment.

In Chapter 8 Gourd suggests how richness of learning can be documented to make the invisible visible, to celebrate the richness of the child's achievement in whatever area that may be. She argues for cursory attention to be given to documenting learning against specific developmental outcomes and a prioritising of the documenting of the richness of the unique child, the child who grows in self-esteem, resilience, self-worth and curiosity through excellent relational practice.

In Chapter 9 Lea takes the stance that practitioners need to develop agency in change through critical reflective practice and use their professional knowledge to facilitate the flourishing of the child. Lea reminds us that until we have a greater understanding and commitment to tackle inequality then we will always have a society where some flourish and others do not. The early years practitioner can make a difference to children's lives through the development of the promotion of equality rather than inequality, but in order to do this the practitioner needs to be able to identify and recognise their own unequal practices, which are often part of a hidden 'regimes of truth'.

Futures

In the final chapter we debate quality and how that relates to the current debates. We again try to suggest ways in which practitioners can try to take back the ground that has been lost in recent years through the limiting constructs of quality indicators and other systems that seek to measure and compare settings. We echo the message of previous chapters when we make a call for self-belief among professionals of the legitimacy of their own knowledge and relational practice.

What comes across in all of these chapters is how, within the contemporary early years sector, the policy landscape has concentrated on the neo-liberal agenda of marketisation and value for money. This driver is a relatively new phenomenon for early years practice. This agenda has been forwarded through the techno-rational approach that seeks to measure and assure quality through measurable defined and limiting outcomes. This approach, rather than forwarding the creation of the flourishing of the child, family and practitioner, has indeed alienated many, caused stress and worry and feelings of failure among parents and indeed in the early years of school children themselves. This is witnessed by the very concerning growth in child and teenage mental health problems. The relational has been forgotten in pursuit of the quantifiable outcome. What hopefully this book encourages is a return to considering what is important in early years practice, namely the flourishing of the children in our care so that they can lead happy and fulfilling lives as individuals. We know through these chapters that the antecedents of flourishing are developed early on, through the attachments that are made, the positive relationships that are formed, the resilience developed and the sense of agency and control that a person feels they have over their own life. None of these things are measureable and we should resist attempts to technologise 'flourishing' programmes. Relational practices are messy and complex; they cannot be reduced to well-being outcomes! Relational practice is inclusive and celebrates the individual as a unique human being and appreciates them within that current moment of being, who they are in the here and now. Childhood is an important and central life phase that needs celebrating in its own right and needs appropriate recognition as a foundation for later happiness, this is the most important aspect of school readiness and life preparation that there can be. The authors here have shown practitioners the importance of taking control, having self-determination to do what is ethically right. The importance of pedagogical documentation and discussion has been foregrounded as one way in which the dilemmas and celebrations of relational practice can be exposed to a wider audience. We need to create new spaces for early years practice that foreground future flourishing and we need to use all the knowledge that we have: professional – gained through experience, psychological – gained through research, and philosophical – gained through reasoning to make our arguments.

Momentum for change

While writing this book there has been a relative sea change in the awareness of parents about the ways in which education is being technologised. This has been largely as a result of the White Paper 2016 Educational Excellence Everywhere in which the minister for education sets out the plan to academise all schools. The government have, however, recently undertaken a U-turn on the introduction of baseline assessment; a test that was to be administered within the first six weeks that a child was in the Reception class. While baseline assessment will not be introduced in the previously agreed format in September 2016 there is likely to be another form of testing brought in to replace it. Concerns about the ever-increasing demands being made on KS1 children have increased, with the debacle of the now cancelled Year 1 spelling, punctuation and grammar tests, which were accidently published online. Such events have propelled the agendas to headline news and opened up the debate over the demands that are being made on young children.

For the first time teacher unions and parents can be seen joining together and creating activist groups, which seek to make their voice heard and the mantra 'enough is enough' is prevalent. Parents generally want their children to be happy and flourish and they can see the harm that current ill-informed policies are doing to their child's happiness and well-being. This brings us back full circle to where we started with the notion that if you ask parents what they want for their children it is to: be confident, to demonstrate happiness, to have good self-esteem and demonstrate contentment (Seligman 2011). Throughout the book we have demonstrated how flourishing supports these attributes and that those that flourish are more likely to achieve them. Therefore, we believe that flourishing is essential and should not be an afterthought within the education system. Instead it should be the central focus, particularly for those working with the youngest children.

References

DfE 2016 White Paper – Educational Excellence Everywhere at www.gov.uk/government/publications/educational-excellence-everywhere (accessed 25/04/2016:19:47)

Seligman, M. (2011) *Flourish: A New Understanding of Happiness and Well-being and How to Achieve Them*. London: Nicholas Brearley Publishing.

Index